Contesting Cosmopolitan Europe

Protest and Social Movements

Recent years have seen an explosion of protest movements around the world, and academic theories are racing to catch up with them. This series aims to further our understanding of the origins, dealings, decisions, and outcomes of social movements by fostering dialogue among many traditions of thought, across European nations and across continents. All theoretical perspectives are welcome. Books in the series typically combine theory with empirical research, dealing with various types of mobilization, from neighborhood groups to revolutions. We especially welcome work that synthesizes or compares different approaches to social movements, such as cultural and structural traditions, micro- and macro-social, economic and ideal, or qualitative and quantitative. Books in the series will be published in English. One goal is to encourage non-native speakers to introduce their work to Anglophone audiences. Another is to maximize accessibility: all books will be available in open access within a year after printed publication.

Series Editors
Jan Willem Duyvendak is professor of Sociology at the University of Amsterdam. James M. Jasper teaches at the Graduate Center of the City University of New York.

Contesting Cosmopolitan Europe

Euroscepticism, Crisis and Borders

Edited by
James Foley and Umut Korkut

Amsterdam University Press

Cover illustration: https://unsplash.com/Maxim Berg

Cover design: Coördesign, Leiden
Typesetting: Crius Group, Hulshout

ISBN   978 94 6372 725 9
e-ISBN   978 90 4855 390 7 (pdf)
DOI   10.5117/9789463727259
NUR   906

Table of Contents

Introduction

James Foley and Umut Korkut

In 2019, the incoming executive of the European Commission nominated a vice-president for migration and security issues bearing the title "Commissioner for Protecting the European Way of Life". This allusion to a continent under attack, and in need of protection, prompted months of controversy about the meaning attached to "European" borders and boundaries. The centre-right European People's Party, who proposed the title, insisted they had not meant to raise the drawbridge against refugees: "this means to rescue people in the Mediterranean [...] not to close harbours" (Zalan, 2019). Yet both supporters and critics saw matters differently and interpreted it as a move designed to absorb xenophobic narratives into the EU's most cosmopolitan structure. Marine Le Pen hailed "an ideological victory"; by contrast, socialist and Green MEPs saw it as surrendering to a notion of an embattled "European civilisation" promoted in the discourses of leaders such as Hungary's Viktor Orbán. The controversy would eventually force a small but crucial change, with "protecting" becoming "promoting" the European way of life. But the polarised reaction had already established a crucial fact about the continent's political identity: today, any talk of a "European way of life" carries new ideological baggage. Where the continent's institutional boundaries and political responsibilities have expanded, so have anxieties about proximity to a non-European "other".

Importantly, this was not always the case. For decades social theorists, commentators and political leaders pictured European institutions – with which the term *Europe* was usually synonymous – as the precursor to a fully cosmopolitan world system (Beck & Grande, 2007; Rifkin, 2013). In contrast to the Washington Consensus mode of globalisation, represented by the coercive force of IMF structural adjustment programmes and the Iraq War, the European project was imagined as prefiguring a consensual, peaceful, and inclusive global order. This comparison often formed an explicit point of rhetorical contrast. Leonard (2005), evoking

Foley, J. and Korkut, U. (ed.), *Contesting Cosmopolitan Europe. Euroscepticism, Crisis and Borders.* Amsterdam: Amsterdam University Press 2022
DOI :10.5117/9789463727259_INTRO

the neoconservative Project for a New American Century, said: "Imagine a world of peace, prosperity and democracy [...] What I am asking you to imagine is the 'New European Century'". For many commentators, Fukuyama (2006) included, Europe as a project had become synonymous with the "end of history", reflecting the triumphant mood of border-crossing that followed the collapse of the Berlin Wall. Even critics tended to endorse this premise, from the other angle, by critiquing a permissively cosmopolitan European superstate.

However, reality has struggled to live up to the rhetoric of an open, borderless world. Indeed, it is sobering to reflect that, since 1989, the EU and Schengen Area states have constructed an estimated 1,000 kilometres of land walls, equivalent to six Berlin Walls, largely in an effort to stop the flight of forcibly displaced people (Akkerman, 2019, 2018). With sea barriers included, a further 4,750 kilometres may be added to that figure. The result has been a death toll of drownings in the Mediterranean which, in the half decade since 2014, approaches 20,000 people. Europe's addiction to walled borders thus arguably exceeds the better publicised efforts of Donald Trump and the American state on the Mexican border.

Meanwhile, a system of detention centres and barbed wire fencing rings the European continent, including satellite states paid by the EU to maintain border control, such as Turkey, Niger, and Libya. Frontex, the EU agency charged with migration control, will command a budget of €11.27 billion for the financial period 2021–2027. Many have thus observed the paradox that the elimination of internal borders within Europe, and the expansion of the European Union to post-Soviet states, has brought both an ideological and an actual hardening of external boundaries. Frequently, this has pivoted on the discourse of a "clash of civilisations" (Huntington, 2000) between the Christian West and Islam, a notion that began in the upper echelons of Anglo-American foreign policy but has become one of the central points of populist mobilisation in Europe, particularly in states on the outer perimeter such as Hungary and Poland, but equally in France, the most unequivocally "European" of states. The result is not simply that there is now a "closed" as well as an "open" narrative of Europe. More disconcertingly, the two continental imaginaries now co-habit and may even be seen as co-dependent. Internal freedom of movement is premised on "security" of external borders, on externalising the problems on Europe's expanding periphery to zones where a lower standard of rights and protection applies. These themes are not new in European politics, but a decade of persistent crises has served to put them at the centre of the continental agenda.

Crisis and Continuity

This book addresses the impact of the politicisation of "Europe" in national politics, particularly though not exclusively through the prism of burgeoning populist right-wing narratives about migration. It adds to a growing literature addressing the impact of crisis, contestation, and public resistance on underlying assumptions about European integration. Since these themes have been focal points of cultural and political mobilisation, our methodology has drawn on ideas from social movement studies. Equally, whereas many studies focus on the experiences of the European core, this study draws on primary research that emphasises, firstly, the peripheral experience of Europe, and, secondly, the growing influence of that peripheral experience on the core narratives of European purpose, as highlighted by the "way of life" controversy. Crucially, it seeks to transcend dichotomies of national sovereignty versus the cosmopolitan outlook the European Commission represents for the populist right in Hungary, Greece, Italy, Poland and UK. Instead, it examines the complex interplay of conflict, coalition, and incorporation between these actors, and how both address their messages to "audiences" at the national and European level. This is our second contribution to studying social mobilisation.

Historically, most theories of European order were devised to explain the puzzle of success (see Haas, 2008; Milward et al., 2000; Moravcsik, 1993). How did the rival interests of post-imperial states, which had twice driven the world to war, end up producing, against all odds, the appearance of a higher mode of social harmony and cosmopolitan order? In the neo-functionalist tradition, the project of integration at the top level would eventually drive cohesion and solidarity at the level of citizens: small steps are taken that imply subsequent and further steps of coordination, with public opinion trailing afterwards. For Milward (2000), in the neo-realist tradition, European integration had "rescued the nation state" from its collapse during the Nazi invasions of the Second World War, allowing political elites to guarantee their citizens security and growing prosperity. For Moravcsik (1993), equally, order is a product of inter-governmental bargaining. These competing theories have radically different emphases in terms of actors and causes, but all are premised on a benevolent cycle involving free trade, economic growth and a "permissive consensus" in public opinion.

In the past decade, researchers, like Europe's leaders, have been forced to reckon with a succession of shocks (Börzel & Risse, 2009; Hooghe & Marks, 2009), beginning with the post-2008 Eurozone crisis, continuing with the rise of external migration following the Arab Spring (the so-called "refugee crisis"), and culminating in the coronavirus pandemic of 2020. As European institutions confronted an unmanageable crisis of currency and capitalism, this conjuncture's ideas were initially shaped by contestation from the left. Negri (2015) was not alone in contrasting "neoliberal Europe" to an emerging "democratic Europe" formed politically of Syriza and Podemos, and concentrated geopolitically in the PIIGS (Portugal, Ireland, Italy, Greece, and Spain) (see also e.g., Badiou, 2012). However, that framing was reversed after Syriza's surrender to the Troika's bailout demands, which, crucially, coincided with rising migration from the Muslim majority countries on Europe's periphery.

The next phase was dominated by contestation from the populist right, with the radical left now feeling obliged – most notably in France – to back pro-austerity candidates to stem the right-wing advance. Public protest at the ballot box was joined by governments explicitly committed to an anti-establishment, anti-immigrant agenda, principally in Eastern Europe and Italy. As early as 2011, European states agreed to suspend the system of passport-free travel within the Schengen Area, in a bid to halt a surge in forced migration following the Arab Spring. Subsequently, the events of 2015, the so-called "refugee crisis", exposed conflicts between the EU's competing commitments for internal open borders and hard external borders. Initially, events such as the drowning of Alan Kurdi prompted outpourings of pro-refugee sympathy, most famously with the German government's response. However, proposals for a Europe-wide quota for relocating asylum seekers provoked conflict both within and between states. Supported by a group of founder EU states, Italy, Germany and France, the Commission president, Jean-Claude Juncker, proposed a system to distribute 160,000 asylum seekers across the continent. A majority decision was taken to accept a similar proposal at a meeting of the Justice and Home Affairs Council, against heavy resistance from the Visegrad Group leaders that involved prime ministers of Hungary, Poland, the Czech Republic, and Slovakia. Orbán went so far as to initiate a referendum of the Hungarian public, which produced a 98.4% rejection of the relocation plan, albeit that the referendum failed to meet the necessary turnout threshold to become legally binding (see e.g., Gessler, 2017). By September 2016 the EU effectively announced the abandonment of the scheme due to non-cooperation.

The effect was to outsource problems of everyday refugee management to Mediterranean border states or to third countries, often run by brutal strongmen. Internally, everyday refugee management has often imposed disproportionately on Greece and Italy, two countries which also suffered the brunt of the Eurozone crisis, where anti-migrant hostility has shaped fluctuations of politics and the rise and fall of governments. Their problems are compounded by the ongoing effect of the Dublin Regulation, an earlier move towards integrating European protection policy, designed to prevent asylum seekers applying in multiple countries but effectively ensuring that applications can only be made in the first European point of entry, meaning that asylum seekers taking the Mediterranean route are barred from applying in the country of their choice. Thus, the system effectively distributes prospective refugees back to overburdened, overpopulated asylum systems where they are guaranteed a rougher mode of justice, and likewise guaranteed to inflame the hostility of local populations.

In retrospect, a crucial turning point occurred when Angela Merkel, having come under pressure for leading a mass acceptance of Syrian refugees, turned to the continent-wide alternative of externalising the refugee problem. During 2015, the Commission signed up to a notorious border policing deal with President Recep Tayyip Erdoğan of Turkey, a leader widely condemned for pursuing oppression against his opponents, leading to a variety of human rights abuses. Critics charged the EU with making a deal that was morally entangled with one of the most oppressive powers on the Eurasian periphery, effectively nullifying its moral authority on wider foreign policy questions. As Guy Verhofstadt remarked, "by signing up to a grubby deal with Turkey, EU leaders have forfeited any right to lecture [...] Erdoğan – and Erdoğan knows it" (Verhofstadt, 2016). By contrast, European Council President Donald Tusk insisted that Turkey offered "the best example in the world" (BBC News, 2016) of how to treat Syrian refugees (this book will offer a contrary perspective in Chapters 4 and 9, based on substantial fieldwork in Turkey). Similar deals were struck with other states, such as Libya and Morocco, with similar consequences. In Morocco, the European Parliament was forced to back the illegal occupation of the Western Sahara; the United Nations, meanwhile, has condemned the consequences of the EU-Libya deal as "inhuman".

The coronavirus pandemic of 2020 further testified to the dysfunctional nature of recent European integration. Initially, the EU was substantially hostile to border closures, before eventually being forced to concede to full closures by late March 2020. Commission President Ursula von der Leyen was forced to issue a public apology to the people of Italy for numerous failings at the level of empathy and solidarity. Controversy centred on the continued imposition of neoliberal spending restrictions at a time when such rules had palpably become a barrier to saving businesses from implosion. On the other side, previously dormant questions about the European Central Bank's role in crisis prevention were reopened by a German Constitutional

Court ruling, stating that the ECB acted illegally in 2015 when it bought up troubled government debt (Tooze, 2020). Coronavirus has thus reprised the twin conflicts over borders and neoliberal economics that dominated the twin crises of 2008–2010 and 2015. At this stage, it remains unclear which political forces will dominate this emerging conjuncture. What is likely, however, is that the European leadership will be less confident about its premises of austerity and open borders than it has been previously. This may not preclude adventurous political responses built around a reimagining of solidarity and internationalism. But it arguably does foreclose any assumptions built on virtuous cycles of economic growth and citizen consent, not to mention the various neoliberal programmes of previous decades that were designed to engineer these ends.

The overall impact of these crises has also left a legacy for social theories of Europe. It has become increasingly impossible to treat the internal workings of the nation-state as a "black box". Conflicts between political parties, between insiders and outsiders, between social classes and ethnic groups, and between voters and political establishments have become central factors shaping the course of European integration. With integration taking an increasingly inter-governmental form, and governments being increasingly wary of their limited platform of consent, interaction within the European elite becomes increasingly centred on the presumed "audience" of the domestic and European public.

Europe: Expansion and Unevenness

From its inception, the boundaries of the European project have expanded significantly, a process which has inevitably brought unevenness and tension. Since the Maastricht Treaty of 1992, the EU has not only jumped from 12 to 28 Member States, it has also assumed a host of new responsibilities, from macroeconomic policy and financial supervision to police cooperation and migration affairs. Until recently, expansion and integration scored apparent successes, which shaped the optimism of most EU theorising. Thus, the inclusion of Spain, Portugal, and Greece in the 1980s was initially controversial: all three had just emerged from dictatorships and their economic systems lagged far behind the European Community mainstream. However, thanks in part to significant structural payments from European taxpayers, all three (and Ireland) had achieved significant convergences with EU averages by the time of the Eastern European "big bang" of 2004. Not just economically, but also institutionally, these countries had become comparable with the core EU countries, exhibiting, for example the stable pattern of government transition between centre-left and centre-right politics. All seemed to share in the hegemonic European value system, a fact which added to the aura of inevitability that surrounded the integration project.

As Habermas (2012) observed, the underlying assumption was that integration would be to the mutual benefit of core and periphery. Political stability, liberal values and economic opportunity would flow to new members, while established members would get the benefits of expanding markets and cheaper labour costs. With each enlargement, the expanding frontiers of Europeanisation would also ensure a secure buffer against encroachments against "European values". But this all presumed, Habermas (2012) noted, "complementary steps of enlargement and consolidation". Each new phase of expansion would be followed by a bedding in process of catching up to European norms.

However, since 2008, notions of Europeanisation built around convergence and assimilation must be heavily qualified. Increasingly, the story has been of fragmentation, both geopolitically and in electorates. The cost of managing the Eurozone crisis has effectively meant that the rich Northern countries that stayed outside of the single currency have been semi-secluded from the costs of integration. Britain, most notably, took the opportunity afforded by the crisis to leave the EU altogether. By contrast, the so-called PIIGS (Portugal, Ireland, Italy, Greece, and Spain), peripheral countries that initially gained from European entry, suffered the brunt of currency crisis shocks (see e.g., Lapavitsas, 2012). After decades of success, their integration went backwards. Many underwent political turmoil precipitated by the austerity programmes demanded by European institutions. The crisis also exposed longstanding tensions between the major powers behind the European project, France, and Germany, with Emmanuel Macron's federalist approach running up against resistance from Merkel's inter-governmental bargaining approach. Underlying this is a basic problem in all European integration since the early 1990s, namely the growing disequilibrium between the two major continental powers that followed from German reunification and the pivoting of the continent's attention to the East.

Compared to earlier phases, eastward expansion has been a turbulent process, in economic, political, and cultural terms. At first, conflict pitted Western European populations against the entrance of poorer Eastern European workers into their labour markets. Significant concessions were made over welfare and migration to compensate for the anxieties of citizens in wealthier European countries. Since 2015, however, anti-immigrant tensions have been focused on external migration towards more easily stigmatised migrants from Muslim majority countries. In this debate, Eastern European governments have emerged as key political actors, often in active collusion with Western European right-populists who, ironically, had previously made political capital by inflaming tensions about migration from Eastern Europe.

Hungary and Poland were initially fast-tracked into NATO and subsequently the European Union as the post-Soviet countries most likely to make a quick transition to Western-style liberal norms. However, not only have they regressed into self-styled "illiberal democracies", they have also exposed the weakness of European sanctions against Member States who violate perceived ethical norms. Aside from pronounced anti-migrant and Islamophobic rhetoric, the Hungarian state under Fidesz has become notorious for attacks on freedom of the press and academic freedom; bigotry and sexism; and numerous violations of the rule of law. However, sanctions have been weak, and Fidesz still technically belongs to the EU's ruling European People's Party, albeit under suspension. Poland's problems were encapsulated by the creation in 2020 of "LGBT-free zones" covering a third of the country and most recently an ongoing conflict with the Commission over the Constitutional Court. While the EU expressed rhetorical objections, sanctions again amounted to little beyond the removal of funding for town twinning programmes for those towns with LGBT-free zones.

Thus, far from convergence towards an assumed set of European norms, there have been cases of rollback. The Southern European periphery has regressed economically and in terms of its Euro-enthusiasm, while the most fêted entrants from Eastern Europe have effectively gone rogue. The former group were disciplined by imposing intense rounds of austerity but disciplining the latter group has proved more difficult. Thus, the establishment has often responded with efforts to meet illiberal sentiment halfway: for critics on both sides of the fence, this is the purpose of the "way of life" agenda.

Politicisation/Depoliticisation/The Rise of Euroscepticism?

Much of the literature on the European Union before 2008 assumed a "permissive consensus", with the public passively accepting the economic benefits of integration without marked enthusiasm for European citizenship. Public audiences were thus subordinate in most theories to questions of functional integration and elite bargaining. This assumption of public indifference was not entirely without foundation: in most countries, opinion polls have always tended to show a broad, moderate majority in favour of

EU membership. Equally, however, on the rare occasions where the public was consulted on further steps of integration, the results were decidedly mixed. Even before the present phase of crisis, EU membership was rejected twice in Norway, twice in Switzerland and once in Greenland; in Sweden, the decision to join was narrow, with just 52% opting for participation. Danish voters rejected the Maastricht Treaty and Euro membership; Swedish voters rejected Euro membership; Irish voters rejected the Treaties of Nice and Lisbon; and French and Dutch voters rejected the European Constitution. With hindsight, it would be misleading to suggest that a passive consensus prevailed even before 2008.

Organised Euroscepticism may have been a marginal political force, studied by an often equally marginal academic cottage industry. But these cases of public resistance arguably had significant and lasting impacts on subsequent integration. Each referendum defeat tended to define the nature of post-Maastricht integration in a less federalist and more intergovernmental direction. Jacques Delors, for instance, was forced to substantially modify his federalist vision for economic integration after the failure of the Danish referendum (and, perhaps more significantly, the very narrow *petit oui* in the French vote). Similarly, the succession of defeats in the 2000s ensured that the EU lacked the federalist powers to manage the range of new contradictions that emerged from the "big bang" of rapid eastward expansion and the single currency. Among other things, this effectively curtailed any prospect of a serious response to the 2008 crisis. A last and important effect of public resistance was to curtail efforts at establishing a mode of European citizenship. Faced with defeats, government elites were less and less inclined to involve the public in any way, particularly where plebiscites were involved (the Brexit referendum being a notable and confounding exception). Tentative approaches to public involvement have been curtailed.

The overall conclusion must be that public mobilisation, even before 2008, has served as a limitation on the federalist ambition of some political elites; and, conversely, other political elites (here, the Danish case is instructive) have mobilised public opposition to extract concessions towards national sovereignty.

Nonetheless, the post-crisis emergence of organised "populist" resistance has made a marked qualitative impact on ideas about Europe. On the one hand, European elites put ever greater emphasis on national public consent and the so-called "constraining dissensus" as a limit to their own power, ambition, and responsibility. An apparent form of self-critique became a key feature of European elite rhetoric. Donald Tusk remarked: "Obsessed with the idea of instant and total integration, we failed to notice that ordinary people, the citizens of Europe, do not share our Euro-enthusiasm". Herman Van Rompuy likewise conceded, "Without public support, Europe cannot go forward [...] This is something I know all leaders, in Brussels and in our member states, realise acutely". Thus, while there has been evidence that structures such as the Eurozone currency will not function effectively without further federalisation, actors at the European level stress their inability to advance the project further.

Conversely, the politicising effect of populist actors may have paradoxically served to restore some measure of legitimacy to EU democracy. For decades, turnout has declined at election after election to the European Parliament, a fact which became synonymous with what Mair (2013) called the "void" separating political elites and voters. However, the elections of 2019, taking place in the shadow of rising populist power and Brexit negotiations, brought a surge of apparent voter enthusiasm, with turnout rising sharply from 42.6% to 50.7%. Part of this can be accounted for by the populists themselves, but their performance, overall, was significantly poorer than expected. Indeed, arguably the biggest successes of the 2019 election belonged to Europhile formations such as the Greens. This lends credence to Taggart's view that politicisation along the so-called "GAL-TAN" spectrum cuts both ways: fear of TAN (traditional-authoritarian-nationalist) sentiment worked to mobilise voters on the GAL (green-alternative-liberation) side (Taggart & Szczerbiak, 2004).

Cutting against this trend was by far the biggest ever practical success for organised Euroscepticism, the United Kingdom's referendum decision to leave the EU. Brexit has seen the loss of the EU's second largest country by population, second largest economy and second largest military, and is clearly a phenomenon of some significance. If nothing else, it served as a reminder that the European project can go backwards as well as forwards: previously, the notion of exit was barely imagined as a possibility, and indeed, Article 50 allowing states to leave was only thought worth enacting in 2009. Nonetheless, the UK's difficult experience of concluding Brexit has arguably served – for now at least – to reinforce continental unity, emphasising to potential imitators the complexities of breaking legal, economic, and cultural ties. This is especially true if Brexit is framed in context with the earlier notion of "Grexit", when Greece's left-wing government confronted European institutions over the country's extreme austerity package, only to find themselves forced to implement yet more radical measures. These twin cases, where European institutions seemed closest to breaking down, may have served to discipline potentially recalcitrant groups of voters and political actors.

Thus, while Mair's "void" between voters and institutions remains, there is also an "abyss" facing those who contemplate breaking apart from European institutions. The UK's ultimate success in breaking with the bloc may eventually serve to shift those calculations, but voters elsewhere have been so far unwilling to contemplate a final break, no matter how severe the burden of EU or Eurozone membership. There may be signs of resilience, and even enthusiasm, in the growing turnout of liberalised younger voters. But, in a more pessimistic analysis, the small successes of Green and liberal parties may simply testify to further polarisation and fragmentation, as the great battalions of European order, social and Christian democracy, continue to fracture.

Euroscepticism Today

An easily forgotten chapter of this story is the motivations and strategies of so-called "Eurosceptics" themselves. Very often they are classified as a public policy nuisance to be addressed rather than distinct agents with their own values, traditions, and conception of "Europe". To add to the problem, they are an increasingly heterogenous group in a confounding array of national contexts, stretching from the mainstream, governing centre-right of the United Kingdom to the far-right Hungarian government and the ideologically eclectic Five Star Movement in Italy; this is before we even consider the range of non-governing parties and movements.

One provisional conclusion from the events of the last decade is that Brexit appears to be an anomaly: the rising profile of populism has not tended towards the collapse or even the dis-integration of European institutions. Instead, as many researchers had predicted, proximity to power and increasing public profile tended to make Euro-critical parties wary of pushing boundaries. Faced with the complexities of Grexit and Brexit, and a public opinion unprepared for a radical break, populist parties tended to revise their stance towards European Union. Ahead of the European elections of 2019, leaders such as Matteo Salvini, Le Pen and Orbán all issued statements formally denying that they would contemplate breaking from European institutions. Salvini, who ran in 2014 under the slogan "No Euro", revised his position to insist that "the Euro is irreversible"; Le Pen likewise promised to "change the EU from within".

However, the above does not necessarily represent an abject surrender to federalists in Brussels. It may instead amount to a strategy of organised subversion. Indeed, populist resistance has taken more organised and ideologically coherent forms, albeit largely on the right-wing of politics (the radical left, since Syriza, having all but disintegrated as an organised component of European politics). Islamophobia, inflamed by the "refugee crisis", has served to unify political blocs with apparently conflicting agendas: Western parties that made their name opposing Eastern European migration can thus find common ground with Orbán or Jarosław Kaczyński; and Orbán, while talking up the legacy of Hitler ally Miklós Horthy, can enter into a near-formal geopolitical alliance with Israel's Benjamin Netanyahu. The EU, lacking democratic legitimacy and serious formal disciplinary powers, has felt the need to incorporate sentiments felt both at public and inter-governmental level. The former European Commission President Jean Claude Juncker even went as far as to call Orbán "a hero" whom he holds "in the highest regard". The tendency, then, has been for Euro-critical elements to accept a measure of incorporation in return for credibility. Discourses of the "European way of life" may represent the culmination of this tendency.

Importantly, our research has demonstrated that supposed Eurosceptics are not merely addressing domestic audiences on issues purely based on national sovereignty. Instead, they have sought to mobilise public opinion more broadly, across Europe. A further finding of our research is that parties and governments critical of the European Union are not necessarily wanting "less Europe", in a crudely quantitative sense. Anti-migrant populists may well demand more Europe-wide intervention on borders, more assistance with managing migration issues, and so on. Anti-austerity critics are as liable to criticise Europe for the absence of federalised mechanisms for economic management as to call for a return to national sovereignty.

The question of Europe thus revolves more around what type of Europe and how Europe is imagined in relation to its "other". Occasioned by rising immigration from Muslim majority and African countries, populist actors have drawn on tropes of European identity that seemed to have been submerged beneath the liberal consensus. The continent is imagined increasingly as a white, Christian civilisation bordered by a hostile rival civilisation which, via immigration, has its own fifth column within Europe's states. This idea has converged with anti-establishment discourses centred on the complicity of cosmopolitan insiders with growing Islamic immigration. For Caldwell, "Europe became a destination for immigration as a result of consensus among its political and commercial elites" (2009). Even relatively respectable commentators with mainstream audiences have complained that "Europe is committing suicide" (Murray, 2017) due to external migration. European identities are thus not inconsistent with xenophobic fears of the external Other, and simply asserting continental unity will increasingly beg the question – unity against what?

Outline of This Book

The book will contribute to three distinct research literatures – on Europeanisation, European integration and Euroscepticism – that occupy the broad field of "European studies". We argue that post-crisis events and processes are working to draw these sub-fields together. In common with the research agenda of postfunctionalism (Börzel & Risse, 2009; Hooghe & Marks, 2009), the most obvious example of the convergence of previously distinct "European" research agendas, we reflect the growing importance of national identities and the normalisation of movements and parties labelled as "Eurosceptic". However, our intention is to consider the added puzzles that emerge when such movements, far from leading to processes of disintegration, are instead normalised in the mainstream of European institutions. The "salience" of these populist movements (Moravcsik, 2018; Mudde, 2012) is increasingly reflected not in institutional ruptures but rather in a framing of "Europe" as a civilisation under threat, perhaps by internal enemies, but, especially, in national and the Commission discourse, by movements of external migration.

Our intention is to explore some of the limits of existing disciplinary and theoretical assumptions about the function of "Europe" in domestic politics and the impact of populist realignments on perceived European norms. The book will particularly add to the debate about the paradoxical impact of enlargement and integration, with contributions looking not just at Europe's periphery, but at the impact of Eastern and Southern politics on the European "core". We aim to transcend divisions between case study, comparative, and transnational research, looking, for example, at the complexities that emerge as populist actors increasingly develop a continental agenda for a "Europe of nations" and at the national politics and imaginary of the European border.

The book's opening section tackles conceptual dilemmas arising from recent crises, with a particular focus on the contradictions of cosmopolitan discourse. Jørgensen's chapter focuses directly on the difficulties of EU institutions and Member States when faced with the 2015 "refugee crisis". His research demonstrates how crises are constructed and the deadlock facing cosmopolitan responses, while concluding on the importance of local responses in preserving a framework of solidarity under crisis conditions. From a socio-legal perspective, Smieszek argues that the legal categories of European citizenship are shaped and limited by deeper categories of identity and otherness. Her chapter likewise takes the occasion of multiple crises to reconsider underlying questions of how discourses of European unity relate to the external world. Meanwhile, Özdüzen and Ianoşev use Twitter methodology to examine the real-time proliferation of anti-cosmopolitan discourses, particularly in response to the 2015 "refugee crisis" in Turkey at the European periphery.

Comparative studies focus on themes of emergency in relation to borders, security and sovereignty. In two chapters in this collection, contributors examine how European states have sought to insulate their own and Europe's borders under the cover of morality. Basbuğoğlu and Korkut show how Orbán and Erdoğan have simultaneously generated their own understanding of humanitarianism to serve their needs of blaming the European Union as the cosmopolitan liberal other while extending their obligation to protect beyond European borders, to defend ethnic or religiously defined affiliates. This chapter demonstrates that populist critics of Europe often tactically respond by extending the seemingly universal boundaries of humanitarian-ism to generate a scale of who needs protection. Foley, Gyollai and Szałańska compare the rhetoric of humanitarianism and solidarity in three countries on Europe's periphery: the UK, Hungary, and Poland. They find a variety of tactical responses to the dominant European discourses, with a complex framing of cosmopolitanism and sovereignty.

The case study chapters address how themes of Europe, crisis and borders have manifested in individual countries. Nicolson explores underlying themes of exclusion in Scotland, where a minority nationalist government has used cosmopolitan and Europhile rhetoric to differentiate itself in UK politics. Josipovic and Reeger explore the impact of migration discourses in Austria, where anti-immigrant and Eurosceptic populism has a longstanding role in shaping government power. Papatzani and Petracou, meanwhile, explore the interaction of two crises in Greece, a nation that experienced the brunt of both the Eurozone crisis and the so-called "refugee crisis". Finally, Hoare examines the one case of a breakaway from the European Union, with the United Kingdom's "Brexit" referendum and its aftermath. Drawing on the theories of Mair, Bickerton and Loughlin, he demonstrates the contradictions of cosmopolitan discourse and argues for the continuing importance of popular sovereignty.

References

Badiou, A. (2012). *The Rebirth of History: Times of Riots and Uprisings*. London: Verso.

BBC News (2016). Turkey "Best Example" of Treating Refugees. *BBC News*, 23 April. Available at: https://www.bbc.co.uk/news/av/world-europe-36122377 (accessed 20 October 2020).

Beck, U., & Grande, E. (2007). *Cosmopolitan Europe Polity.* Cambridge: Polity.

Börzel, T. A., & Risse, T. (2009). Revisiting the Nature of the Beast – Politicization, European Identity, and Postfunctionalism: A Comment on Hooghe and Marks. *British Journal of Political Science, 39*(1), 217–220.

Caldwell, C. (2009). *Reflections on the Revolution in Europe: Immigration, Islam, and the West.* New York: Anchor.

Fukuyama, F. (2006). *The End of History and the Last Man: With a New Afterword.* New York: Free Press.

Gessler, T. (2017). The 2016 Referendum in Hungary. *East European Quarterly, 45*(1–2), 85–97.

Haas, E. B. (2008). *Beyond the Nation State: Functionalism and International Organization.* Stanford, CA: ECPR Press.

Habermas, J. (2012). *The Crisis of the European Union: A Response.* Malden: Polity Press.

Hooghe, L., & Marks, G. (2009). A Postfunctionalist Theory of European Integration: From Permissive Consensus to Constraining Dissensus. *British Journal of Political Science, 39*(1), 1–23.

Huntington, S. P. (2000). The Clash of Civilizations? *Culture and Politics, 72*(3), 99–118.

Lapavitsas, C. (2012). *Crisis in the Eurozone.* London: Verso.

Mair, P. (2013). *Ruling the Void: The Hollowing of Western Democracy.* London; New York: Verso.

Milward, A. S. (2000). *The European Rescue of the Nation-State.* London: Routledge.

Milward, S. A., Brennan, G., & Romero, F. (2000). *The European Rescue of the Nation-State.* London; New York: Psychology Press.

Moravcsik, A. (2018). Preferences, Power and Institutions in 21st Century Europe. *Journal of Common Market Studies, 56*(7), 1648–1674.

Moravcsik, A. (1993). Preferences and Power in the European Community: A Liberal Intergovernmentalist Approach. *Journal of Common Market Studies, 31*(4), 473–524.

Mudde, C. (2012). The Comparative Study of Party-Cased Euroscepticism: The Sussex versus the North Carolina School. *East European Politics, 28*(2), 193–202.

Murray, D. (2017). *The Strange Death of Europe: Immigration, Identity, Islam.* London: Bloomsbury Publishing.

Negri, A. (2015). The New Left in Europe Needs to Be Radical – and European. *The Guardian,* 27 February. Available at: http://www.theguardian.com/commentisfree/2015/feb/27/new-left-europe-greece-democratic-capitalism-nato (accessed 3 February 2021).

Rifkin, J. (2013). *The European Dream: How Europe's Vision of the Future is Quietly Eclipsing the American Dream.* New York: John Wiley & Sons.

Streeck, W. (2016). Scenario for a Wonderful Tomorrow. *London Review of Books*, *38*(7), 7–10.

Taggart, P., & Szczerbiak, A. (2004). Contemporary Euroscepticism in the Party Systems of the European Union Candidate States of Central and Eastern Europe. *European Journal of Political Research*, *43*(1), 1–27.

Tooze, A. (2020). The Pandemic Has Ended the Myth of Central Bank Independence. *Foreign Policy*, 13 May. Available at: https://foreignpolicy.com/2020/05/13/european-central-bank-myth-monetary-policy-german-court-ruling/ (accessed 4 February 2021).

Verhofstadt, G. (2016). The Turkey Refugee Deal: Europe Sells Out. *Social Europe*, 12 May. Available at: https://www.socialeurope.eu/the-turkey-refugee-deal-europe-sells-outeurope-sells-out (accessed 4 February 2021).

Zalan, E. (2019). Defending the "European Way of Life" Name Splits MEPs. *Euobserver*, 17 September. Available at: https://euobserver.com/political/145976 (accessed 3 February 2021).

1 'The Never-Ending Crisis'

Europeanisation of Crisis Management and the
Contestation of Solidarity

Martin Bak Jørgensen

Abstract

This chapter outlines the background of the "refugee crisis" and responses by the international community in terms of refugee management. It looks at the national attempts to manage refugee-flows and the inclusion of refugees into the European Union framework and the member-states. It aims to investigate how a particular framing of the crisis has legitimised restrictive policies at the national level, which emerge against the EU regulations, but in its own particular way points to convergence of crisis management among the Member States. This movement is not characterised as institutional Europeanisation at EU level, but Europeanisation at the national level. The chapter ends with a discussion of the role of municipalism and social mobilisation as a response to the crisis.

Keywords: Refugee crisis, Europeanisation, solidarity, frame analysis, asylum policies

1.1 Introduction

When does a phenomenon become a crisis? The framing of recent controversies around migration to Europe offers crucial insights into this classic theoretical riddle. "We will only save Schengen by applying Schengen", said Dimitris Avramopoulos, EU Commissioner for Migration, Home Affairs and Citizenship in February 2016 (Migration and Home Affairs, 2016). Fourteen days previously, Avramopoulos had said that: "All Member States have to play the game and show more solidarity" (Speaking points from the meeting with the LIBE Committee, 14 January 2016). Some states followed the call

Foley, J. and Korkut, U. (ed.), *Contesting Cosmopolitan Europe. Euroscepticism, Crisis and Borders.* Amsterdam: Amsterdam University Press 2022
DOI :10.5117/9789463727259_CH01

for solidarity – but not for long, because what was known as the "refugee crisis" was erupting at the centre of European politics.

Germany and Austria did open their borders. Likewise, Sweden for a long time received and welcomed a large share of the newly arrived refugees. However, the political realities show us that the initial moment of "opening" immediately was followed by multiple "closures", including border controls, tightening of asylum law and deterrence policies (Agustín & Jørgensen, 2019). Europe indeed was – and perhaps still is – facing a crisis. It becomes more complicated, however, when we try to deconstruct the crisis framings and examine what underpins them. Although we may agree that Europe is in crisis, there is less consensus as to what kind of crisis it is. We now see a proliferation of interchangeable discourses, framings, and narratives.

The aim of this chapter is to investigate how a particular framing of the crisis has legitimised a movement towards restrictive policies on the national level, which emerge against the EU regulations, but in its own way points to convergence of crisis management among the Member States. Such a movement is not characterised as institutional Europeanisation on EU level, but Europeanisation on the national level.

While the refugee crisis framing has been the dominant one, we also find framings such as the "migrant crisis" (expanding the crisis not only to deal with the refugee situation but migration to Europe in general) or the "humanitarian crisis" which, contrary to focusing on the human conse-quences, also emphasises victimisation and creates distinctions between wanted and unwanted migrants and, ultimately, is linked to a 'crisis of the asylum system' and/or a "crisis of the European border" and border control (De Genova et al., 2015, pp. 7–14). The collapse of border regimes also turned the crisis into a "crisis of the EU", of "the Schengen zone" and ultimately a "crisis of the political idea of Europe" (Agustín & Jørgensen, 2019). On a European level, the inability to solve the crisis (or crises) and establish viable and sustainable solutions has turned it into a "crisis of legitimacy" where the EU project of peace, prosperity, and integration is far from becoming a reality. Prem Kumar Rajaram argues that "the refugee crisis in Europe is fabricated" (2015). The crisis can, then, be seen as a representation or as a particular framing. Representations are not devoid of realities, but how Europe and the European Member States respond to these realities depends on their framing/representation.

My main argument in this chapter is twofold. Firstly, I argue that the refugee management we have seen developing since 2015 is connected to the framing(s) of the crisis; and secondly, that the way both the EU as an institution and the Member States have framed the crisis has led to a management focusing on securitisation and militarisation established to face a perceived state of exceptionalism and emergency. Overall, this constitutes a new form of Europeanisation of crisis management. I argue that a "race to the bottom" in terms of setting up deterrence policies and restrictive border regimes, to avoid responsibility and burden-sharing with the EU and the Member States, has led to a stalemate where no sustainable solutions to deal with the continuing effects of the refugee crisis can be identified at the international institutional or national levels. The latest attempt to foster support for the EU Commission's New Pact on Asylum and Migration vividly illustrates this tendency. I end the chapter with a brief discussion of the role of municipalism and social mobilisation as more viable responses to the crisis.

1.2 Understanding and Theorising Representations of Crisis

Research on the refugee crisis has been developing rapidly in the last years. My chapter is positioned within the group of studies conceptualising and analysing crisis (see e.g., De Genova, 2016; Rajaram, 2015). I build on this literature and emphasise how particular framings of the crisis carry political actions, which again have consequences for the people who are governed along the lines of a given framing. To understand how framing leads to action I draw on Benford and Snow's (2000) conceptualisation of collective action frames. According to Benford and Snow (2000, p. 615), these frames have different characteristic features. Here I focus on the core framing tasks, which comprise diagnostic framing, prognostic framing, and motivational framing. Core framing tasks concern the action-oriented function of collective action frames. Diagnostic framing refers specifically to problem identification and attributions. Prognostic framing involves "the articulation of a proposed solution to the problem or at least a plan of attack, and the strategies for carrying out the plan" (Benford & Snow, 2000, p. 616). Finally, motivational framing evokes agency and mobilises support. Benford and Snow's framework is more complex than the outline given here but I employ a simplified version, as my aim in this article is to engage in a discussion of how various framings of the "refugee crisis" since 2015 have led to both convergent and divergent policy responses within the EU, among the Member States, and increasingly between local governance levels and national authorities.

What is important to stress here for analytical purposes is that a particular framing (Benford & Snow) or representation (Rajaram) can and will legitimise particular policy interventions. Rajaram argues, with reference to the refugee issue in Europe, that "crisis mobilises specific types of intervention" as the "reading of a crisis at a state's border sets up a politics of state-led intervention centred on border control" (2015). Consequently, describing something as a crisis underlines the alleged exceptionality of the event/situation/condition. Exceptionality indicates that the issue at stake is not "normal", is something out of the "ordinary" and something which signals emergency. Emergency, therefore, can legitimise governmental and EU measures aimed at enhancing and expanding border control, enforcing, and policing new measures such as externalisation, outsourcing and marketisation of border control (De Genova, 2016). It could also open for new politics and practices of humanitarianism (Agustín and Jørgensen, 2019), as a felt emergency could push for abolishment of restrictive practices. Consequently, words matter, and a particular framing that opens up the prospect of governing through exception has consequences for people governed through this.

As Kasparek (2016) has noted, "emergency management" stands out as a real unifying thread running through European interventions and measures in face of the crisis of the border regime. This led to the Europeanisation of crisis management, where Europeanisation can be defined as "a set of processes through which EU political, social and economic dynamics become part of the logic of domestic discourses, identities, political structures and public policies" (Getimis & Grigoriadou, 2004, p. 6). In this context, it takes a paradoxical shape through the (temporary) dismissal of joint EU regulations as a "race towards the bottom" to deter refugees from entering the countries. This is perhaps a controversial or unorthodox understanding of Europeanisation, but nevertheless a tentative attempt to capture the movement towards policy and governance convergence within Europe in the absence of a strong institutional EU governance. Cantat (2015) described the tensions between the EU level, the intergovernmental level, and the Member States as a "politics of Europeanism". The production of European identity has relied on exclusionary mechanisms. To trigger a sense of allegiance within the populations of the Member States, the EU has pitted populations against the figure of the "foreign other" (Cantat, 2015, p. 3). As Cantat (2015, p. 4) argues, rather than making nationalism obsolete, EU integration is instead crafting a form of hyper-nationalism. European identity is thus created at its external and internal borders – in its regime of visa and residence permits, in its retention centres, in its discriminatory policies against migrants within Member States.

These exclusionary dynamics also become tools of the Member States during the "refugee crisis", where, steered by a narrative of exceptionalism, they drive states to develop near identical policy responses aimed at protecting the nation-state. This leads to convergence towards national exceptionalism and less interference from the European Commission and common regulations.

1.3 Framing the Crisis in Europe

When analysing framings, one problem is that it is difficult to understand the developments of policy interventions from a vertical governance perspective. The EU as an institution may push for one framing and thus point to one set of policy tools; Member States may push other framings and pursue alternative policy interventions. This rival prerogative may prove detrimental to the goals of the EU. What we see is a constant interrelation between the EU and the Member States where the actions of one actor leads to a response from another. In what follows, I will therefore shift between the governance levels and rather try to follow the chronological order of events and actions than structuring the analysis according to the policy actors. The aim of this analysis is to show how the dismissal of a joint European approach led to national responses of deterrence, restrictions, and exclusions.

In earlier phases, the framing of the situation as a crisis was not predominantly used. The numbers of people crossing into Europe were nonetheless high. The year 2011, for instance, set a record with more than 58,000 people reaching Europe via the Mediterranean, which marked a sevenfold increase of the figures for 2010. The death of more than 400 people, caused by two major shipwrecks in 2013, compelled Italy to act, appealing to humanitarian principles and disengaging from the ordinary management of irregular migration by launching the rescue-at-sea programme, Mare Nostrum (Gattinara, 2017). The programme was also a call for European solidarity as Italy at the time received a large proportion of the irregular migrants coming to Europe. It was closed and reintroduced in a less costly – and less comprehensive – manner in 2014. The main framing here is not one of exceptionality or emergency. The EU reacted to the Italian approach, which they considered was not tackling the problem properly. Rather than stopping unwanted migration, it allegedly indirectly promoted it. Ferrucio Pastore claims that (2017: 31) Mare Nostrum was a "technical success but a political failure", as the programme was criticised not only within Italy but also by European countries that saw it as indirectly encouraging and even facilitating migration. The humanitarian framing in this way was challenged by a counter-frame stressing border protection. However, it was not regarded as something that was out of control or that called for suspension of existing policy frameworks.

1.4 Triggering Events – The Emergence of the Crisis

Three events in 2015 inaugurated what has since been described as the refugee crisis (Agustín & Jørgensen, 2019). The first occurred on 19 April 2015, when a ship transporting over 800 migrants and refugees capsized en route from Tripoli to Italy and nearly all aboard drowned or went missing. The second incident was the response to the images of the drowned Syrian child Alan Kurdi, who was found on 3 September near Bodrum in Turkey after a failed attempt to reach the Greek island of Kos with his family. The third event happened the day after 4 September. Thousands of migrants and refugees had camped at the Budapest Keleti railway station, and the Hungarian police had started to deny them access to the trains, rerouting them towards detention camps outside the city (De Genova, 2016). These incidents represent a particular spatialised version of the crisis. If we look at the development from the perspective of Greece, the crisis enters a new stage with the closure of the Balkan corridor. For the Northern countries, the crisis was an abstract event until hundreds of refugees started marching on the Danish highways towards Sweden (Agustín & Jørgensen, 2019). What unites these examples is the framing of a situation being both unprecedented (not necessarily in reality as much as in the perception) and uncontrollable.

It is difficult to find any institutionalised humanitarianism on a European level, which would be indicative of a Europeanisation of solidarity. The Member States on their own initiatives abolished the common regulations. In Hungary, the authorities capitulated and, with opportunistic motivations, assisted those marching towards Austria and Germany subsequently declared their borders to be open. A few months previously, in May 2015, the European Commission had launched the European Agenda on Migration. At the top of the agenda was fighting human "trafficking". The diagnostic framing of the refugee issue on the agenda was to reduce the incentives for irregular migration, which could then pave the way to a managed asylum procedure based on solidarity among the Member States. The motivational framing of this issue failed, however, as the Member States on their own initiative suspended the Dublin Procedure, as they all believed that the EU system could not handle the circumstances. Examining the different framings of the crisis, no one pays much attention to the people at stake, the people on the move who are being governed along the lines of a "disaster".

The way the crisis was framed and dealt with had dire consequences for such people, but from the perspective of the Member States the consequences discussed relate to the consequences for the Member States themselves and less to the circumstances of the people on the move, that is, the migrants/refugees.

The refugee crisis caused a "domino effect" when groups of migrants/refugees advanced from the Southern and Southeast part of Europe towards Central and Northern Europe. Within a very short time, most of the EU Member States claimed that they were unable to cope with the situation, and they found themselves in states of emergency, which called for – but also allowed for – exceptional measures that breached the principles of the Schengen Agreement (Agustín & Jørgensen, 2019). The main framing here is not only based on securitisation but on exceptionality. The situation caused problems, which could not be solved with regular policy means. Each Member State framed the issue from the perspective of the country's own interests and not from the perspective of EU solidarity. The convergence here is not based on common EU regulations, but on the logic of "each country on its own", which nevertheless emerges as sets of very similar regulations and measures. We can argue that, although there clearly was (and is) a need for an efficient common European asylum system and mechanisms for fair burden-sharing, the actions taken by the Member States point to a lack of solidarity and collaboration. What we see as an outcome of the refugee crisis are re-bordering practices and preventive measures. The EU had lost its legitimacy and was met by a lack of trust in combination with a reluctance of governments to cooperate with one another (Agustín & Jørgensen, 2019).

1.5 Institutional Solidarity – The Relocation Programme as a New Attempt at Europeanisation

In 2015 the EU launched a refugee relocation scheme aiming to transfer 160,000 refugees who had arrived in Italy and Greece to other Member States. By any measure, the scheme was a failure and it was terminated in September 2017 (according to plan). In September 2017, only 27,695 refugees had been relocated and some EU members, led by Hungary and Poland, refused to take part, even though their participation was supposed to be mandatory. EU efforts to solve the situation were based on a frame of burden-sharing, but most Member States lacking geographical proximity to the Mediterranean Sea or being first recipient countries in other ways had little interest in supporting the scheme. Moreover, responsibility for the failure of the scheme was placed on the refugees, who were accused of not having displayed the necessary patience and trust in cases where they had instead tried to move away from Greece and Italy. The French refugee coordinator Kléber Arhoul said to the Guardian: "the official relocation system, which is slow, demanding and restrictive [...] and the option to try to move freely to Germany, Austria, Sweden or France" has ended up "completely undermining the effectiveness" of the EU scheme (quoted in Henley, 2016). The relocation caused strife both between Member States and between the MEPs and national governments. Before voting on a resolution on relocation in May 2017, some MEPs accused national governments of "dragging their feet on refugee transfers" (European Parliament, 2017a) and saw what they considered a "scandalous lack of political will". One Belgian MEP, for instance, called for a respect for the Dublin rules and blamed Greece and Italy: "[They] are not managing to organise the inflow of refugees" (European Parliament, 2017a).

The general framing used by the EU (Commission, many MEPs) diagnoses the problem as lack of solidarity. Not having such will lead to a failure of common efforts and to the breakdown of the Dublin Regulation and Schengen Agreement. Hence, the motivational call here is to get things back on track by demanding that the Member States live up to their obligations by accepting the number of allocated refugees destined for relocation in other EU Member States.

1.6   The Permanence of Crisis and Contestation of (EU) Solidarity

"We are facing the biggest refugee and displacement crisis of our time. Above all, this is not just a crisis of numbers; it is also a crisis of solidarity. [...] We must respond to a monumental crisis with monumental solidarity" (UN, 2016). This call for action was given by UN Secretary-General Ban Ki-moon in April 2016. The refugee crisis is here framed as a crisis of solidarity; hence, the solution, for Ki-moon, was to let solidarity be the guiding principle for policymaking. Looking at the situation in European today (writing in the early winter of 2020), it is difficult to see any evidence of Ki-moon's pledge having been taken up. The EU did try to establish a common framework for dealing with the refugee situation. On 18 March 2016, EU Heads of State or Government and Turkey agreed on the EU-Turkey Statement. The agreement was guided by the same framing as the previous migration agenda: the goal was to "end irregular migration flows from Turkey to the EU, ensure improved reception conditions for refugees in Turkey and open up organised, safe and legal channels to Europe for Syrian refugees" (EC 2018). Under the heading "game changer", the Commission, two years after the agreement was implemented, declared it to be a success (EC, 2018, p. 1).

The number of refugees entering from Turkey had indeed decreased and in that sense the self-declared success can be seen as warranted. However, if we look at the agreement from the perspective of Greece, which has to deal with thousands of refugees who are stuck and unable to go anywhere, the success is meagre. Even in 2015, the Greek authorities could not keep up with managing incoming populations, not only in terms of a complete registration, but also with regard to means of transportation to the mainland and providing for basic needs such as shelter, food, and medical care. Makeshift registration venues were set up in ports as well as in parking lots and other available open spaces. Many of those makeshift registration venues would function as de facto accommodation "camps". After some time, some camps were discontinued, and some functioned as official centres of Greek and European "response" hosting screening centres operated by the Greek Police and Frontex – later to be named "Hotspots". The Hotspots can be said to undermine the human rights of migrants; the conditions have led to an array of dire health consequences, including suicide attempts, and human smugglers have been capitalising on the chaos and insecurity existing in these camps.

From a Spanish perspective, however, this agreement would not be seen as success. In 2018 57,000 people – that is, more than half of all undocumented migrants who made the Mediterranean crossing – came to Spain (Víudez, 2019). That number surpassed the previous peak of 2006, which saw around 39,000 undocumented migrants arriving in Spain (Víudez, 2019). Moreover, the agreement did not establish any institutional solidarity between Member States. The reinstalling of border controls is still the norm and hence a strong example of convergence on national level, but not on the EU level. The Migration and Home Affairs Committee (2019) writes that the Schengen Borders Code provides Member States with "the capability of temporarily reintroducing border control at the internal borders in the event that a serious threat to public policy or internal security has been established" and further makes it clear that:

> The reintroduction of border control at the internal borders must remain an exception and must respect the principle of proportionality. The scope and duration of such a temporary reintroduction of border control at the

internal borders is limited in time and should be restricted to the bare minimum needed to respond to the threat in question. (The Migration and Home Affairs Committee 2019)

Despite a reduction in numbers of people arriving by sea and by land, a number of countries deem it necessary to go for the "last resort". Here the production of statistics and numbers plays a crucial role in producing the crisis and in immigration policymaking.

1.7   Spectacle of Statistics – As a Driver of National Exceptionalism

Writing two and a half decades before the refugee crisis, Deborah Stone argued "the most common way to define a policy problem is to measure it. Most policy discussions begin with a recitation of figures purporting to show that a problem is big or growing, or both" (1988, p. 127). The crisis, so to speak, is dependent on politics of counting. De Genova et al. (2015) have termed this "the spectacle of statistics". People may not necessarily know if a number is "high" or "low" – if it is unprecedented or not, how the number is produced, what is included in it or not. Nevertheless, numbers and statistics inform most of the representations of the crisis and establish the sense of emergency.

Data released by the European Parliament (EP) informs us that in 2017 there were 728,470 applications for international protection in the EU, a figure which represents a decrease of 44%, compared to 2016 when there were close to 1.3 million applications (European Parliament, 2017b). Furthermore, the EP reveals that the European Border and Coast Guard Agency collecting data on illegal crossings of the EU's external borders in 2015 and 2016 registered more than 2.3 million illegal crossings (European Parliament, 2017b). In 2017, the Agency reports that the total number of illegal border-crossings into the EU dropped to 204,700, the lowest it had been in four years (European Parliament, 2017b). The EP (2017b) emphasised that "one person can go through a border more than once, so the number of people coming to Europe is lower". IOM data shows that while 390,432 arrived by sea or land in 2016 and 186,768 in 2017, the number fell to 144,166 in 2018 (IOM, 2019). The tendency seems to have continued in 2019. Hence, data shows that 15,316 people have arrived in Europe as of 4 April 2019 (IOM 2019). The same tendency, then, can be traced in the individual Member States, especially when taking into account that in 2018 alone Spain received 57,000 of the total stock. If anything, these numbers and tendencies would seem to indicate a decline in the number of refugees into Europe and, following from this, less of a sense of emergency. Nevertheless, six Member States (Austria, Denmark, France, Germany, Poland, Sweden) have found it necessary to temporarily reintroduce border controls in the period from November 2018 to May 2019 due to issues of security and threats (The Migration and Home Affairs Committee, 2019). None of these countries except for Poland has external borders with non-EU countries. Most of them legitimised their re-bordering decision on the grounds of security issues. Taking Denmark as just one example, we see a development where, having received 21,000 asylum-seekers in 2015, the number declines in subsequent years to 6,235 in 2016 and 3,559 in 2017, and more or less the same number in 2018 (Danmarks Statistik, 2020). Throughout 2019, "only" 2,716 people applied for asylum; thus, the decline seems to continue. The question is: how can so few refugees legitimise as drastic a solution as breaching with the Schengen regulations and reinstalling border control? Since 2016, the European Council has sought to restore normal functioning of the Schengen Zone and has adopted the Commission proposal on the lifting of temporary internal border controls. Yet, three years later, the list of Member States who have introduced border controls has gone from five countries to eight (EC, 2016; The Migration and Home Affairs, 2019).

1.8   Beyond the Crisis – A European Solution?

Considering the development and tendencies outlined above, we could ask if Europe is still facing a refugee (or migration) crisis? In 2019, the Commission's position on this was already very clear: No! In a publication titled "Debunking myths about migration", the Commission dismissed the first of these myths: the idea that "Europe is no longer in crisis mode" (EC, 2019a). The extraordinary situation, the exceptionality, the emergency – all that defines a crisis – is gone. In a press release from 6 March 2019, First Vice-President Frans Timmermans stated that:

> In very difficult circumstances, we [EU] acted together. Europe is no longer experiencing the migration crisis [that] we lived in 2015, but structural problems remain. [...] Continuing to work together through a comprehensive approach, in solidarity, and with a fair sharing of responsibility, is the only way forward if the EU is to be equal to the migration challenge. (EC, 2019b)

Elsewhere in the press release it is stated that "arrivals figures have been steadily falling, and current levels are a mere 10% of what they were at their peak in 2015" (EC, 2019b). The crisis, in other words, is over. The main framing of the crisis is that EU managed to deal with the situation and control the external borders – a frame which counters the assumed lack of security by, on the contrary, insisting that the EU was responsible for the re-securitisation of Europe. The crisis is dealt with in the past tense. The key lesson to be learned from the migration crisis – as seen from the perspective of the Commission – is "the need to overhaul the EU's asylum rules and establish a system that is fair and fit for purpose and could manage any future hike in migratory pressure" (EC, 2019b; author's italics). "Overhaul" is a fairly weak term given the internal critique within the EU Member States and the deep fault lines caused by the refugee crisis within Europe. An example of this division is Italian far-right leader Matteo Salvini's attempt in April 2019 to create a populist alliance within the European Parliament, with the aim of forming the biggest group in the European Parliament after the elections. The counter-frame of Salvini and the members of the alliance was one that did not identify a Europe that was out of the migration crisis but a Europe in continuous crisis, hence the motivational framing of the need for a strong Eurosceptic, right-wing alliance in the Parliament. Again, it should also be emphasised that framing the crisis in the past tense was a political discursive construction. For the refugees stuck in camps, waiting for decisions on their claims for asylum and increasingly facing deportation, the crisis is not a thing of the past but very much what defines their everyday lives. The way the crisis has been dealt with has had dire or even catastrophic consequences on these people's lives, and nothing indicates that this situation will change in a near future.

In September 2020 a fire in Moria refugee camp on Lesvos in Greece, the largest in Europe, burned down the camp. It was both a tragic human incident and a dramatic episode in the failing European Union refugee policy (Agustín and Jørgensen 2020). The actions that followed were also symptomatic of the lack of coherence between the EU Commission and the Member States. The political leaders of EU Member States quickly adopted a rhetoric of "solidarity" in response to the humanitarian crisis, like the Greek Prime Minister Kyriakos Mitsotakis, who demanded that "Europe must move from words of solidarity to acts of solidarity. We must place the migration crisis at the heart of our discussions and be much more concrete" (cited in Tidey, 2020). Countries like Germany and France encouraged other

European countries to take responsibility and host unaccompanied minors living in the Moria camp. However, the number of relocated children is far from impressive, as some countries have refused to provide shelter. The European Commission reacted promptly to the Moria case by announcing its New Pact on Asylum and Migration. The impetus to show "solidarity and responsibility", already drawn up in the Commission's response in 2015, should be concretised through specific mechanisms of solidarity (Agustín & Jørgensen 2020). It should imply a model that does not impose quotas on Member States (Chadwick & Monella 2020) and avoids of "solidarity à-la-carte", as it was labelled by former European Commission President Jean-Claude Juncker, and instead implement solidarity as a two-way street. There is little evidence for this happening, though. The new Pact could instead contribute to the uneven geographical development within the EU. Member States are expected to contribute according to their GDP and population rather than their spending power. This in turn will deepen the economic divide and the existing geographical imbalances regarding migration and asylum by privileging the capabilities of the richest countries and reducing the pressure on frontline EU states only in part (Agustín & Jørgensen 2020).

These divisions or even ruptures within Europe and between the Member States present a paradox for the Commission. When the Commission offers one diagnosis and following from that a prognosis stipulating what needs to be done, in this case a comprehensive framework, burden-sharing, and institutional solidarity, (some) Member States see things differently and depict solutions coming only from less, not more, horizontal and vertical collaboration within the EU. In this sense, the immigration/refugee issue comes to resemble what Horst Rittel and Melvin M. Webber (1973) termed "wicked" problems, that is, public policy problems for which the requisites for a solution are unclear or lacking. The paradox is embedded in the institutions of the EU. EU-wide policies are already in place and designed to handle incoming refugees. The Dublin Regulation sets the guidelines for handling the problem. However, at the same time, the institution is not necessarily fair as it de facto places responsibility on the EU countries receiving most of the migrants by land and sea due to their geographic position, which are also the countries with – at least currently – weaker economies (Italy and Greece). Without the necessary mechanisms for burden-sharing or political will on the part of other Member States for mechanisms like the relocation scheme, it is difficult to see the contours of a fair system.

1.9   Solidarity From Below – Social Mobilisation and Municipalism as Response to the Crisis

If solidarity in not developed at an institutional level, we will have to look elsewhere for alternatives. The welcome refugee movement across Europe played a big role in welcoming and assisting people on the move during the "refugee crisis" (see Agustín & Jørgensen, 2019). So far, I have discussed the Europeanisation of crisis management through the actions taken by Member States; however, we can also turn the perspective towards the local governance level and identify a turn towards solidarity among cities within the EU that have sought to provide tangible solutions to a crisis-stricken Europe.

Throughout the world, cities have responded to the disjuncture between exclusionary national migration and residency policies, and the need to be inclusive at the local level. The refugee crisis is not a "national" issue seen from the perspective of the local level. It is cities that must find a way to secure access to legal residency, social protection, and cultural belonging and accept the physical presence of illegalised migrants (Agustín & Jørgensen, 2020) – often in a contentious relationship with national authorities, as it is national governments who hold the right to issue visas, permits, residence, and so on. Yet the new municipalist surge demonstrates that the municipality is becoming a strategically crucial site for the organisation of transformative social change (Roth & Russell, 2018). If we turn an analytical gaze to the local level and to local-level responses to the refugee crisis, we can see how the crisis was framed in local particular settings. The examples of progressive municipalities point towards a growing movement of translocal solidarities between cities that have produced counter-frames for the crisis as well as alternative solutions (Agustín & Jørgensen, 2020).

One example is the Barcelona Refugee City Plan. In May 2015 Barcelona en Comú, a citizen platform created less than one year before the elections, won the municipal elections. Combining a strong social justice agenda with citizen participation, the platform emerged in opposition to the political and economic establishment. Later the same year, the City Council launched the "Barcelona's Refugee City Plan" conceived as "a citizen space to channel urban solidarity and to set up coordinated ways of participating in its application" (Barcelona Ciutat Refugi, n.d.). The Plan was a reaction against the restrictive politics towards refugees carried out by the Spanish government (Agustín & Jørgensen, 2020). The idea of "Refuge Cities" has evolved into the establishment of a national network in Spain and European Networks. Today several cities have entered networks such as "Fearless cities", "Solidarity cities", "Euro-cities", and other networks. Mayors in different cities stand together and call for action to address a problem that they are not only already facing but also that they are capable of coping with. The state is still the main decision-maker in asylum policies, but municipalism entails a new space in which to do everyday politics and to challenge the absolute lack of a humanitarian approach by national governments. An example outside Spain but comparable to the position of Barcelona is a story from Italy in January 2019, when mayors of several Italian cities refused to obey Italy's new anti-migrant law (DW 2019). The new decree (the so-called Salvini decree) strips humanitarian protection for migrants not approved for refugee status, but who at the same time cannot be deported.

1.10   Conclusion – "The Endless Crisis as an Instrument of Power"

In a 2013 interview, Giorgio Agamben argued that the endless crisis is an instrument of power (2013). Here he did not refer to the refugee crisis but to the debt crisis, the crisis of state finance, and the crisis of the EU. He went on to argue that "today crisis has become an instrument of rule. It serves to legitimise political and economic decisions that in fact dispossess citizens and deprive them of any possibility of decision", adding that "[t]he citizens of Europe must make clear to themselves that this unending crisis – just like a state of emergency – is incompatible with democracy" (Agamben, 2013). Can we, then, trace this logic to the current crisis and use it to understand the policy responses towards the refugee crisis?

The answer seems to be both yes and no. At one level, the policy logics seem to be different from the former crisis. Where the financial crisis legitimised a politics of austerity as necessary both from the perspective of the EU and from national governments, the policy responses to the refugee crisis diverge. This has to do with different framings of the crisis. However, at another level, we can also see similarities between the crises. Like the financial crisis, the European refugee crisis has also been exploited for political and economic purposes (Franck, 2018). It has led to restrictive and securitised immigration and border regimes alongside a commercialisation where, in Anja Franck's words (2018, p. 199), "commercial actors have secured profits through providing technology and infrastructure to strengthen border enforcement, but also through providing services that have aided states to house, to feed, to administer, to detain, and eventually also to deport, arriving refugees". The lived experiences and human consequences of the people met with protracted austerity politics and refugees are perhaps more similar than we would assume. Even though the number of migrants involved in the search-and-rescue operations is limited, it is an illustrative case for understanding how the refugee crisis is framed on different levels. For the EU, it is about controlling the external borders. As mentioned above, the EU did not want to maintain the costly Italian sea-rescue programme and replaced it with the less costly Triton programme. The EU's main aim is to reduce the number of incoming refugees by controlling the Eastern, Central, and Western Mediterranean routes through externalisation and commercialisation of the asylum process. This suggests that the exceptional situation that caused the refugee crisis is over. For national governments, it is not. In most countries, we can still see the strong attraction of deterrents and restrictive policies. For most national governments in the Member States, it is a matter of not wanting the migrants. For those with borders on the Mediterranean, it is matter of unjust burden-sharing. For most of the Member States, the refugee crisis is never-ending as they still claim to face exceptional challenges justifying restrictive and preventive policy measures. Here we see the new policy convergence: not driven by a Europeanisation of asylum and border policies from the EU Commission, but from a Europeanisation from the national level aiming to protect the given Member State and, in reality, making the aim of European solidarity an impossibility.

Only at a local level do we see a framing responding to the pledge of Dimitris Avramopoulos and Ban Ki-moon. However, if Europe is to be "saved", one could argue that it must happen at the municipal level. Cities cannot disregard refugees in the same manner that national politicians tend to do, because refugees are already there. We need to learn from the local-level experiences and identify best practices.

References

Agamben, G. (2013). The Endless Crisis as an Instrument of Power: In Conversation with Giorgio Agamben. *Verso Blog*, 4 June. Available at: https://www.versobooks.com/blogs/1318-the-endless-crisis-as-an-instrument-of-power-in-conversation-with-giorgio-agamben (accessed 14 January 2021)

Agustín, Ó., G., & Jørgensen, M., B. (2019). *Solidarity and the "Refugee Crisis" in Europe*. Cham: Springer.

Agustín, Ó. G., & Jørgensen, M., B. (2020). On Transversal Solidarity: An Approach to Migration and Multi-Scalar Solidarities. *Critical Sociology*, 47(6), 857-873

Barcelona Ciutat Refugi (n.d.) El plan. Available at: http://ciutatrefugi.barcelona/es/el-plan (accessed 14 January 2021).

Benford, R. D., & Snow, D. A. (2000). Framing Processes and Social Movements: An Overview and Assessment. *Annual Review of Sociology, 26*, 611–639.

Cantat, C. (2013). Contesting Europeanism: Migrant Solidarity Activism in the European Union. *INTEGRIM Online Papers* N 8/2015. Available at: https://citeseerx.ist.psu.edu/viewdoc/download?doi=10.1.1.1084.466&rep=rep1&type =pdf (accessed January 15, 2021)

Chadwick, L. & Monella, L. M. (2020). What is the EU's New Migration Pact and How Has it been Received? *Euronews.* 8 October. Available at: https://www.euronews.com/2020/09/24/what-is-the-eu-s-new-migration-pact-and-how-has-it-been-received (accessed January 14, 2021).

Danmarks Statistik (2020). Laveste antal asylansøgninger siden 2008. Available at: https://www.dst.dk/da/Statistik/nyt/NytHtml?cid=30283 (accessed 14 January 2021).

De Genova, N., Casas-Cortes, M., Cobarrubias, S., Garelli, G., Grappi, G., Heller, C., Hess, S., Kasparek, B., Mezzadra, S., Neilson, B., Peano, I., Pezzani, L., Pickles, J., Rahola, F., Riedner, L., Scheel S., & Tazzioli M. (2015). New **Keywords:** Migration and Borders. *Cultural Studies, 29*(1), 55–87. https://doi.org/10.1080/09502386.2014.891630

De Genova, N. (2016). The "Crisis" of the European Border Regime: Towards a Marxist Theory of Borders. *International Socialism, 150*, 31–54.

DW. 2019. Italian Mayors Rebel against Salvini Migrant Laws. *DW*, 4 January. Available at: https://www.dw.com/en/italian-mayors-rebel-against-salvini-migrant-laws/a-46963415 (accessed 14 January 2021).

EC. (2019a). Facts Matter: Debunking Myths About Migration. March 2019. Available at: https://ec.europa.eu/home-affairs/sites/homeaffairs/files/what-we-do/policies/european-agenda-migration/20190306_managing-migration-factsheet-debunking-myths-about-migration_en.pdf (accessed 14 January 2021).

EC. (2019b). European Commission – Press release. The European Agenda on Migration: EU Needs to Sustain Progress Made over the Past 4 Years. Brussels, 6 March 2019.

EC. (2016). European Commission – Press release. Back to Schengen: Council Adopts Commission Proposal on Next Steps towards Lifting of Temporary Internal Border Controls. Brussels, 12 May 2016.

EC. (2018). EU-Turkey Statement Two Years On. April 2018. Available at: https://ec.europa.eu/home-affairs/sites/homeaffairs/files/what-we-do/policies/european-agenda-migration/20180314_eu-turkey-two-years-on_en.pdf (accessed 14 January 2021).

European Parliament. (2017a). EU Refugee Crisis: "Relocation is our Shared Moral Duty." News, 16 May. Available at: http://www.europarl.europa.eu/news/en/headlines/society/20170515STO74806/eu-refugee-crisis-relocation-is-our-shared-moral-duty (accessed 14 January 2021).

European Parliament. (2017b). EU Migrant Crisis: Facts and Figures. News, 30 June. Available at: http://www.europarl.europa.eu/news/en/headlines/society/20170629STO78630/eu-migrant-crisis-facts-and-figures (accessed 14 January 2021).

Franck, A. K. (2018). The Lesvos Refugee Crisis as Disaster Capitalism. *Peace Review*, *30*(2), 199–205.

Gattinara, P. (2017). The "Refugee Crisis" in Italy as a Crisis of Legitimacy. *Contemporary Italian Politics*, *9*(3), 318–331.

Getimis, P., & Grigoriadou, D. (2004). The Europeanization of Urban Governance in Greece: a Dynamic and Contradictory Process. *International Planning Studies*, *9*(1), 5–25.

Henley, J. (2016). EU Refugee Relocation Scheme is Inadequate and Will Continue to Fail. *The Guardian*, 4 March. Available at: https://www.theguardian.com/world/2016/mar/04/eu-refugee-relocation-scheme-inadequate-will-continue-to-fail (accessed 14 January 2021).

IOM (2019). Flow Monitoring [n.d., dynamic update]. Available at: http://migration.iom.int/europe?type=arrivals (accessed 14 January 2021).

Kasparek, B. (2016). Routes, Corridors, and Spaces of Exception: Governing Migration and Europe. *Near Futures Online* 1, "Europe at a Crossroads".

LIBE Committee. (2016). Speaking Points from the Meeting with the LIBE Committee, 14 January 2016. Available at: https://avramopoulos.gr/en/content/speaking-points-commissioner-avramopoulos-meeting-libe-committee-1412016 (accessed 14 January 2021).

Pastore, F. (2017). *Beyond the Migration and Asylum Crisis*. Rome: Aspen Institute.

Rajaram, P. K. (2015). Beyond Crisis: Rethinking the Population Movements at Europe's Border. Available at: http://www.focaalblog.com/2015/10/19/prem-kumar-rajaram-beyond-crisis/ (accessed 14 January 2021).

Rittel, H. W., & Webber, M. M. (1973). Dilemmas in a General Theory of Planning. *Policy sciences*, *4*(2), 155–169.

Roth, L., & Russell, B. (2018). Translocal Solidarity and the New Municipalism. *ROAR*, *8*(Autumn), 80–93.

Stone, D. A. (1988). *Policy Paradox and Political Reason*. Northbrook, IL: Scott Foresman.

The Migration and Home affairs. (2016). Commission Adopts Schengen Evaluation Report on Greece and Proposes Recommendations to Address Deficiencies in External Border management. 2 February. Available at: https://ec.europa.eu/commission/ presscorner/detail/hr/IP_16_211 (accessed 14 January 2021)

The Migration and Home Affairs. (2019). Temporary Reintroduction of Border Control, Available at: https://ec.europa.eu/home-affairs/what-we-do/policies/borders-and-visas/schengen/reintroduction-border-control_en (accessed 14 January 2021).

Tidey, A. (2020). Moria Camp Fire: France and Germany Urge EU States to Welcome Migrants. *Euronews*, 10 September. Available at: https://www.euronews.com/2020/09/10/moria-camp-fire-france-and-germany-urge-eu-states-to-welcome-migrants (accessed 15 January 2021).

UN. (2016). UN Secretary-General Ban Ki-moon. Available at: https://www.un.org/press/en/2016/sgsm17670.doc.htm (accessed 16 January 2021).

Víudez, J. (2019). Spain Sees New Record in Migrant Arrivals in 2018. *El País*, 2 January. Available at: https://elpais.com/elpais/2019/01/02/inenglish/1546421799_623057.html (accessed 17 January 2021).

About the Author

Martin Bak Jørgensen is Associate Professor of Democracy, Migration and Society (DEMOS) at Aalborg University, Denmark. He works within the fields of sociology, political sociology, and political science, and has recently published Solidarity and the "Refugee Crisis" in Europe (Palgrave, 2019) with Óscar García Agustín.
Email: martinjo@hum.aau.dk

2   A Meta-View Psychology of Legal Categories

Rights, Identity, and Inclusiveness in Europe

Magdalena Smieszek

Abstract

Mindful of the multiple crises in Europe and the world, a meta-view interdisciplinary perspective considers how categories of Self and Other entrenched in laws influence the European identity, as part of a social psychology that creates ingroups and outgroups. The assertion is that this intersection of psychology and legal categorisation gives human beings either hierarchical or equal social value via status, identity, and rights, whether as European citizens, intra-EU migrants, or non-Europeans seeking asylum. Moving beyond these category distinctions to a cosmopolitan human-self-identity expands what it means to be European both from a legal and psychological perspective. In this process, new movements in Europe concerning its future can bring European institutions into dialogue with European citizens, migrants, and newcomers to the EU in efforts to co-create a post-national Europe.

Keywords: European identity, legal categorisations, European citizens and migrants, human rights and dignity, social and economic rights, social psychology and law

2.1   Europe's Identity Meta-crisis

The multiple increasing, intersecting, and seemingly never-ending crises facing Europe and the world all conspire to create, or rather, to reveal, a meta-crisis of identity. To address the unfolding crises, a different kind of inquiry needs to take place – a deeper, interdisciplinary analysis of the

Foley, J. and Korkut, U. (ed.), *Contesting Cosmopolitan Europe. Euroscepticism, Crisis and Borders.* Amsterdam: Amsterdam University Press 2022

DOI :10.5117/9789463727259_CH02

psychology of identity and how the narrative of Europe is affected by the human rights of Europeans and non-Europeans in a way that ultimately creates a measurement of human value reliant on membership of an "ingroup". In this respect, Postelnicescu (2016) and Nougayrède (2016) have suggested that what came to be called the migration or refugee crisis in Europe was in fact a reflection of Europe's own identity crisis. The makings of that identity crisis go back further to factors including internal EU migration, Europeanisation in previous decades, the shifting of borders, and the establishment of new legislative systems as a union of states. In a broader sense, crisis is a psychological response to perceived threats, amplified when intersecting systems and values are overwhelmed. As reflected across this volume, this sense of threat increasingly applies in Europe: as Guild aptly observes, "identity in Europe is in flux. The differentiation between the citizen and the foreigner as rights holders is the site of struggles at national and supranational levels" (2004, p. 252).

In this chapter, I build on my earlier work in applying a social psychology lens to legal categories of Europeanness in relation to citizen and migrant's rights. My research has shown that these legal categories have social psychological underpinnings and implications (Smieszek, 2021). Here I extend this focus to European citizens who are intra-EU migrants from Central and Eastern Europe, continue to consider categories of non-Europeans seeking refuge in Europe, and propose that an expansion of rights within legal categories is connected to both jurisprudential and social movements in Europe. A reflection on the interrelation of social psychology and law provides insights into the contestations of cosmopolitanism at a time of crisis. Within all this, migration is a central issue from a meta-perspective because of its relationship to European identity. As an example, Virdee and McGeever (2018) and Krzyanowsk (2019) showed that Brexit was premised on resentments against perceived threats from migration that helped spur an identity crisis. When Covid-19 hit Europe, the Hungarian government closed its borders, with Viktor Orbán (2020) suggesting that "foreigners brought in the disease" and that he was "fighting a two-front war" – namely, migration on the one hand, and coronavirus on the other – with a "logical connection between the two". Likewise, the climate change crisis is raising fears about new influxes of migrants coming into Europe from the global south.

To pull these interdisciplinary threads together, the discussion here first considers relevant social psychology theories on identity, categorisation, and threat-perception, which serve to inform the meta-view reflection about legal discourse and policy developments. Having established that theoretical background on the psychology side, I move on to consider political theory concepts of citizenship as providing definitions that include psychological elements of status, recognition, and identification with community membership that ultimately includes rights. Turning the focus to European citizenship further points to some of the psychological expressions embedded in laws. This forms the basis for discussing the rise of labels in regard to migration, including EU migrants, asylum seekers, and refugees. I claim that the legal categories within European policies are entwined with general views about migration more broadly, particularly as they concern perceptions of migrants' worthiness, taking note of exclusionary views and policies aimed at EU migrants from Central and Eastern Europe. Taking a closer look at social and economic rights of both the citizen and the non-citizen in Europe further reveals the differentiated valuation between the categories. Finally, and most importantly, I propose that new conceptualisations about human rights, an identity based on human dignity, and new social movements in Europe have emerged to redefine Europeanness.

2.2 The Social Psychology of Identity Categorisation

Although it is not always explicit, numerous scholarly disciplines have explored a social psychological element in establishing that the process of defining the "Self" involves identifying an "Other". In applying this Self–Other conceptualisation to international relations, the European Union has been referred to as "an enlarged in-group" in which Member States define themselves as a social group to gain psychological significance (Ongur, 2015, p. 1). Dovidio et al. (2005) explain that this view is in line with social psychology's Common In-Group Identity Model, which states that when members of different groups enter into a single superordinate group, perceptions of previous outgroup members become more positive. The recategorisation into a higher-level category of inclusiveness – which EU membership attempts to achieve – can change the biases that attach to nationalities. However, more resistant biases may even increase to re-establish group distinctiveness (Dovidio et al., 2005, pp. 253–256). Space for holding multiple identities, which European citizenship aims for, can moderate group status and social values. In this sense, identities have been described as complex constellations of "We-groups" consisting of the "Self/We" which, according to Flockhart (2006, p. 94), are often placed in hierarchies between the "Significant We" and the Other. In this case, the EU has been described as the Self/We, an ingroup that provides its members with higher self-esteem by heightening their political and economic standing, as well as providing "a better cognitive point of social comparison" through a European identity that is a higher level of social identity (Ongur, 2015, p. 80).

Other theories in social psychology analyse this mode of ingroup formation by looking specifically at categorisation. Social Identity Theory names social categorisation as the first of three mental steps, alongside social identification and social comparison (Tajfel & Turner, 1979; Tajfel, 1981, p. 254). Social categorisation refers to the basic distinction between the group containing the Self and other groups, followed by social identification in which the identity of the group is adopted by conforming to behaviours and norms. This process comes with emotional attachments in which group members develop a sense of worth. In the third stage of the process, social comparison involves a relationship and contrast with other groups that ensures one's ingroup is viewed positively (Tajfel & Turner, 1979; Tajfel, 1981, p. 254). Furthermore, Self-Categorisation Theory suggests that individuals create categories of identity at different levels of abstraction. At the highest level of abstraction is identifying as human, while the lower levels are the individual self and the group categories to which the individual belongs (Turner, 1985). Social psychology further explains that ingroup categories are created by cognitively minimising differences between ingroup members while exaggerating differences from outgroups (Tajfel, 1969; Abrams, 1985). Not only does the value given to an ingroup create more positive feelings, but studies also show that the memories of group members become more positive, and that members are more helpful to one another and less trusting of outgroup members (Park & Rothbart, 1982; Wilder, 1981; Howard & Rothbart, 1980; Worchel et al., 1998; Insko et al., 2001; Otten & Moskowitz, 2000; and Hogg & Hains, 1996).

Threat-perception is also a key component in categorisations of ingroups and outgroups that underlie social exclusion (Abrams, Hogg, & Marques, 2005). The othering of foreigners as threats has been explained by Inter-Group Threat Theory, also referred to as Integrated Threat Theory, where group members perceive another group as potentially harmful and prejudices are formed (Stephan & Stephan, 2000). Applied to migration, these theories have led to numerous studies showing how perceived threats about migrants and social identity perceptions related to group status correlate with exclusionary anti-migrant attitudes (Smynov et al., 2020; Nyla et al., 1999). Since the psychological perceptions of threats can be linked to policy responses both at the national and European level, laws and policies have been referred to as "identity technologies" because they construct collective identities facilitated by political figures (Karolewski, 2000, p. 47). Karolewski (2000, p. 47) further notes that political figures solidify collective identities through political practices because they "categorise and classify people by assigning them to categories which are associated with consequential identities" (also see Prentoulis, 2001).

2.3   The Category of European Citizenship

Categories of citizenship have social psychological underpinnings (Stevenson et al., 2015; Condor, 2011). Within citizenship, there are observable psychological components of social categorisation, self-categorising as a common ingroup, and perceiving threats from outsiders (Smieszek, 2021). Heater (2004, p. 1) described citizenship as a sociopolitical identity in which the individual has "a status, a feeling about the relationship". That status must be recognised by others to give a person value, equal or otherwise, under the law. Recognition of individuals' citizenship, therefore, is a process of identification in that what is recognised is other people's attributes or properties as either identical or similar, just as in the psychological process of establishing commonalities and minimising of differences (Isin, 1999, p. 19). This view of citizenship as a reflection of identity has been described as a "feeling of belonging", referring to the "affective ties of solidarity with a group" (Lister & Pia, 2008, p. 74). The identity-based feeling of belonging and solidarity in turn creates expectations of duties and entitlements within the group that are enforced by reciprocity in the form of institutionalised rights within a given community (Smieszek, 2021). It is therefore this reciprocal connection of rights and duties as a member of a political community of belonging that has defined the concept of citizenship as a status of having rights.

Extending the concept of citizenship to the supranational level, European citizenship is therefore an enlarged identity formation that involves recognition of the European Self that comes with a status and a set of rights (Smieszek, 2021). It aims to create a common European ingroup by giving legal value to this status category and its members. Within the social group categories of European citizenship and national citizenship, when contrasted with non-members, a higher valuation via legal rights is intended and can have the effect of a higher emotional and cognitive valuation, and therefore stronger social cohesion. In fact, European citizenship is said to have been created as an attempt to instil a positive feeling of belonging to a preconceived construct of Europe (Martinello, 1995, p. 46). While the positive effect is not guaranteed, the assertion can have cognitive and emotional value that can serve to boost the self-esteem of those recognised and included as European if the value of that ingroup is deemed positive (Karolewski, 2000, p. 19). Legal categories entrench this valuation through the content of rights, with a visible discrepancy between the categories of nation-state citizen, European citizen, and non-citizen. At times, the unequal valuation among the categories clashes with the equalising objective of human rights, contradicting the values that purportedly serve as the foundations of a European identity.

In fact, the very origin of European citizenship is rooted in migration and the socioeconomic aspects of inter-group relations, going back to the European Economic Community Treaty of 1957 that extended free movement rights to migrant workers in another Member State, referring in Article 51 to the necessity for states to adopt social security measures to ensure such rights and freedoms. Non-discrimination and freedom of movement for workers was thus embedded in the legal framework from the outset. Moreover, the psychological concept of reciprocity becomes evident here in connecting cross-border movement, labour, and rights. Labour, viewed as a contribution to the (national or transnational) community, is exchanged for rights and protection. This exchange creates a social value of a person based on what the community perceives that the individual contributes to the community versus what is perceived as being taken (Smieszek, 2021). That is, a psychology is present in ascertaining deservingness of shared benefits coupled with human rights (Hafer, 2011). The legal concept of European citizenship therefore taps into that psychology in aiming to create a common level of rights between separate nations in order to limit rivalries and create mutual benefit, with a presumption of equality.

2.4   The Social Value Through Rights

Based on the principle of non-discrimination, European citizenship should offer social protection to non-nationals from other EU Member States – that is, a European social citizenship. However, the Maastricht Treaty of 1992, while giving legal recognition to European citizenship, only provided for a limited set of rights, chiefly civil and political, granted by provisions regarding free movement, elections, diplomatic protection, and petitions. Economic and social rights are missing in this delineation, arguably a critical element in establishing an inclusionary European identity, since rights confer social value. The rights of EU citizens were extended by the Lisbon Treaty in 2007 and the EU Charter of Fundamental Rights and Freedoms in 2000, giving European citizenship a standing of equality before the law in which

Member States are obliged to grant social benefits to citizens from other Member States (Guild, 2004, p. 240). The rights of EU migrants – European citizens in another EU country – are therefore intended to be post-national.

Nonetheless, as Guild (2014, p. 423) suggests, EU Member States seem to fear that European citizenship creates an identity that may seduce away their citizens; even more critically, there has been a perception that incoming EU migrants could impose a burden on the state. This fear of outsiders posing a socioeconomic burden, an example of psychology's Inter-Group Threat Theory noted above, has resulted in curtailing of certain rights within European citizenship, inevitably meaning that social rights of EU migrants are made provisional (Seeleib-Kaiser, 2015, p. 5). Access to socioeconomic rights for an EU migrant not only varies by country; it also depends on residency and/or registration requirements, as well as Member States' disposition to implement rules that limit rights for EU migrant citizens (Seeleib-Kaiser, 2015, p. 30). Because EU Member States have differing rules on welfare, a uniform meaning of social rights is lacking (Seeleib-Kaiser, 2015, p. 5). Consequently, EU migrants have been part of "a theatre of conflict" where the Member State aims to protect its welfare system from claims of "outsider insiders" that want equal treatment as EU citizens (Kostakopoulou, 2014, p. 430). The issue has been contested within the European Court of Justice (ECJ), with the highest number of ECJ rulings on social benefits as it relates to citizenship (Leiberd and Pierson, 1995, p. 54; Vonk, 2012, p. 6). The contestation concerns solidarity and an expanded social value through rights, wherein European citizens who are EU migrants demand the same entitlements as nationals (Guild, 2014, pp. 421–422).

Psychologically, there is a link between perceived contributions to economy and the perception of being deserving of social support – that is, a perception of economic or other threats versus perceived benefits gained by identifying with group membership, both of which are built into the legal system. An inclusive European citizenship with a broader spectrum of rights for the enlarged ingroup is yet to fully extend to migrants from Central and Eastern Europe moving to work in Western European countries. EU migrants coming from the east continue to be viewed as outsiders and stereotyped. There are examples of mainstream British media and supporters of Brexit having portrayed EU migrants from Central and Eastern Europe as an external economic threat, as criminals and diseased, and representing them with dehumanising language (Allen, 2016; Spigelman, 2013; Myslinska, 2020). This legitimised differentiated levels of citizenship, observed across the EU with political references to intra-EU mobility as "benefit tourism" and "poverty immigration", with jobseekers referred to as "welfare-scroungers" (Drzewiecka, Hoops, & Thomas, 2014; Galgóczi, Leschke, & Watt, 2011, p. 5; Poptcheya, 2014, p. 1). Such views reflect a legacy of Othering of Eastern Europeans and fear of the Others' access to social benefits without their contribution through taxes. In reality, there is evidence that overall, EU migrant citizens are contributors, as a group putting in more through taxes and social insurance than they take out in benefits, even over-fulfilling their duty in the Member State of destination (Seelib-Kaiser, 2019, p. 232; Martinsen & Rotger, 2017; Dustmann & Frattini, 2014; Vargas-Silva & Sumption, 2019). The EU's Fundamental Rights Agency (2018) outlines the areas, and related legal cases, where EU migrants face discrimination in accessing housing, employment, banking services, and education. Related to these inequalities, Seeleib-Kaiser (2019, p. 234) asserts that EU citizenship needs to evolve beyond differentiating EU migrants as economically active and non-active and that residence requirements should be abolished.

However, a "creeping process of retrenchment" has been observed, since policy strategies in some Member States that are changing the idea of free movement of persons to just another form of "immigration" based on exclusion, restriction, and sovereign control (Barbulescu & Favell, 2020). As Europe's multiple crises have unfolded, access to welfare for EU citizens has been reshaped. Barbulescu and Favell (2020) reflect on the UK and Germany as examples of two countries that have "the largest populations of free moving EU nationals" as well as having "distinct welfare state and labour market contexts". They are also said to have been leaders in dismantling non-discrimination for EU citizens, thereby undermining the post-national aspect of European citizenship (Barbulescu & Favell, 2020, p. 152). Moreover, Barbulescu and Favell also claim that these countries have pulled "the rest of Europe towards restriction on free movement rights that will largely terminate cosmopolitan claims of freedom of movement rights" (Barbulescu & Favell, 2020). One of the methods these states use is conditionality with rules of residence to impose restrictions on access to benefits – such as the UK curbing welfare by imposing "tests" that target primarily migrants from Central and Eastern Europe (Barbulescu & Favell, 2020, pp. 154–155; Bruzelius, Chase, & Seelib-Kaiser, 2015; Dwyer et al., 2019). Germany had also unilaterally reduced or restricted access to welfare benefits for EU citizens, while both UK and Germany showed evidence of increasing incentives, or otherwise not limiting them, for highly skilled and employable migrants (Barbulescu & Favell, 2020, pp. 157–161).

Thus, legal categorisations for granting or withholding access to social and economic rights can be used as expressions of psychological exclusionary sentiments. The devaluing of EU migrants has also been observed within legal discourse of European institutions. There are examples of the ECJ shifting towards a restrictive interpretation of EU social citizenship, upholding the common suspicion of non-national welfare claims as illegitimate (Barbulescu & Favell, 2020, p. 153; Menendez, 2019; Blauberger et al., 2018). Transnational social citizenship becomes expressed in EU case law as one that must be "earned" through economic activity (Kramer, 2016). Myslinska (2020) scrutinises the discourse of the ECJ jurisprudence regarding EU migrants from Central and Eastern Europe, observing a prioritisation of the values of Western European Member States. She notes that in the EU legal discourse, negative assumptions and an image of Central and Eastern European nationals that is "socially and economically inferior to westerners, as not belonging to the proper EU polity and as not quite deserving of EU law's protections" (Myslinska, 2020, p. 1). In this assessment, she also shows that the ECJ contributes to Western-centric EU identity and policies, noting that the ECJ has become more responsive to arguments based on fears of welfare tourism in which EU migrants from Central and Eastern Europe are said to be attracted by generous welfare policies (Myslinska, 2020; Bauberger et al., 2018). These migrants are found to be portrayed in the ECJ rulings as "having little knowledge, limited education and insufficient financial resources, and as lacking the ability to conform to proper middle-class behavioural practices" (Myslinska, 2020, p. 26). The ECJ jurisprudence may even be propagating antagonistic statements about Central and Eastern European nationals.

There are also observable differences, evident from political manoeuvres, in how EU Member State leaders from the East and West represent the idea of Europe and the view of migration. Insecure identities of the Central and Eastern European countries within the EU may be among the culprits. In Western Europe, there are leading proponents of deeper European supra/ post-national integration and multiculturalism. On the Eastern side, leaders advocate a nation-based, even Christian-focused identity that manifests as migration-fearing, Brussels-blaming nationalism. These identity insecurities, and therefore rejection of what is deemed as supranational imposition, can be reasonably traced to a history of Central and Eastern European states being subject to domination, most recently under the Soviet Union, hence the existential fear targeted at the EU that Brussels will be the "new Moscow" (Gallon, 2019). Thus, resistance to supranational identity, and emphasis on self-determination, likewise manifests in a perception of national identity and related rights as being degraded by migratory newcomers. Gallon (2019) suspects this existential vulnerability is validated even further by high emigration of European citizen from Eastern countries, who are then treated as second-class citizens in other parts of the EU.

Europe-wide statistics show some regional discrepancies in how Europeans feel about Europe, the EU, and European citizenship. Data from across Europe, based on respondents with sociodemographic differences, suggests that persons with lower incomes and less education feel less attached to the EU (Standard Eurobarometer, 2018, p. 16). Notably, in all parts of the EU, respondents are more attached to Europe than the EU (Standard Eurobarometer, 2018, p. 14). Divergences between Member States show up in the data, with Eurozone respondents feeling more European than those outside the eurozone (Standard Eurobarometer, 2018, p. 36). There is a socioeconomic class divide in attitudes to European cosmopolitanism and this supports the oft-cited notion of European identity as an elite-led project. In turn, elites perceive threats to a cohesive Europe as coming from nationalism and socioeconomic differences, varying between those from founding EU Member States and those from post-socialist states (Matonyte & Morkevicius, 2012). In his reflections on citizenship and collective identity in Europe, Karolewski (2010, p. 78) notes that in the EU "deliberation is discussed primarily as argument-based reasoning among experts within the political elite". Hence, the legitimacy of the EU is drawn from "the efficiency and effectiveness of elite-driven decision-making in the EU" rather than collective, free, and consensual exchange (Karolewski, 2010, p. 78). The sentiment that certain populations are excluded from political discourse and decision-making is why new movements already underway for more inclusive, participatory, and deliberative democracy are imperative. As the elected policymakers ultimately legislate the sets of rights for European citizenship, the participatory process can have a particular effect on determining how the social valuing of members within the category of European citizenship.

2.5   The Categories of Non-Europeans

In addition to categories of European citizen and EU migrants, numerous categories of non-European migrants, the so-called third-country nationals, have emerged in the process of Europeanisation. Like all categories, these labels express a psychological evaluation and social value through provision and denial of rights (Smieszek, 2021). In particular, the public and legal discourse gets muddled in the differentiation between the migrant and the refugee, two terms that have a tangled history related to distinctions based on economic criteria, one category denoting economic self-reliance and the other related to humanitarian assistance (Long, 2013). Migrants are seen as taking voluntary action seeking economic betterment: they are therefore illegitimate if they pursue an application for asylum, whereas refugees are viewed as having been forced to act due to persecution outside of socioeconomic grounds, and as such are seen as genuine asylum applicants. The category of *refugee* is seen as qualifying one for protection and therefore as deserving it, while the category of *economic migrant* is "commodified as labour subordinated to the economic needs of the host country or otherwise viewed as an economic or identity-based threat" (Sajjad, 2018, p. 47; Wilson & Mavelli, 2017, p. 11). On the other hand, the vulnerable asylum seeker can be viewed as undeserving and fraudulent if part of their trajectory is seeking economic benefit. The "benefit" sought by the state is not in question by policymakers – indeed, it is deliberate policy to seek out good migrants for the community who are seen to contribute, as opposed to bad ones who are perceived to be dependent. These "victims versus threats", "costs versus benefits", and "deserving and underserving" constructs are embedded in policies that propagate the discourse about the European Self vis-à-vis the non-European Other (Sajjad, 2018).

This rhetoric has a long history, going back to the negotiations of the 1951 Refugee Convention where the drafters struggled with the wording of the refugee category, debating passionately whether it should apply only to persons displaced "in Europe" or be of a more universal and inclusive nature. The psychological tension existed between compassionate calls for a broader definition in line with humanitarian and human rights principles, and, conversely, fears about "undesirable elements" from outside of Europe (Smieszek, 2021). This back and forth continues to reverberate within the European Union, a "long established dance", with established moves – that is, calls for primacy of national interests with warnings of unrestrained migration versus appeals for moral and humanitarian duties towards innocent victims (Hawes, 2018).

The result is an asylum system that is, at all levels – international, regional, national, local, and certainly individual – premised on the process of categorisation. Moreover, the refugee category under international law has been susceptible to interpretations that amount to psychological evaluations about identities, labels, and worthiness for recognition and assistance. In the evolution of the European laws that led to the formation of the European Union, reference to refugees was largely absent in terms of rights, an antipathy that was in evidence from the beginning of the EU project, and exclusionary measures were slowly introduced as the European common system was taking shape (Guild, 2006, p. 633). The psychological factors in post-war Europe that permitted liberal admissions were overturned from the 1970s onwards, with new categories emerging when European states created screening processes for refugee status from which came the category of "asylum-seekers" as a separate notion from refugees (Sztucki, 1999, p. 70). From the 1990s, restriction measures in Europe became even more stringent (Sztucki, 1999, p. 71).

The Common European Asylum System, which emerged at the turn of the millennium, has in it an embedded European social identity and hierarchical categorisations of non-Europeans. One of the main pieces of legislation within this asylum acquis has been the Qualification Directive providing the direction on determining refugee status or another categorisation (Directive 2011/95/EU). This process applies only to non-Europeans, in spite of the sharp criticism that this limitation has received for positioning non-Europeans as "socially and economically inferior to westerners, as not belonging to the proper EU polity and as not quite deserving of EU law's protections" (McAdam, 2007, p. 60). The Directive, proposed to be later replaced with a regulation, applies to those applicants that "legitimately seek protection in the Union" and has as its main objective ensuring that Member States apply common criteria for identifying persons as genuinely in need of international protection (Directive 2011/95/EU). These references to seeking asylum "legitimately" and "genuinely" place applicants under suspicion as to their motives and thus implies a threat (Smieszek, 2021). This is all the more the case as one of the main objectives of the Qualification Directive is to limit the secondary movement of applicants between Member States.

Within this EU legislation, two legal categories are defined: refugee status and subsidiary protection which makes such a person a "beneficiary of international protection". The category of subsidiary protection within European law extends to a person that does not qualify as a refugee could face real risk of suffering serious harm if they returned to their country of origin or former habitual residence. The categorisation of *refugee* and *subsidiary protection holder* has been criticised for creating a two-tier system owing to unequal treatment between the categories, which created a hierarchy (European Commission, 2009). The recast directive of 2011 made some corrections to its predecessor, but a two-tier system has persisted, with differences in recognition rates and the nature of protection and assistance. Indeed, socioeconomic benefits related to employment, social welfare, healthcare, and integration facilities are left to the discretion of the Member States "within the limits set out by international obligations" (Directive 2011/95/EU). The discretionary approach within national practice in Member States has resulted in the level of rights for persons granted subsidiary protection being lower when compared to those recognised as refugees, "often as far as EU law would allow" (European Council on Refugees and Exiles, 2016, p. 7). The categorisation of the statuses results in "dramatic disparities vis-à-vis most rights and entitlements" (European Council on Refugees and Exiles, 2016, p. 24).

The refugee categorisation, with its related sub-categories and labels, are clearly not value neutral (Sajjad, 2018, pp. 42–46). They are malleable in accordance with context, linked to "ideas of citizenship, the state, and understandings of the 'self' and 'other' in any given period of time" (Sajjad, 2018). The social psychological view of the non-European can bypass labelling and change status when there is a perceived act of solidarity with the European ingroup. A case in point is Mamouda Gassama from Mali, who scaled a building in France to save a four-year-old child from falling from a balcony. Upon the act of bravery that caught the media's attention, his status quickly changed from an "undocumented migrant" who was living incognito (he had crossed the Mediterranean from Libya and had papers in Italy but went to France to join his brother, where he stayed illegally) to being fast-tracked for residency and French citizenship, offered a job, and granted a personal meeting with President Macron in which he received a medal "signed by the police prefect and declaring the French Republic's gratitude" (Willsher, 2018). Likewise, in France, doctors who are refugees from Syria, Libya, and Somalia were hailed for risking their lives to volunteer in overwhelmed hospitals dealing with Covid-19, where they used their particular skills acquired from providing medical care in warzones (Perrier & Alasaad, 2020). UN reporting (UN News, 2020) noted that although refugee workers in Europe face obstacles and delays in joining the labour force, despite having expertise, there are newly introduced schemes to fast-track acceptance of their qualifications, which permits health services that are otherwise highly regulated to benefit from these needed skills.

Indeed, identities themselves are not fixed and often reliant on context and time. Refugees are not only refugees by virtue of their migratory path, but persons with stories as members of communities, professions, and families, much of which aligns well with notions of European membership. The status of legal category provides a conceptual category, and vice versa, which feeds into perceived ideas about identity. Simply put, the stories of migratory human beings cannot be easily squeezed into conceptual categories, often making the laws in place unequipped to respond to these complex trajectories. Categories that simplify the multi-layered reasons for migration have the effect of undermining the human rights of migrants

(Bakewell, 2011; Zetter, 2015). The hierarchies of classifications based on worthiness, legitimacy, and genuineness lead to justifications of restrictive migration policies (Adelson, 2004; Diop, 2014). Moreover, the migrant or refugee categories can limit or expand access to rights since "labels transform realities", determining perceptions of who deserves inclusion and in what form (Sajjad, 2018, p. 41).

2.6   The Human-self Identity

As the evidence in this book shows, there are numerous contestations of a narrative of cosmopolitan Europe. This chapter affirms this with reference to legal categorisations as part of that phenomena, which embed within European and national law the human psychological inclinations to group and separate as a means of identity-making. However, there is yet another identity categorisation that transcends the categories of citizen, migrant, refugee, asylum-seeker, or any other "Other". That is the category of human being with dignity – protection of which is a perceived European value enshrined in constitutions and the Charter of Fundamental Rights of the European Union. This legal notion of dignity extends to all persons, including persons with the least access to social and economic rights, such as rejected asylum seekers, as is being increasingly the case in European jurisprudence. Thus, the proposal herein is that this "dignity as human self-identity" is largely based on human shared values and psychological experiences of suffering, humiliation, vulnerability, and empathy, which crises also tend to reveal, in parallel with the experience of fear.

A notion of a human self-identity can be found within the concept of dignity not only because dignity is well-established in European and international law, but also because it corresponds to the highest level of abstraction that is proposed by the Self-Categorisation Theory within social psychology (Smieszek, 2021). This theory, as noted, presents a model in which human beings categorise themselves first as individuals, second as part of groups with a social identity, and third within the category of the human at the highest all-encompassing level. Importantly, social psychology studies further inform us that the sense of oneself as a human being first, as opposed to one's national identity, directly corresponds to how inclusive one is towards those in migrant and refugee categories (Nickerson & Louis, 2008).

Moreover, dignity and human rights more broadly are purportedly the foundational concepts of European identity. The Treaty of Amsterdam in its Article 6 claims that the "EU is founded on the principles of liberty, democracy, respect for human rights and fundamental freedoms, and the rule of law". According to Williams (2004, pp. 137–138), this is meant as a declaratory statement of interpretation of what has always been the case, "a fundamental precept underpinning the whole European Project and the institutions that have given it form". The Lisbon Treaty went on to reinforce human dignity as the first foundational value of the European Union (Article 2 TEU). In response to the controversy around "the European way of life" in 2019, the European Commission President, Ursula von der Leyen, made repeated references to dignity and human rights as foundational European values that need to be promoted or protected. Likewise, Margaritis Schinas, as the designate of the title for promoting the European way of life, stated to the European Parliament that being European at its core means "protecting the most vulnerable in our societies [...] It means access to healthcare, welfare and having the same opportunities" (Gotev, 2010; Timsit, 2019). The takeaway, therefore, is that dignity, as this foundational value of European identity with which to create social and economic equality across Europe, is part of the mandate to overcome the disparities created by legal and conceptual categorisation.

2.7 New Movements and Narratives Emerging Out of Crisis

The unfolding meta-crisis has the potential to strengthen all the above-mentioned identities and their corresponding legal categories: the human self-identity reliant on the concept of dignity and the European identity via European citizenship, as well as creating a stronger hold on national and local identities. This means that the categories can either come into further conflict with one another or they can be transcended and included within a "multiple identities" objective. Ultimately, the value of the human being in all its various attachments – via social, economic, and other sets of rights – is at stake. Theoretically speaking, social psychology would support any one of the outcomes.

The social psychology of human beings is both enduring and malleable, as are laws and institutions. In that sense, the result of crisis can be unpredictable. For example, while there has been observable rise of populism in Europe, a recent study suggests that it may be on the decrease as a result of Covid-19 (Sas & Daniele, 2020; Daniele et al., 2020). Moreover, although nationalist movements based on perceived threat of the non-European Other or EU migrant have certainly affected the European narrative and categorisations within law, there are new social movements emerging that counter right-wing populism. One such social movement that can be observed is the transition from human rights as foundational for European identity because of constitutional and institutional grounding to persons having more of a direct relationship with their rights-based identities. One of many examples is the civil rights organisation New Europeans, which has a large and growing transnational network that aims to create a new Europe based on principles of solidarity. The focus within the organisation is on mobile EU citizens who have found a home in another EU Member State, as well as a focus on responsibilities toward non-EU nationals. New Europeans provides a platform for local communities and regional networks to be engaged on matters concerning the future construction of Europe, and the focus is on the triad of EU citizens, migrants, and refugees.

A spurring of European movements through more online transnational connections and dialogue can also be seen in the coalition that forms Citizens Take Over Europe, created during the first wave of Covid-19 in 2020. This vast alliance of Europe-focused organisations and individuals coalesces around the idea that an EU conference on the future of Europe should have representation from citizens and in general be citizen-centred. The invitation is particularly significant considering the noted regional differences. Considering the interplay of social psychology and policies, political leaders should aim to understand the feelings of European citizens, reconcile the perspectives, and build environments of trust. Within these movements, there is an emphasis on "co-creation" with the citizens in a governance process. This includes proposals towards the use of citizen assemblies, including a transnational European Citizens' Assembly, for participatory decision-making on polarising issues during crises (Mommers & Rovers, 2020). Thus, while there may be a rise in contestation over the meaning of Europe, it may not necessarily be anti-EU, but instead a countermove towards a co-creation among Europeans citizens and the institutions at the European, national, local, and even global levels – one that is ultimately more inclusive in refining its self-definition. The initiatives expand inclusiveness by inviting diversity of voices – including those persons whose legal status categories fall outside of national and European citizenship but who are very much part of the co-creation of Europe in accordance with its human dignity ideals.

Within all this, a reflection on the European laws can give indications as to how the legal categories and their underlying psychology intertwine. European laws are part of an ongoing identity-forming exercise, struggling between individual, local, and national inclinations towards self-determining distinctions, pan-European ones towards a superordinate solidarity, and even broadly inclusive ones towards a self-identity based on human rights. The differentiation of legality and access to the economic space, expressed through socioeconomic rights, are related to social valuation and proving of ingroup membership. In short, creating value within ingroups and outgroups, the We and the Other, with a hierarchical or equality-based outcome, involves a psychological process that is revealed in the provision and denial of identity, status, and rights. In this process, the European systems and their underlying psychology shows an identity conflict: though they are cosmopolitan and solidarity-driven, members are compelled to defend their internal systems and external boundaries from outgroups perceived in various degrees as threats, whether this applies to non-Europeans or fellow European citizens. The interdisciplinary connections between the mechanics of international law and those of social psychology provide a wider reflection and meta-perspective through which to better understand the broader social discourse and the psychological experience of the construct of Europe – and its future.

References

Abrams, D. (1985). Focus of Attention in Minimal Intergroup Discrimination. *British Journal of Social Psychology, 24*(1), 65–74.

Abrams, D., Hogg, M. A., & Marques, J. M. (2005). *The Social Psychology of Inclusion and Exclusion*. New York: Psychology Press.

Adelson, W. (2004). Economic Migrants and Political Asylum Seekers in the United Kingdom: Crafting the Difference. *The Michigan Journal of Public Affairs, 1*, 1–23.

Allen, L., W. (2016). *A Decade of Immigration in the British Press*. Oxford: Migration Observatory.

Bakewell, O. (2011). Conceptualizing Displacement and Migration: Processes, Conditions and Categories. In Koser, K., & Martin, S. (eds.), *The Migration–Displacement Nexus: Patterns, Processes and Policies* (pp. 14–28). Oxford: Berghan Books.

Barbulescu, R., & Favell, A. (2020). Commentary: A Citizenship without Social Rights? EU Freedom of Movement and Changing Access to Welfare Rights. *International Migration, 58*(1), 151–165.

Blauberger, M. (2018). ECJ Judges Read the Morning Papers: Explaining the Turnaround of European Citizenship Jurisprudence. *Journal of European Public Policy, 25*(10), 1422–1441.

Branscombe, N. R., Schmitt, M. T., & Harvey, R. D. (1999). Perceiving Pervasive Discrimination Among African Americans: Implications for Group Identification and Well-Being. *Journal of Personality and Social Psychology, 77*(1), 135–149.

Bruzelius, C., Chase, E., & Seelin-Kaiser, M. (2015). Social Rights of EU Migrant Citizens: Britain and Germany Compared. *Social Policy and Society, 5*(3), 403–416.

Condor, S. (2011). Towards a Social Psychology of Citizenship? Introduction to the Special Issue. *Journal of Community & Applied Social Psychology, 21*(3), 193–201.

Dennison, J., & Geddes, A. (2018). Brexit and the Perils of "Europeanised" Migration. *Journal of European Public Policy, 25*(8), 1137–1153.

Diop, P. M. (2014). The "Bogus" Refugee: Roma Asylum Claimants and Discourses of Fraud in Canada's. *Refuge, 30*(1), 67–80.

Directive 2011/95/EU of the European Parliament and of the Council of 13 December 2011 on Standards for the Qualification of Third-Country Nationals or Stateless Persons as Beneficiaries of International Protection, for a Uniform Status for Refugees or for Persons Eligible for Subsidiary Protection, and for the Content of the Protection Granted (recast). Available at: http://data.europa.eu/eli/dir/2011/95/oj.

Dovidio, J. F., Gaertner, S. L., Hodson, G., Houlette, M. A., & Johnson, K. M. (2005). Social Inclusion and Exclusion: Recategorization and Perception of Intergroup Boundaries. In Abrams, D., Hogg, M. A., & Marques, J. M. (eds.), *The Social Psychology of Inclusion and Exclusion* (pp. 245–264). New York: Psychology Press.

Drzewiecka, J. A., Hoops, J. F., & Thomas, R. J., (2014). Rescaling the State and Disciplining Workers in Discourses on EU Polish Migration in UK Newspapers. *Critical Studies in Media Communication, 31*(5), 410–442.

Dustmann, C., & Frattini, T. (2014). The Fiscal Effects of Immigration to the UK. *The Economic Journal, 124*(580), 593–643.

Dwyer, P. J., Scullion, L., Jones, K., & Stewart, A. (2019). The Impact of Conditionality on The Welfare Rights of EU Migrants in UK. *Policy & Politics, 47*(1), 133–150.

European Commission. (2009). Proposal for a [recast Qualification Directive] – Explanatory Memorandum. Brussels: Commission of European Communities.

European Council on Refugees and Exiles. (2016). Refugee Rights Subsiding? Europe's Two-tier Protection Regime and its Effect on the Eights of Beneficiaries. *Refworld. org*, 2016. Available at: https://www.refworld.org/docid/58e1fc8e4.html (accessed 28 October 2020).

European Commission. (2018). Standard Eurobarometer 89 "European Citizenship" Report. Survey Carried Out by Kantar Public Brussels on Behalf of TNS Opinion & Social at the Request of the European Commission, Directorate-General for Communication.

Flockhart, T. (2006). "Complex Socialization": A Framework for the Study of State Socialization. *European Journal of International Relations* 12(1), 89–118.

FRA. (2018). Handbook on European Non-Discrimination Law. 20 March. Available at: https://fra.europa.eu/en/publication/2018/handbook-european-non-discrimination-law-2018-edition (accessed 21 September 2020).

France24. (2020). Hungary's Orban Blames Foreigners, Migration for Coronavirus Spread. *France 24.com*, 13 March. Available at: https://www.france24.com/en/20200313-hungary-s-pm-orban-blames-foreign-students-migration-for-coronavirus-spread (accessed 28 December 2020)

Galgóczi, B., Leschke, J., & Watt, A. (2011). Intra-EU Labour Migration: Flows, Effects and Policy Responses. 17 May, ETUI Working Paper 2009.03 (update Spring, 2011). Available at: https://papers.ssrn.com/sol3/papers.cfm?abstract_id=226404 (accessed 22 October 2020).

Gallon, J. (2019). For Eastern Europe, Brussels is the New Moscow. *Foreignpolicy.com.*, 11 October. Available at: https://foreignpolicy.com/2019/10/11/eastern-europe-eu-brussels-soviet-union-moscow/ (accessed 22 September 2020).

Gianmarco, D. et al. (2020). Winds of Change? Experimental Survey Evidence on Covid-19 Shock and Socio-Political Attitudes in Europe. CESfifo Working Paper No. 8517, Munich 2020. Available at: https://www.cesifo.org/en/publikationen/2020/working-paper/wind-change-experimental-survey-evidence-covid-19-shock-and-socio (accessed 20 December 2020).

Gotev, G. (2010). Schinas Puts on Good Performance but MEPs want "European Way of Life" Title Ditched. *Euractiv.com with Reuters*, 4 October. Available at: https://www.euractiv.com/section/future-eu/news/schinas-puts-up-good-performance-but-meps-want-european-way-of-life-title-ditched/ (accessed 23 October 2020).

Guild, E. (2004). *The Legal Elements of European Identity: EU Citizenship and Migration Law.* The Hague: Kluwer Law International BV.

Guild, E. (2014). Migration, Security and European Citizenship. In Isin, E. F., & Nyers, P. (eds.), *Routledge Handbook of Global Citizenship Studies* (pp. 418–426). Abingdon: Routledge.

Guild, E. (2006). The Europeanization of Europe's Asylum Policy. *International Journal of Refugee Law, 26*(1), 630–651.

Hafer, L., C. (2011). *The Psychology of Deservingness and Acceptance of Human Rights.* In Kals, E., & Maes, J. (eds.), *Justice and Conflicts* (pp. 407–427). Berlin; Heidelberg: Springer.

Hawes, D. (2018). Refugees in Europe 1919–1959: A Forty Years' Crisis? *Journal of Contemporary European Studies, 26*(1), 137–139.

Heater, D. (2004). *A Brief History of Citizenship.* Edinburgh: Edinburgh University Press.

Hogg, M. A., & Hains, S. C. (1996). Intergroup Relations and Group Solidarity: Effects of Group Identification and Social Beliefs on Depersonalized Attraction. *Journal of Personality and Social Psychology, 70*(2), 295–309.

Howard, J. W., & Rothbart, M. (1980). Social Categorization for In-group and Out-group Behaviour. *Journal of Personality and Social Psychology, 38*(2), 301–319.

Insko, C. A. (2001). Interindividual-Intergroup Discontinuity Reduction Through the Anticipation of Future Interaction. *Journal of Personality and Social Psychology*, *80*(1), 95–111.

Isin, E. F., & Wood, P. K. (1999). *Citizenship and Identity*. Politics and Culture series. London: Sage.

Jenkins, R. (1996). *Social Identity*. London: Routledge.

Karolewski, I. P. (2010). *Citizenship and Collective Identity in Europe*. London; New York: Routledge.

Kostakopoulou, D. (2014). European Union Citizenship Rights and Duties: Civil, Political and Social. In Isin, E. F., & Nyers, P. (eds.), *Routledge Handbook of Global Citizenship Studies*, (pp. 427–436). Abingdon: Routledge.

Kramer, D. (2016). Earning Social Citizenship in the European Union: Free Movement and Access to Social Assistance Benefits Reconstructed. *Cambridge Yearbook of European Legal Studies*, *18*, 270–301.

Krzyżanowsk, M. (2019). Brexit and the Imaginary of "Crisis": A Discourse-Conceptual Analysis of European News Media. *Critical Discourse Studies*, *16*(4), 465–490.

Leibfried, S., & Pierson, P. (1995). *European Social Policy: Between Fragmentation and Integration*. Washington, DC: Brookings.

Lister, M., & Pia, E. (2008). *Citizenship in Contemporary Europe*. Edinburgh: Edinburgh University Press.

Long, K. (2013). When Refugees Stopped Being Migrants: Movement, Labour and Humanitarian Protection. *Migration Studies*, *1*(1), 4–26.

Martinello, M. (1995). "European Citizenship, European Identity and Migrants: Towards the Post-National State?" In Miles, R., & Thränhardt, D. (eds.), *Migration and European Integration: The Dynamics of Inclusion and Exclusion* (pp. 37–52). London: Pinter Publishers.

Martinsen, D. S., & Rotger, G. P., (2017). The Fiscal Impact of EU Immigration on the Tax-financed Welfare State. *European Union Politics*, *18*(4), 620–639.

Matonytė, I., & Morkevičius, V. (2012). "The Other Side of European Identity: Elite Perceptions of Threats to a Cohesive Europe." In Lengyel, G., & Verzichelli, L. (eds.), *The Europe of Elites: A Study into the Europeanness of Europe's Political and Economic Elites* (pp. 94–121). Oxford: Oxford University Press.

McAdam, J. (2007). *Complementary Protection in International Refugee Law*. Oxford: Oxford University Press.

Menéndez, A. J., (2019). Which Citizenship? Whose Europe?: The Many Paradoxes of European Citizenship. *German Law Journal*, *15*(5), 907–933.

Mommers, J. & Rovers, E. (2020). Democracy is in Decline. Here's How We Can Revive It. *The Correspondent*, 27 October. Available at: https://thecorrespondent.com/766/democracy-is-in-decline-heres-how-we-can-revive-it/41228418-9590f2a6 (accessed 15 December 2020).

Myslinska, D. R. (2020). Not Quite Right: Representations of Eastern Europeans in ECJ Discourse. *International Journal of Politics, Culture, and Society, 34*, 271-307

Nickerson, A. M., & Louis, W. (2008). Nationality Versus Humanity Personality, Identity and Norms in Relation to Attitudes Toward Asylum Seekers. *Journal of Applied Social Psychology, 38*(3), 796–817.

Nougayrède, N. (2016). Refugees Aren't the Problem. Europe's Identity Crisis Is. *The Guardian*, 31 October Available at: https://www.theguardian.com/commentisfree/2016/oct/31/refugees-problem-europe-identity-crisis-migration (accessed 25 November 2020).

Ongur, H. O. (2015). *Minorities of Europeanization: The New Others of European Social Identity*. London: Lexington Books.

Otten, S. & Moskowitz, G. B. (2000). Evidence for Implicit Evaluative In-Group Bias: Affect-based Spontaneous Trait Inference in Minimal Group Paradigm. *Journal of Experimental Social Psychology, 36*(1), 77–89.

Park, B., & Rothbart, M. (1982). Perception of Out-Group Homogeneity and Levels of Social Categorization: Memory for the Subordinate Attributes of In-Group and Out-Group Members. *Journal of Personality and Social Psychology, 42*(6), 1051–1068.

Perries, G., & Alasaad, D. (2020). Meeting Syrian Doctors on the Covid-19 Frontline in France, *France24*, 12 June. Available at: https://www.france24.com/en/france/20200612-meeting-syrian-doctors-on-the-covid-19-frontline-in-france (accessed 20 September 2020).

Poptcheva, E-M. (2014). *Freedom of Movement and Residence of EU Citizens: Access to Social Benefits*. Brussels: DG for Parliamentary Research Services.

Postelnicescu, C. (2016). Europe's New Identity: The Refugee Crisis and the Rise of Nationalism. *Europe's Journal of Psychology, 12*(2), 203–209.

Prentoulis, N. (2001). On the Technology of Collective Identity: Normative Reconstructions of the Concept of EU Citizenship. *European Law Journal, 7*(2), 196–218.

Sajjad, T. (2018). What's in a Name? "Refugees", "Migrants" and the Politics of Labelling. *Race & Class, 60*(2), 40–62.

Sas, W., & Danielle, G. (2020). How Covid is Shaping the Way Europeans Think About Politicians. *The Conversation*, 28 October. Available at: https://theconversation.com/how-covid-19-is-shaping-the-way-europeans-think-about-politicians-146895 (accessed 20 December 2020).

Seeleib-Kaiser, M. (2019). EU Citizenship, Duties and Social Rights. In Bauböck, R. (ed.), *Debating European Citizenship* (pp. 231–234). Cham: Springer Open.

Seeleib-Kaiser, M. (2015). Social Rights of EU Migrant Citizens: A Comparative Perspective. *BEUCITIZEN*, 15 July. Available at: file:///C:/Users/tbasb/Downloads/Deliverable_6.1_final.pdf (accessed 25 November 2020).

Semynow, M., Raijman, R., Tov, A. Y., & Schmidt, P. (2004). Population Size, Perceived Threat, and Exclusion: A Multiple-Indicators Analysis of Attitudes Toward Foreigners in Germany. *Social Science Research, 33*(4), 681–701.

Smieszek, M. (2021). *The Evolving Psyche of Law in Europe: The Psychology of Human Rights and Asylum Frameworks.* Cham: Springer.

Spigelman, A. (2013). The Depiction of Polish Migrants in the United Kingdom by the British Press after Poland's Accession to the European Union. *International Journal of Sociology and Social Policy, 33*(1/2), 98–113.

Stephan, W. G., & Stephan, C. W. (2000). An Integrated Threat Theory of Prejudice. In Oskamp, S. (ed.), *Reducing Prejudice and Discrimination* (pp. 23–45). Mahwah, NJ: Lawrence Erlbaum Associates.

Stevenson, C., Hopkins, N., Luyt, R., & Dixon, J. (2015). The Social Psychology of Citizenship: Engagement with Citizenship Studies and Future Research. *Journal of Social and Political Psychology, 3*(2), 192–210.

Sztucki, J. (1999). Who is a Refugee? The Convention Definition: Universal or Obsolete? In Nicholson, F. & Twomey, P. (eds.), *Refugee Rights and Realities: Evolving International Concepts and Regimes* (pp. 55–80). Cambridge: Cambridge University Press.

Tajfel, H. (1969). Cognitive Aspects of Prejudice. *Journal of Social Issues, 25*(4), 79–97.

Tajfel, H. (1981). *Human Groups and Social Categories: Studies in Social Psychology.* Cambridge: Cambridge University Press.

Tajfel, H., & Turner, J. C. (1979). An Integrative Theory of Intergroup Conflict. In Austin, W. G., & Worchel, S. (eds.), *The Social Psychology of Intergroup Relations* (pp. 33–47). Monterey, CA: Brooks/Cole.

Timsit, A., Your Questions About the New EU Job for Protecting Our European Way of Life, Answered. *Quartz,* 3 October. Available at: https://qz.com/1721178/the-eu-job-for-protecting-our-european-way-of-life-explained/ (accessed 28 October 2020).

Turner, J. C. (1985). Social Categorization and the Self-concept: A Social Cognitive Theory of Group Behaviour. In Lawler, E. J. (ed.), *Advances in Group Processes, 2* (pp. 77–122). Greenwich, CT: JAI Press.

Turner, J. C. (1987). *Rediscovering the Social Group: A Self-Categorization Theory.* London: Blackwell.

Turner, J. C. (2010). Social Categorization and the Self-concept: A Social Cognitive Theory of Group Behaviour, In Postmes, T., & Branscombe, N. R. (eds.), *Rediscovering Social Identity (Key Readings in Social Psychology)* (pp. 243–272). Abingdon: Psychology Press.

UN News. (2020). From the Field: How Refugees are Helping Overwhelmed Health Systems. *UN News,* 27 April. Available at https://news.un.org/en/story/2020/04/1062642 (accessed 22 September 2020).

Vargas-Silva, C., & Sumption, M. (2019). The Fiscal Impact of Immigration in the UK. *The Migration Observatory at the University of Oxford*, 18 February. Available at: https://migrationobservatory.ox.ac.uk/resources/briefings/the-fiscal-impact-of-immigration-in-the-uk/ (accessed 25 October 2020).

Virdee, S., & McGeever, B. (2018). Racism, Crisis, Brexit. *Ethnic and Racial Studies*, *41*(10), 1802–1819.

Vonk, G. J. (2012). *Cross-border Welfare State: Immigration, Social Security and Integration*. Cambridge: Intersentia.

Wilder, D. A. (1981). Perceiving Persons as a Group: Categorization and Intergroup Relations in Cognitive Processes. In Hamilton, D. L. (ed.), *Stereotyping and Intergroup Behaviour* (pp. 213-257). Hillsdale, NJ: Erlbaum.

Williams, A. (2004). *EU Human Rights Policies: A Study in Irony*. Oxford: Oxford University Press.

Wilson, E. K., & Mavelli, L. (2017). The Refugee Crisis and Religion: Beyond Conceptual and Physical Boundaries. In Wilson, E. K., & Mavelli, L. (eds.), *The Refugee Crisis and Religion: Secularism, Security and Hospitality in Question* (pp. 1–22). Lanham, MD: Rowman and Little.

Willsher, K. (2018). "Spider-Man" of Paris to Get French Citizenship After Child Rescue. *The Guardian*, 29 May. Available at: https://www.theguardian.com/world/2018/may/28/spider-man-of-paris-to-get-french-citizenship-after-rescuing-child (accessed 28 October 2020).

Worchel, S., Rothgerber, H., Day, E. A., Hart, D., & Butemyer, J. (1998). Social Identity and Individual Productivity with Groups. *British Journal of Social Psychology*, *37*(4), 389–413.

Zetter, R. (2015). *Protection in Crisis: Forced Migration in a Global Era*. Washington, DC: Migration Policy Institute.

About the Author

Magdalena Smieszek is a human rights practitioner, researcher, and educator. She has a doctorate in juridical science from the Central European University, focusing on international law, as well as degrees in international relations and human rights law from the universities of Oxford, Windsor, and Calgary.
Email: magdalena.e.smieszek@gmail.com

3 Towards a Political Theory of Brexit

Sovereignty, Cosmopolitanism and Member State Theory

George Hoare

Abstract

In this chapter I examine the role and function of "Europe" in British domestic politics from the point of view of member-state theory. This analytical perspective sees European integration as above all a process of state transformation, specifically from a nation-state to a member state of the European Union, under conditions of a hollowing-out of the institutions of representative democracy. I first outline the key claims of member-state theory before using it as a frame through which to interpret both the events of the Brexit process and the arguments over identity, cosmopolitanism, and sovereignty around Brexit. I conclude with some reflections on the meaning of popular sovereignty and member-statehood after Brexit.

Keywords: Brexit, sovereignty, cosmopolitanism, European Union, member-state theory, state transformation

3.1 Introduction

In this chapter[1] I examine the role and function of "Europe" in British domestic politics through the lens of the Brexit process. The central theoretical framework of the chapter is that of "member-state theory", which sees European integration as above all a process of state transformation, specifically from a nation-state to a member state. From this perspective, the workings of "Europe" are not simply "over there" in "Brussels", in the

1   I would like to thank Philip Cunliffe, Lee Jones, Peter Ramsay, Anshu Srivastava, and Sally Turner for comments on earlier versions of this chapter.

Foley, J. and Korkut, U. (ed.), *Contesting Cosmopolitan Europe. Euroscepticism, Crisis and Borders.* Amsterdam: Amsterdam University Press 2022
DOI :10.5117/9789463727259_CH03

workings and politics of the European Union (EU), but also, and perhaps more importantly, "over here". The overlap between European integration and the decline of representative democracy is real but complex.

The widespread failure to recognise this meant that the contestation of "Europe", as witnessed through the Brexit process, treated the EU not as a political structure but rather an object onto which a range of narratives, assumptions, prejudices, and domestic political claims could be projected (Streeck, 2017a). Britain's peripheral status with respect to "Europe" offers a clear vantage point for highlighting how the characteristic views of Europe advanced in the Brexit process either tended to be limited or highly particularistic, and to have little connection (in the main) with the deeper questions of representative government that emerged at the outset of the Brexit process and remain importantly unanswered today.

This chapter starts by outlining the key claims of member-state theory, focusing on the relationship between the processes of member-state transition and the increasing hollowing-out of the institutions of representative government experienced in the neoliberal period (Bickerton, 2012; Cunliffe, 2020b; Heartfield, 2006b, 2013). Next, the framework of member-state theory is used as a lens through which to interpret the Brexit process. In particular, I argue that this "void" of representative politics (Mair, 2013) explains not only the origins of Brexit but also the protracted nature of the process, as well as conditioning the emergence of a political ideology that I tentatively term "Remainism" and whose contours I aim to map. Finally, I offer some brief reflections on the implications for our understanding of "popular sovereignty" of understanding the function of "Europe" in British politics in terms of a deeper process of state transformation and the crisis of representative democracy.

3.2   Context: The Politics of the Void and Member-statehood Prior to the Brexit Referendum

In the run-up to the 2016 Brexit referendum and after, the debate over the UK's membership of the European Union was founded on implicit assumptions about the nature of the EU and, by implication, the function of "Europe" in British domestic politics (Bickerton, 2016). For many, particularly on the right, the EU was portrayed as some sort of super-state, tending to trample on national democratic freedoms. The left, on the other hand, tended to see the EU as a gateway to, or even an instantiation of, a "social Europe" that could act as a protector of workers' rights (Davis, 2018). For others, the EU was painted as a historical peace project that looked to realise the hopes of devastated Europeans in the immediate post-war period. Each of these stereotyped views of the EU is, though, mistaken. Respectively, they ignore the small size of the EU administration and the role of national governments in EU politics; the ways in which the EU constrains national governments' responses to neoliberalism; and the real developments in the EU's relations with the rest of Europe and beyond (such as controversies over "Fortress Europe" and the EU's hard Mediterranean border) (see e.g., Kouvelakis, 2018; Lapavitsas, 2012).

To advance beyond these often somewhat simplified pictures of the EU, a network of theorists including James Heartfield (2006b, 2013) and Chris Bickerton (2012) have developed a wider theory of state transformation based the concept of "member-statehood" that has aimed to capture the process through which European nation-states have transformed into EU member-states.[2] From this perspective, each of the accounts of the EU given above are essentially looking in the wrong place for the effect of "Europe". European integration, from the perspective of member-state theory, is not primarily a process of international or supranational cultural or economic convergence, but rather of domestic state transformation. A nation-state, as one of the typical constructs of political modernity, is best described as a vertically integrated political unit, entrenching the relationship between political elites and citizens that gives the state both its political direction and, crucially, its legitimacy. Member-states, on the other hand, are horizontally integrated political units, where legitimacy and policy direction are increasingly drawn from elites' relations with their European counterparts (Bickerton, 2012).

The movement from nation-statehood to member-statehood, and the democratic deficit that it entails, was not created by the EU. Instead, it is a deeper process with its ultimate roots in the structural changes of European democratic politics since the Second World War, with those changes accelerating from the late 1970s onwards (Bickerton, 2018). The EU is more accurately seen as an outgrowth of the withering of political representation within the nation-state (Bickerton, 2012; Heartfield, 2013). As voter turnout, party membership rates (with few exceptions), rates of party identification, and stability of partisan preferences all fell in the

---

2   The analysis in this section draws on the work of the Full Brexit group of scholars, whose steering group comprises Chris Bickerton, Philip Cunliffe, Mary Davis, Maurice Glasman, Lee Jones, Costas Lapavitsas, Martin Loughlin, Danny Nicol, Peter Ramsay, Anshu Srivastava, and Richard Tuck, as well as the author of this chapter.

(particularly Western) Europe of the later twentieth century, a widespread distrust of politics and politicians pervaded nation-states (Mair, 2013). Often, the blame for a lack of political engagement and trust was put on citizens themselves, attributed variously to increased consumerism, globalisation, or the pernicious effects of media, with a general moral panic about apathy emerging as particularly marked in the mid-2000s (see e.g., Hay, 2007 and Stoker, 2006 for analyses).

However, as Mair (2013) points out, it was clear that this period was defined not just by the disengagement of citizens, but also by the withdrawal of elites into an official world of public offices and the declining capacity of political parties to play any mediating role between the people and their representatives. As elites increasingly abandoned their task of aggregating, organising, and representing distinctive and opposed social forces, the parties they led became increasingly "catch-all" parties appealing to the "centre-ground". Unable to offer voters distinctive alternatives or substantive policy differences, parties lost their appeal to voters, who increasingly withdrew into private life. As Hobsbawm (1994) had already noted, declining rates of trade union membership and church membership attested to the decline of a wider associational life and the undermining of the social bases of politics; older models of politics as the representation of social interests, such as the classic account of Lipset (1960), came to be increasingly untenable.

Consequently, elites increasingly searched for legitimacy in sources other than the mass participation of the citizenry. Their need to adapt to declining popular sovereignty explains a whole range of characteristic modes of neoliberal governance (Crouch, 2004, 2020; Streeck, 2017b). Just as the responsibility for decision making has shifted to unelected bodies, such as courts, regulators, or quangos, so too has policy inspiration increasingly come from a range of transnational policy networks (Leys, 2003; Flinders & Buller, 2006). The latter work characteristically through the creation of a series of overlapping transnational regulations (rather than, say, the creation of supranational bodies), which member-states then enact on domestic populations, transforming themselves in the process (Hameiri & Jones, 2016).

Member-state theory considers that the withdrawal of elites and citizens across Europe was mutual and came in time to be a self-reinforcing process: elites looked away from disinterested citizenries to other elites, with citizens becoming even more disillusioned by an increasingly remote and unresponsive elite. As this dynamic unfolded, this period also saw the completion of a longer-term dynamic: the virtual wrapping-up of the era of party government and its modes of popular sovereignty. Although the old vehicles remained, the 1990s and 2000s had seen them divest themselves of their substantive function of organising social conflict and structuring political division. In the words of Peter Mair (2013, p. 1) "The age of party democracy has passed. Although the parties themselves remain, they have become so disconnected from the wider society, and pursue a form of competition that is so lacking in meaning, that they no longer seem capable of sustaining democracy in its present form". We arrived at the beginning of the Brexit period, then, with exhausted and disintegrated political parties.

The disconnection between the citizenry and established political vehicles was and is not a uniquely British phenomenon. It is possible to see this tension reproduced in the politics of many European states, especially as the delayed consequences of the Global Financial Crisis have re-politicised polities across the continent (Streeck, 2017b; Hochuli et al., 2021). One of the clearest symptoms of this has been in the range of new vehicles that have looked to address the distance between "politics" and "the people". The notion of "digital parties" advanced by Gerbaudo (2018) captures this trend well: facilitated by social media and other digitised forms of communication, parties look to reduce the distance between politicians and voters. By mobilising supporters in a series of votes on party policy, any mediation between the leader and the base is reduced. Paradoxically, for all their democratic rhetoric, digital parties are reliant on prominent leaders, who come to stand in for a whole web of associations within civil society that "traditional" parties may have established. Digital parties, from a range of Pirate Parties in Northern Europe to the 5-Star Movement in Italy (or even Bernie Sanders' presidential bids in 2016 and 2020) all look to boost participation from ordinary members through a range of online mechanisms that seem a world away from older modes of party organising (Gerbaudo, 2018). In this sense, digital parties are not fundamentally in contradiction with the post-political modes of governance to which they ostensibly offer an alternative, as the 5-Star Movement illustrates, combining new modes of participation and more established modes of self-appointed or expert-driven governance (Bickerton & Invernizzi Accetti, 2018).

In summary, then, member-state theory provides a perspective on the UK's membership of the EU that focuses on the effects of European integration on domestic politics, and in particular a shift in the sources of legitimacy and policy direction of Member States. The underlying explanation of this shift lies in a deeper, structural crisis of representative politics in which the popular component of democracy – mass participation as catalysed and organised through political parties – has steadily eroded. In the next section of the chapter, I apply this understanding of the relationship between "Europe" and British domestic politics to the Brexit process.

3.3   Reading the Brexit Process Through Member-state Theory

Member-state theory also offers a clear reading of the origins of Brexit referendum process. On this account, it was precisely the "void" between rulers and ruled that generated complaints that politicians were "out of touch" or "all the same" and took no notice of popular concerns; the hollowing of democracy was perceived, particularly by working class citizens, as a loss of sovereignty (Lapavitsas, 2019). Citizens, therefore, turned increasingly to populist parties: in Britain's case, particularly, the United Kingdom Independence Party (UKIP). The threat UKIP posed to the Conservative political base prompted David Cameron's government in February 2016 to call a referendum on EU membership with the aim of pacifying UKIP's key appeal. In this sense, rather than being a "ruling class" or "Tory" project, Brexit actually began as a symptom of political decay; without the void generating UKIP, the cosmopolitan Conservative Party leadership would not have felt the need to even risk a Leave result in the referendum.

In the referendum of 23 June 2016, on a turnout of 72.2%, 51.9% voted to Leave and 48.1% to Remain. The vote saw several key splits within the electorate. First, in terms of region, England (outside London) voted by 242 districts to 52 to Leave, and Wales by 17 districts to 5. London voted 28 districts to 5 for Remain, and all Scottish districts voted to Remain. Although districts do not map exactly onto Parliamentary constituencies, it is estimated that 61% of Labour constituencies and 75% of Conservative constituencies (with a total of 64% of all constituencies) voted Leave (Hanretty, 2017), while only 158 out of 650 had, prior to the vote, declared their intention to do so (BBC, 2016). Further analysis has shown that voting Leave was correlated with lower occupational status (64% of those from C2DE socioeconomic backgrounds voted Leave), and even more so with educational inequality: other things being equal, support for Leave was 30 percentage points higher among those with only GCSE qualifications or below than it was for people with a degree (Goodwin & Heath, 2016).

Brexit was an unexpected result that did not fit in with the expectations and outlook of the political class. The Remain campaign had included the vast majority of parliamentarians, had the support of some key sections of the state apparatus (which sent a pro-Remain brochure to every household), and enjoyed a high level of support within academia. Among cultural and political elites, there was a general presumption that a Leave vote was unthinkable, or at the very least very unlikely (see e.g., Toynbee, 2016); the result was consequently a massive political and cultural shock to the liberal establishment and their supporters (Hochuli et al., 2021).

Although the referendum had an enormous effect on British politics, in and of itself the referendum result did nothing to alter the fact that British state still functioned as a member-state. Accordingly, it lacked both the technical capacity and the political authority required to implement and to take responsibility for a decision like that of the Brexit referendum (Bickerton & Tuck, 2018; Tuck, 2020). Over the previous decades decision-making had been hived off to technocratic, depoliticised forms of national and trans-national regulation with an emphasis on ensuring the smooth operation of market mechanisms and promoting international competitiveness (Cerny, 1997); there was little experience of management or implementation of a political decision whose implications did not fit this model. This led to an extended, tortuous, and frequently rancorous period of British politics as Theresa May's weak Conservative governments, ostensibly accepting of the result but dominated by Remainers and having little enthusiasm to represent the popular will, struggled to make any progress (Jones, 2018). The central limitation of the Brexit process, from the point of view of democratic theory, is that Brexit remained a democratic moment without a democratic movement (Jones & Ramsay, 2016; Hoare, 2020). That is, while the referendum itself expressed a moment of mass democratic participation, there was no corresponding democratic movement capable of subordinating political representatives to its will. After a long period of atomisation and demobilisation, the June 2016 result in one sense merely presented a crude political aggregate of 17.4 million individual votes, rather than a coherent or developed set of demands or any political party willing and able to organise or catalyse the political claims underlying the Leave vote.

Eventually, The Brexit Party emerged as precisely as a populist challenger with no emphasis on party democracy and only a thin political programme, prompting the Conservatives to replace Theresa May with a more pro-Brexit leadership (Jones, 2019; Ramsay, 2019). The political deadlock was then broken in 2019 when sections of traditionally Labour-working working-class voters lent their support to Boris Johnson's Conservatives, who promised to "Get Brexit Done" (Cunliffe, 2019). However, even Johnson's handling of Brexit still displayed the hallmarks of the processes of state transforma-tion associated with member-statehood, as described by Bickerton (2012), Heartfield (2006b, 2013) and others. The UK's future relationship with the EU was negotiated entirely in secret, with parliament eventually forced to ram through the Trade and Cooperation Agreement without any serious debates (Hoare, 2020). Much as it was within the EU itself, control over large parts of economic policy continues to be subject to secretive diplomatic negotiation. To be clear, the process of state transformation traced in this chapter is a long-term one and cannot be reversed overnight – another reason why the UK was never going to be able straightforwardly to escape the gravitational field of the EU through the right trade deal.

3.4   Debates Over Brexit: Identity, Remainism, and Cosmopolitan Supranationalism Versus Illiberal National Sovereignty?

From the perspective of member-state theory, one of the most striking aspects of the Brexit process was the extent to which the debates over Brexit in the years following the referendum dealt tangentially, if at all, with the key questions of political representation, state transformation, and the nature of the EU. Instead, there was a great confusion and casting about for explanations and accounts of this unexpected political event, focusing more on identity or cultural concerns than questions of the political structure of the EU. In other words, the void of representative democracy made itself felt through the lack of organised, party-centric responses and the divides within parties on the issues of Brexit. Moreover, it also gives some explanation of why the debate over Brexit quickly became an "identity" issue, particularly around a successful and relatively coherent Remain identity and associated "Remainism" ideology.

Indeed, the months and years after June 2016 witnessed a process through which a large majority of the political class, along with the intellectual and cultural establishment, came to embrace a position at odds with the referendum result. For some, this expanded into a concerted political project of "Remain and Reform" (or even "Remain, Reform, Revolt"). Although there was no uniformity of anti-Brexit positions, it is still worth attempting to group together some of the key determinants of the Remain position, which we can tentatively call "Remainism". This developing ideology proved incredibly influential, gaining sufficient traction within the Labour Party to influence the direction of the party's unsuccessful 2019 general election bid towards an increasingly more pro-Remain or second referendum position.

First, Remainism was in an important sense a (defensive) response to the success and appeal of the Leave campaign. Exit polls suggested that for those who voted Leave, the major concern was "the principle that decisions about the UK should be taken in the UK" (49%), but immigration was also a key issue, with 33% of Leave voters saying that their main reason for backing Brexit was that leaving "offered the best chance for the UK to regain control over immigration and its own borders" (Ashcroft, 2016).[3] Moreover, the Leave campaigns, particularly the unofficial Leave EU strand led by Nigel Farage, made a direct appeal to concerns around immigration. This was not simply a cynical mobilisation of racism or xenophobic sentiment to win the referendum. There was a direct connection between the EU and immigration, since immigration, enabled by the free movement of labour within the EU, was the one of the main ways in which the vast majority of British people had actually experienced the practical consequences of EU membership (Aber et al., 2018; Hall, 2018). Alongside the experience of immigration, there was the related experience of elite unresponsiveness, unaccountability, and aloofness (Heartfield, 2013; Mair, 2013). To many voters, this aloofness manifested in the reluctance of any of the main parties to engage in a sustained way with questions of immigration and associated changes to communities. Consequently, first the BNP (British National Party) and then UKIP were able to "own" the political issue of immigration, gaining varying levels of votes (but much lower levels of representation) prior to 2016.

It was also this combination of the experience of change and a feeling of political powerlessness (not least through a lack of mainstream political representation) that also enabled the Leave campaign to connect powerfully with voters through the "Take Back Control" slogan. The appeal of the "Take Back Control" slogan (which never had an effective counterpart from the Remain side), and its direct link to experiences of immigration, is easy to grasp from a class perspective. The defeat of the organised labour movement in the 1980s has deprived most working people of the collective organisations that would have helped them to make sense of the relentless neoliberal attack on their communities, their stagnating living standards, and a dwindling supply of public services (Heartfield, 2006a). Abandoned and feeling betrayed by the Labour Party, they were able to find in the right a framework (with questions of immigration central) through which to interpret their experiences (Winlow et al., 2017). In sum, the Leave campaign articulated a politics that combined ideas of sovereignty and immigration, to which an inchoate Remainism began to respond.

3   The major concern for Remain voters was "the risks of voting to leave the EU looked too great when it came to things like the economy, jobs, and prices", with 43% of respondents giving this as the major reason for voting Remain (Ashcroft, 2017).

However, because of their alienation from working-class communities especially, the Remain establishment tended not to grasp this dynamic in political terms, instead predominantly interpreting the result through a cultural lens. That is, the role played by immigration in the referendum campaign – punctuated by the murder of Jo Cox MP by a supporter of the far right – was seen as signifying a groundswell of racist, xenophobic, and nationalistic sentiment. As their basic outlook was that any challenge or change to the status quo could only be irrational, it is understandable that they could only explain the referendum result as the triumph of irrational sentiment (Hochuli et al., 2021).

Consequently, the result was quickly understood in terms of a clash over cultural preferences, entailing a division between the "bad", irrational Leavers and the "good", rational Remainers. In a typical article, Laurie Penny described the vote as a "referendum on the modern world", in which those with a "frightened, parochial lizard-brain" had triumphed (Penny, 2016). Polls showing that Leave voters tended to espouse conservative social values, and vice-versa, were immediately seized upon to provide a cultural explanation of the result. Much academic analysis contributed to this interpretation through arguments that Brexit had been driven by racism and imperial nostalgia, or a "cultural backlash" against progressive, modern values (see for instance Virdee & McGeever, 2018, or Norris & Inglehart, 2019). This inspired and legitimised resistance to enacting the result, which emerged almost immediately after the referendum. The moralisation of a hard-line Remain position also sparked an outraged response among many Leave voters, affronted at being branded racist, fascist and so on. In a context where party identification had withered over decades, it was rapidly overtaken by "Brexit identity", such that by mid-2018 only 6% of people did not identify with either Leave or Remain, compared to 21.5% with no party identity (UK in a Changing Europe, 2019).

Remainism as an identity had a relatively minimal conceptual structure, with two related key elements. The first element, which was structurally core, was the counterposing of "Europe" to "the nation", with the former elevated and the latter associated with nationalism and xenophobia. Importantly, the EU was then directly identified with "Europe". Streeck (2017a, p. 21) attributes the success of this identification to a deliberate "European narrative" that equated the two, confusing "a set of political institutions aligning a selection of European nation-states in a neoliberal common market with Europe as an international community of jointly produced diversity, a way of life, a civilisation, a culture, and if you will a home". Streeck (2017a) sees in this process a moral core, based in the "sacralisation" of Europe, and the coding of Brexit as "anti-European".[4] Accordingly, "Europe" is understood as open, while the nation is closed and exclusionary. The EU is linked, in this understanding, with the moral goods of cosmopolitanism (as a form of supranationalism) and freedom of movement, with the latter, in particular, seen as a moral absolute. It is worth underscoring here that this identification is something that emerged after the referendum, since fewer than one in ten (9%) remain voters gave "a strong attachment to the EU and its shared history, culture and traditions" as their main reason for voting (Ashcroft, 2017). The depth of enthusiasm for Europeanism after the referendum in this sense is best understood in part as a projection of the values that Remainers saw as under threat from their own compatriots (as explored in the discussion of the Leave campaign above). Both cosmopolitanism and freedom of movement have their function within Remainism as paradigmatically liberal ideas, linked to conceptions of "the human" and "human rights" that are not constrained to national boundaries (Cunliffe, 2020a). By contrasting Europe with the nation, Remainers portrayed themselves as "open", both to outsiders and to new ideas, while situating Leavers as "closed", inward-looking, and parochial. Emily Thornberry, way before her embrace of the EU's blue and gold, let the mask slip by presenting St George's flags in Rochester as self-evident symbols of a closed, nationalistic working-class community.

Adjacent to this core of Europeanism was an articulation and defence of the interests of the poor. That is, Remainers argued that Brexit would inflict most harm on the worst-off in society. This was always a highly contradictory element of Remainism, given that many poorer citizens had actually voted Leave (Clarke, Goodwin, & Whiteley, 2017). Again, alienated from working-class communities and so unable to understand why they might have made this political choice, Remainers could only see this as a "monumental act of self-harm which will bewilder historians" (Ashdown, 2017).[5] Particularly, poorer Leave voters then tended to be portrayed as either motivated by racism and xenophobia or manipulated by powerful right-wing elites using propaganda or online messaging techniques (see e.g., Flynn, 2017; Khalili 2016). Either perspective entailed contempt for

4   Streeck (2017a, p. 22) does however argue that Brexit may be considered a pro-European act to the extent that it both undermines an EU that does not instantiate European principles while also representing the European normative political principle that citizens are entitled to disagree with the structure of the state governing them.
5   We can note that Brexit was described, with different emphases, as an act of national or economic "self-harm" by figures as Tony Blair, John Major, Simon Schama, and Leo Varadkar, among many others.

working class voters, but leavened, in the latter case, with traces of pity and charitable concern.

This aspect of Remainism, which was not put in strictly class terms, came to be a counterposing of the working class as an object of politics with the working class as a subject of politics. The traditional socialist view included the welfare of the working class as an objective goal of politics alongside an attempt to develop the capacity of working-class people for self-government as political subjects. Within a Remain identity, the working class came to be seen primarily as the object of politics, defined above all by their vulnerability to market forces and social change. This is understandable at least in part as a defensive reaction to the Brexit result, and to concerns about the material and economic costs of exiting the EU. One of the clearest expressions of this approach can be seen in Labour's 2017 election slogan "For the Many, Not the Few"; for the many, of course, is not by the many. Seeing the working class as the object of politics was allied with a redefining of political processes as mechanisms of charity, and in particular as a very real concern for the worst off in society – those, that is, who would be most impacted by a No Deal Brexit or five more years of Conservative rule. As the front-page headline of the Daily Mirror pleaded with on election day on 12 December 2019, "Do it for them" – "them" being a series of impoverished and marginalised individuals depicted in heart-rending photographs. By viewing the working class as objects of politics or charity, rather than as subjects with political agency capable of demanding and enacting political change, the Remain identity is grounded in a sympathy for the working class, not a commitment to its self-government (cf. Tuck, 2019, pp. 67–68). More importantly, a commitment to the welfare of the working class allowed those advocating a Remain position to present themselves as charitable, and again as morally good.

Ultimately, Remainism was mostly successful in framing the debate in terms of a dichotomy between cosmopolitan supranationalism and illiberal national sovereignty, such that claims for the latter could be dismissed on the basis of an imputed racism, xenophobia, or economic nationalism. However, from the perspective of democratic theory it is clear that the notion of cosmopolitan supranationalism excludes any idea of popular sovereignty (Cunliffe, 2020b). Without a clear focus on the decline of popular sovereignty that demarcates a specific and delimited (through relation to the nation-state) political community over which citizens' votes have a binding say, any form of cosmopolitanism ultimately folds into a defence of the four freedoms of the EU (Streeck, 2020, p. 127). The next steps for democratic theory at the present juncture seem to lie in the unpacking of the relationship between national sovereignty and popular sovereignty. Brexit represents the first blow against the EU and against the associated conditions of member-statehood. The question remains open the extent to which this will allow a movement (back) towards nation-statehood, or a transition to a new political form.

3.5 Conclusions: Popular Sovereignty and Member-statehood After Brexit

One of the key implications of this crisis of representative democracy that the Brexit process clearly revealed lies in its implications for our understanding of "sovereignty". As Mair notes in his *Ruling the Void* (2013), a familiar theme in the political science of the 1960s was that the people could end up being "semi-sovereign" to the extent that they could not exert control over political decision-making. This theme returns for Mair with added force in an empirical survey of actual levels of political engagement. Mair also goes considerably further, contending that a conception of democracy without a necessary popular component has emerged, highlighting either the importance of procedural checks and balances on power or putting as central a notion of human rights. In very broad terms, these two understandings can be linked to two of the great political traditions of modernity, with an understanding of democracy as popular sovereignty linked with the history of socialism and an understanding of democracy as protections for the individual and society against the concentration of power or the tyranny of the majority associated with history of liberal thought.

What conclusions can be drawn, then, from the Brexit process in relation to this understanding of democracy as popular sovereignty? The first point to make, in developing a case for representative democracy and a parliamentary form of popular sovereignty, is that in contrast to Tory Euroscepticism, an analysis grounded in member-state theory sees the EU not as a foreign imposition on British democracy but rather as a domestic evasion of accountability, specifically through a process in which members of parliament acquiesced in their exclusion by the executive from processes of law-making (Bickerton & Jones, 2018). A key implication of that is that leaving the EU means for British democrats a potential step forward, to the extent that room to evade accountability for domestic representatives (i.e., by invoking external constraints associated with the EU) is reduced. The issue of popular sovereignty also raised its head in the question of a second referendum. From the perspective of democratic theory, a second referendum had not just the more straightforward potential risk of annulling or undermining the first referendum result, but also a larger one of undermining parliament's political authority, which is ultimately derived from its electoral mandate (Tuck, 2019).

A more reflective point can also be made. The majority of parliamentarians, and the political class more generally, were not receptive to these arguments grounded in democratic theory. Instead, there was a consistent questioning of the 2016 referendum result and quite concerted efforts to overturn certain aspects of the result, or even the vote *in toto*. We can, though, move beyond a populist opposition of the people and parliament ("they don't represent us") to make the more foundational point that this action by parliamentarians revealed a deep lack of authority and even a defence of the trapping of member-statehood. Although the 2019 election saw in one sense a defeat of anti-Brexit forces (on the issues of Brexit itself and on the second referendum), the Trade and Cooperation Argument maintains a core EU mechanism of secret intergovernmental rulemaking (Full Brexit, 2020).

As we move to a post-Brexit settlement, there are few signs that the mechanisms for a revival of popular sovereignty are close to hand. Most obviously, during 2020 and 2021, Covid lockdowns have demobilised the population and made associational political activity either extremely difficult or illegal. Revealingly, at the outset of the Covid outbreak, MPs were prepared themselves to demobilise and to declare their work in parliament not to be essential. In these conditions, it is unclear where the impetus for democratic renewal will come from. The Conservative Party, having dealt with populist challengers and discharged as much residual democratic energy as possible by "getting Brexit done", is in a strong position to govern for the next decade. Facing little threat from a left demoralised by Corbyn's 2019 election defeat and sidelined in Keir Starmer's Labour party, the Conservative challenge will be to maintain a coalition between the supporters who won them the 2019 election and their more traditional base. Given large spending commitments (even prior to the outbreak of Covid) that suggest a clear and irreversible break from austerity, a Conservative project that shares some similarities with a state capitalist one seems likely to predominate for some time to come (Hoare, 2021b).

The future of the principle of representative government is less certain. On the one hand, the broader condition of democracy is firmly on the agenda, including a likely constitutional crisis around the Union with Scotland after the Scottish Nationalist Party victory after the Scottish elections in May 2021. On the other, as argued above the Brexit process revealed a deep ambivalence towards the popular sovereignty aspect of democracy on the part of many Remainers and much of our political class. Accordingly, we can predict an upsurge in interest around a sort of "moral minoritarianism" that celebrates participatory but non-binding or non-majoritarian political mechanisms, such as sortition, deliberative democracy, and citizens' assemblies, that look to generate political legitimacy outside of traditional majoritarian processes (Hoare, 2021a).

References

Aber, J., Jones, L., and Tuck, R. (2018). Why Does the British Left Love the EU? *The Full Brexit*, 11 June. Available at: https://www.thefullbrexit.com/why-does-the-british-left-love-the- (accessed 19 January 2021).

Ashcroft, L. (2016). How the United Kingdom Voted on Thursday [...] and Why. *Lord Ashcroft Polls*, 24 June. Available at: http://lordashcroftpolls.com/2016/06/how-the-united-kingdom-voted-and-why/ (accessed 20 January 2021).

Ashdown, P. (2017). Brexit is a Monumental Act of Self-Harm which Will Bewilder Historians. *The Independent*, 27 March. Available at: https://www.independent.co.uk/voices/article-50-brexit-theresa-may-eu-negotiations-paddy-ashdown-monumental-self-harm-bewilder-historians-a7656306.html (accessed 20 January 2021).

BBC. (2016). EU Vote: Where the Cabinet and other MPs Stand. *BBC News*, 22 June. Available at: https://www.bbc.co.uk/news/uk-politics-eu-referendum-35616946 (accessed 13 January 2021).

Bickerton, C. (2012). *European Integration: From Nation-States to Member States.* Oxford: Oxford University Press.

Bickerton, C. (2016). *The European Union: A Citizen's Guide.* London: Penguin.

Bickerton, C. (2018). Beyond the European Void? Reflections on Peter Mair's Legacy. *European Law Journal, 24*(4), 268–280.

Bickerton, C., & Invernizzi Accetti, C. (2018). "Techno-populism" as a New Party Family: The Case of the Five Star Movement and Podemos. *Contemporary Italian Politics, 10*(2), 132–150.

Bickerton C., & Jones, L. (2018). The EU's Democratic Deficit: Why Brexit is Essential for Restoring Popular Sovereignty. *The Full Brexit*, 11 June. Available from: https://www.thefullbrexit.com/the-eu-s-democratic-deficit (accessed 19 January 2021).

Bickerton C., & Tuck, R. (2018). Why is Brexit Proving So Difficult to Implement? *The Full Brexit*, 11 June. Available at: https://www.thefullbrexit.com/why-implementing-brexit-difficult (accessed 13 January 2021).

Cerny, P. (1997). Paradoxes of the Competition State: The Dynamics of Political Globalization. *Government and Opposition, 32*(2), 251–274.

Clarke, H., Goodwin, M., & Whiteley, P. (2017). *Brexit: Why Britain Voted to Leave the European Union.* Cambridge: Cambridge University Press.

Crouch, C. (2004). *Post-Democracy.* Cambridge: Polity.

Crouch, C. (2020). *Post-Democracy After the Crises.* Cambridge: Polity.

Cunliffe, P. (2019). Who Shall Rouse Him Up? Brexit: The World Turned Upside Down. *The Full Brexit*, 4 February. Available at: https://www.thefullbrexit.com/brexit-revolution (accessed 19 January 2021).

Cunliffe, P. (2019). The Workers' Revolt Against Labour. *The Full Brexit*, 18 December. Available at: https://www.thefullbrexit.com/workers-revolt-against-labour (accessed 20 January 2021).

Cunliffe, P. (2020a). *Cosmopolitan Dystopia: International Intervention and the Failure of the West.* Manchester: Manchester University Press.

Cunliffe, P. (2020b). *The New Twenty Years' Crisis: A Critique of International Relations, 1999–2019.* London: McGill-Queen's University Press.

Davis, M. (2018). The Chimera of Workers' Rights in the EU. *The Full Brexit*, 15 July. Available at: https://www.thefullbrexit.com/labour-rights-eu (accessed 23 January 2021).

Flinders, M., & Buller, J. (2006). Depoliticisation: Principles, Tactics and Tools. *British Politics*, *1*(3), 293–218.

Flynn, P. (2017). What Brexit Should Have Taught us about Voter Manipulation. *The Guardian*, 17 April. Available at: https://www.theguardian.com/commentisfree/2017/apr/17/brexit-voter-manipulation-eu-referendum-social-media (accessed 21 January 2021).

Full Brexit. (2020). The UK-EU Trade and Cooperation Agreement: Minimum Brexit. *The Full Brexit*, 30 December. Available at: https://www.thefullbrexit.com/uk-eu-deal (accessed 18 January 2021).

Gerbaudo, P. (2018). *The Digital Party: Political Organisation and Online Democracy.* London: Pluto.

Goodwin, M., & Heath, O. (2016). The 2016 Referendum, Brexit and the Left Behind: An Aggregate-level Analysis of the Result. *Political Quarterly*, *87*(3), 323–332.

Hall, S. (2018). When the Left Abandons Workers, they are Easy Prey for the Right. *The Full Brexit*, 28 June. Available at: https://www.thefullbrexit.com/edl (accessed 21 January 2021).

Hameiri, S., & Jones, L. (2016). Global Governance as State Transformation. *Political Studies*, *64*(4), 793–810.

Hanretty, C. (2017). Areal Interpolation and the UK's Referendum on EU Membership. *Journal of Elections, Public Opinion and Parties*, *27*(4), 466–483.

Hay, C. (2007). *Why We Hate Politics.* Cambridge: Polity.

Heartfield, J. (2006a). *The Death of the Subject Explained.* Sheffield: Sheffield Hallam University Press.

Heartfield, J. (2006b). *European Union: A Process without Subject*. In Bickerton, C., Cunliffe, P., and Gourevitch, A. (eds.), *Politics without Sovereignty: A Critique of Contemporary International Relations* (pp. 131–149). London: Routledge.

Heartfield, J. (2013). *The European Union and the End of Politics*. Winchester: Zero.

Hoare, G. (2020). Brexit Britain Still Acts Like a Member State of the EU. *The Full Brexit*, 17 December. Available at: https://www.thefullbrexit.com/post/brexit-britain-still-acts-like-a-member-state-of-the-eu (accessed 13 January 2021).

Hoare, G. (2021a). Moral Minoritarianism from the Ashes of Left Populism. *Damage*, 13 January. Available at: https://damagemag.com/2021/01/13/moral-minoritarianism-from-the-ashes-of-left-populism/ (accessed 13 January 2021).

Hoare, G. (2021b). After Left Populism, Part Two: Pro-Worker Conservatism in the UK. *The Full Brexit*, 3 February. Available at: https://damagemag.com/2021/02/03/after-left-populism-part-two-pro-worker-conservatism-in-the-uk/ (accessed 3 February 2021).

Hochuli, A., Hoare, G., & Cunliffe, P. (2021). *The End of the End of History: Politics in the Twenty-First Century*. Winchester: Zero.

Jones, L. (2018). The Brexit Party: Creature of the Void. *The Full Brexit*, 13 May. Available at: https://www.thefullbrexit.com/brexit-party-creature-of-the-void (accessed 19 January 2021).

Jones, L. (2019). British Politics in Chaos: Brexit and the Crisis of Representative Democracy. *The Full Brexit*, 12 December. Available at: https://www.thefullbrexit.com/british-politics-chaos (accessed 13 January 2021).

Jones, L., & Ramsay, P. (2016). Representative Democracy, Populism, and Technocracy. *The Current Moment*, 31 July. Available at: https://thecurrentmoment.wordpress.com/2016/07/ (accessed 23 January 2021).

Khalili, L. (2016). After Brexit: Reckoning with Britain's Racism and Xenophobia. *Truthout*, 30 June. Available at: https://truthout.org/articles/after-brexit-reckoning-with-britain-s-racism-and-xenophobia/ (accessed 23 January 2021).

Kouvelakis, S. (2018). Borderland: Greece and the EU's Southern Question. *New Left Review*, 2(110), 5–33.

Lapavitsas, C. (2012). *Crisis in the Eurozone*. London: Verso.

Lapavitsas, C. (2019). *The Left Case Against the EU*. Cambridge: Polity.

Leys, C. (2003). *Market-Driven Politics: Neoliberal Democracy and the Public Interest*. London: Verso.

Lipset, S. M. (1960). *Political Man: The Social Bases of Politics*. New York: Doubleday.

Hobsbawm, E. (1994). *The Age of Extremes: The Short Twentieth Century, 1994–1991*. London: Michael Joseph.

Mair, P. (2013). *Ruling the Void: The Hollowing of Western Democracy*. London: Verso.

Norris, P., & Inglehart, R. (2019). *Cultural Backlash: Trump, Brexit, and Authoritarian Populism*. Cambridge: Cambridge University Press.

Penny, L. (2016). I Want my Country Back. *New Statesman*, 24 June. Available at: https://www.newstatesman.com/politics/uk/2016/06/i-want-my-country-back (accessed 20 January 2021).

Ramsay, P. (2018). The Brexit Party: Vital Stop-Gap, But No Solution. *The Full Brexit*, 13 May. Available at: https://www.thefullbrexit.com/brexit-party-stopgap (accessed 19 January 2021).

Stoker, G. (2006). *Why Politics Matters: Making Democracy Work*. London: Palgrave Macmillan.

Streeck, W. (2017a). Caution: European Narrative. Handle with Care! In Amin, A., & Lewis, P. (eds.), *European Union and Disunion: Reflections on European Identity* (pp. 14–22). London: British Academy.

Streeck, W. (2017b). *Buying Time: The Delayed Crisis of Democratic Capitalism*. London: Verso.

Streeck, W. (2020). *Critical Encounters: Democracy, Capitalism, Ideas*. London: Verso.

Toynbee, P. (2016). On Friday I'll Get My Country Back. Britain will Vote Remain. *The Guardian*, 21 June. Available at: https://www.theguardian.com/commentisfree/2016/jun/21/friday-britain-remain-leave-campaign-foreigners (accessed 20 January 2021).

Tuck, R. (2019). Parliament has No Sovereignty Higher Than a Popular Mandate. *The Full Brexit*, 3 September. Available at: https://www.thefullbrexit.com/parliamentary-sovereignty (accessed 18 January 2021).

Tuck, R. (2020). *The Left Case for Brexit: Reflections on the Current Crisis*. Cambridge: Polity.

UK in a Changing Europe. (2019). Brexit and Public Opinion 2019. Available at: http://ukandeu.ac.uk/wp-content/uploads/2019/01/Public-Opinion-2019-report.pdf (accessed 21 January 2021).

Virdee, S., & McGeever, B. (2018). Racism, Crisis, Brexit. *Ethnic and Racial Studies*, *41*(10), 1802–1819.

Winlow, S., Hall, S., & Treadwell, J. (2017). *The Rise of the Right: English Nationalism and the Transformation of Working-Class Politics*. Bristol: Bristol University Press.

About the Author

George Hoare is an independent researcher based in London. His books include (with Nathan Sperber) *An Introduction to Antonio Gramsci: His Life, Thought, and Legacy* (Bloomsbury, 2016) and (with Alex Hochuli and Philip Cunliffe) *The End of the End of History: Politics in the Twenty-First Century* (Zero, 2021).
Email: gthoare@gmail.com

4 Responsibility to Protect European Identity

How Do Orbán and Erdoğan Expand Europe's Boundaries of International Protection?

Tarik Basbugoglu and Umut Korkut

Abstract

Turkey and Hungary have become two important cases through which to investigate the development of anti-European Union narratives. In this case study, we try to express how the Turkish and the Hungarian political elite sought to construct their humanitarian narratives to criticise the European Union during the Syrian refugee crisis. First, we explain how the Turkish political elite aimed to construct a Muslim self to vicariously identify with the Syrian Sunni Arabs. Second, we show how the Hungarian political elite sought to create a Christian self, so as to consider Middle Eastern Christians and European citizens as an extension of the Hungarian populace. In this chapter, we use speeches by members of the Turkish and Hungarian political elite as our data to investigate how these elites appealed to their domestic public audiences from 2011 to 2020.

Keywords: Turkey, Hungary, migration, periphery, Orban, Erdoğan

4.1 Introduction

This chapter explores themes of Europe, humanitarianism, and cosmopolitanism framed by two Eurosceptical political leaders in Turkey and Hungary. The selection of Turkey and Hungary to explore these three themes is particularly crucial considering that the former is located at Europe's periphery and the latter is at the EU's periphery. However, both states have played a significant role in the way Europe has responded to the abrupt

Foley, J. and Korkut, U. (ed.), *Contesting Cosmopolitan Europe. Euroscepticism, Crisis and Borders.* Amsterdam: Amsterdam University Press 2022
DOI :10.5117/9789463727259_CH04

increase in the number of migrant arrivals in 2015 and afterwards. What makes the selection of these two cases even more interesting is that, while the two countries diverged in the way that they responded to external migration, they converged in branding themselves as the true humanitarians in comparison with the way the European Union protected and received migrants. Turkey has operated an open-door policy towards the Syrian migrants from the inception of the Syrian Civil War until recently, while Hungary adopted a security-focused migration policy with highly limited humanitarian protection. Yet, by branding themselves as humanitarian, both Turkey and Hungary used the "migration crisis" as a political tool to appeal to their domestic public audiences. Their respective interpretation of humanitarianism, therefore, presents us with an interesting take on questions of Europe and cosmopolitanism, viewed from the periphery and usurped by populist political leaders to justify migration politics.

Our chapter concentrates on AKP (Justice and Development Party) and Fidesz (Hungarian Civic Alliance), and how their respective leaders set the Turkish and Hungarian narratives of humanitarianism in a manner designed to shame Europe for its failure to deliver the same. In order to understand Turkish and Hungarian politics, one needs to read the politics and discourses of Turkish President Tayyip Erdoğan and Hungarian Prime Minister Viktor Orbán very closely. In this chapter, we therefore reflect on their speeches to trace their audience-making, using external migration to present Turkey and Hungary as the true humanitarians.

In terms of theory, we take as our point of departure ontological inse-curity (Kinnvall, 2004), examining its exploitation by the political elite to consolidate a domestic public audience. Kinnvall (2004, p. 746) states that "ontological security refers to a "person's fundamental sense of safety in the world and includes a basic trust of other people". Kinnvall (2004, p. 749) further suggests that if individuals feel ontologically insecure, they look for a stable identity to offset their anxieties. In this sense, narratives can shape both the self and the other (Steele & Homolar 2019, p. 215) while they remain "integral to individual and collective memory, something that relates not only to the past, but also to the present and future" (Steele & Homolar, 2019, p. 216). Considering how the political elite can consolidate public insecurities through their manipulation of humanitarianism narrative, we explore how the elite of AKP and Fidesz used the "Syrian refugee crisis" as a narrative tool to blame the EU, in an effort to control the ontological insecurity of Turkish and Hungarian public.

In this narrative, the AKP represented Turkey and their government as the protector of Syrian refugees by pointing to the EU's moral inadequacy in response to the plight of the refugees. Equally, they foregrounded the superiority of their nation vis-à-vis the EU. The Fidesz government, meanwhile, depicted themselves as the defender of European Christianity while noting that the EU has failed on that score with its humanitarian practices, not only with regard to Middle Eastern Christians but also as an enabler of refugees' "perilous journeys" to Europe with false promises of integration. In this manner, they also reflected on Hungary's historical role as the defender of Christianity at the borders of Europe. Meanwhile, the Turkish government praised its "open-door" policy towards the Syrians as a reflection of its true humanitarianism, in comparison to the EU, which had closed its borders to refugees. Taking these positions as starting points, this chapter expresses how the Turkish and Hungarian political elites fostered a "Western other" that had failed in its humanitarianism in order to mobilise their domestic public audiences around the success of their own migration politics, even if they diverged from them extensively. In this way, they have also used claims of humanitarianism to redress the ontological insecurity that their respective populations may experience in the face of the EU and its cosmopolitanism.

To this extent, the AKP and Fidesz governments also looked for an external self with which to vicariously identify themselves, using religion, history, and culture as their narrative tools. For the AKP political elite, their extended selves were the Sunni Syrians, and for Fidesz it was the Middle Eastern Christians. Browning (2018, p. 251) defines vicarious identification as "living through" others' experiences, identified in those moments when people actually appropriate others' stories as their own as if they happened to them". Subotic and Zarakol (2013, p. 915) highlighted that cultural intimacy between nations provided insiders with a sense of national comfort and ontological security. Thus, as we discuss how the Turkish and Hungarian elites depict Europe with its failures of humanitarianism, we also trace how both Turkish and Hungarian political elites referred to their religious, cultural, and historical characters in order to emphasise their humanitarian superiority vis-à-vis the EU. We also analyse their politics of foregrounding their own national virtues, which presumptively informed their humanitarianism, as an expression of their criticism towards the EU.

Methodologically, this chapter draws its data from the narratives of Prime Minister Viktor Orbán of Hungary, Turkey's President Tayyip Erdoğan, and ex-Minister of Foreign Affairs and former Prime Minister Ahmet Davutoğlu regarding refugees and the EU. Our analytical tools are rooted in Critical Discourse Analysis (CDA), which helps to uncover the hidden meanings of elite narratives. In Wodak and Meyer's (2009, p. 7) terms, CDA aims to produce and convey critical knowledge that enables human beings to emancipate themselves from forms of domination through self-reflection. In addition, they (2009, p. 9) explain that CDA uses narratives to analyse the power of ruling elite, stating, moreover (2009, p. 10) that "language can be used to challenge power, to subvert it, to alter distributions of power in the short and the long term". Taking this as our cue, we demonstrate how both Turkish and Hungarian political leaders constructed their "powerful self" to challenge the cosmopolitanism represented by the EU. To this extent, we explore Turkish and Hungarian political elite narratives from 2011 to 2020.

The first section of our chapter underlines how the AKP leadership adopted narratives to show themselves as a responsible regional power in comparison to the EU, in order to manage the ontological insecurity of Turkish public. The second section of this chapter expresses how the Fidesz administration pursued migration politics to depict themselves as the vanguard of European Christianity against the migrants, and in this way sought to manage the ontological insecurity of Hungarian public. The final section summarises our findings, considering how nationalist leaders have usurped humanitarian discourses, sought to mobilise publics against the EU to cater to their own ontological insecurity, and finally converged in presenting themselves as the true humanitarians while diverging extensively in their own migration politics.

4.2 Turkish "Humanitarianism" and Open-door Policy Towards Migrants

After the demise of Ottoman Empire, Turkey's Republican leadership sought to be recognised as a Western nation by the European elites. The elite set EU membership for Turkey as a proof of having become a "Western" and "civilised" nation. This can be theorised as an attempt to redress the ontological insecurity of Turkish public. Capan and Zarakol (2019, p. 269) argue that Turkey sought to leave its Eastern identity, which symbolised being traditional and underdeveloped, to embrace the Western identity, which meant being modern and developed. However, the Turkish public and political elite continued to feel "othered" by EU nations due to their identity. Rumelili (2003, pp. 221–222) wrote that although Turkey was a member of Western institutions such as NATO and the Council of Europe, the EU continued to consider Turkey as the "other" due to its Asian and Muslim identity. Moreover, Buzan and Diez (1999, p. 46) state that the EU started to withdraw its full membership promise to Turkey after the end of the Cold War. This arguably contributed to the Turkish public feeling ontologically insecure for being non-Western, facing the EU nations.

The Republican Turkish political elite also sought to exploit the so-called "Sèvres Syndrome" to appeal to the ontological insecurity of Turkish public audience, presenting Europeans as dangerous due to the bitter memories of the last period of Ottoman imperial rule. In that sense, the Sèvres Treaty[6], signed between the Ottoman Empire and the European powers in 1920 at the end of the First World War, remained a source of permanent ontological insecurity among the Turkish public. Hale (2007, p. 50) and Guida (2008, pp. 38, 44, 47–49) stated that the Turkish public and political elite drew upon Sèvres Syndrome to promote the idea that the nation was surrounded by a Western-backed enemy powers seeking to divide the Turkish lands. Kirisci (2018, p. 113) suggests that the Islamist political ideology in Turkey also considered the EU as the most recent version of Christian Europe's Crusaders, who aimed to drive the Islamic civilisation from Europe. Sèvres Syndrome thus allowed the Turkish elite to depict the Europe and the EU as the dangerous "other" for Turkish identity.

Building upon these insecurities, the AKP has sought to criticise EU nations for remaining silent in the face of the violence in Syria and the plight of the Syrian refugees. They have used humanitarian narratives to underline their moral superiority in comparison to the EU nations. This also serves as a cover for their own failures in meeting high democratic standards and respect for human rights. Howell (2002, p. 11) argued that the narrative of Europeanisation encouraged accountability and democracy in constructing a common European identity. Human rights and rule of law are perceived as part of the Europeanisation discourse (Morozov & Rumelili, 2012, p. 38) and the Europeanisation process supports the protection of universal rights of refugees (Lavenex, 2001, p. 852). However, Ferris and Kirisci (2016, pp. 66–67) state that the EU promised to pay Turkey to prevent the "illegal arrivals" of Syrian refugees instead of facilitating their reception and protection in the EU. Moreover, they suggest (2016, p. 112) that the EU nations were lacking in solidarity when responding to humanitarian crises like the drowning of Syrians in the Mediterranean. In that sense, the AKP political elite, who failed to meet EU human rights criteria for membership, blamed the

6   In 1920, the European imperial powers (Britain, France and Italy) pushed the Ottoman Empire to sign the "Sèvres Treaty", which demanded the partition of what remained of the Empire between European powers and their proxies (Greece and Armenia).

EU nations for being bystanders to the Syrian crisis and the human rights violations that it involved.

Davutoğlu, the ex-Foreign Minister and the Prime Minister until 2016, depicted the Turkish protection of refugees as an "open door" policy that the ongoing Syrian conflict necessitated. The AKP leadership thereafter extended protection to 3.7 million Syrian refugees into Turkey (UNHCR, p. 2020). Korkut (2016, p. 630) states that "the refugee crisis in the aftermath of the Syrian crisis paved the way for pragmatism, as the Turkish government almost welcomed Syrian refugees hoping that this would enhance an international attention to the crisis in Syria". The Turkish government established refugee camps at the border towns to create shelters for Syrians who had fled the civil war (Can 2017, p. 179; Cop & Zihnioglu 2015, p. 35). Ambramowitz and Edelman (2013, p. 30) emphasised that the Turkish government tried to convince the Western nations to support the Syrian National Council, which represented the Syrian opposition. Moreover, Bowen (2012) and Phillips (2012) stated that the Turkish government pressured their Western partners to build safe zones to deter the Assad regime's bombing campaign against Syrian civilians. That was how Turkey sought to present itself to the EU as a regional power in Syria, with generous humanitarian practice and protection policies. The then Prime Minister Recep Tayyip Erdoğan (2011) used the chaotic situation in Syria not only to appeal to the Turkish public but also reflected on its weakened neighbour to appeal to the EU nations as follows: "We do not see the Syrian issue as an external issue, Syrian civil war is our domestic issue".

In particular, the AKP used humanitarian ideology to brand Turkey as a conscientious power in comparison to the anti-humanitarian indifference of Europeans. Numerous times both Erdoğan and Davutoğlu referred to Sunni Islam and Ottoman history to support their humanitarian narratives and to enable the Turkish self to vicariously identify with the Sunni Syrians. In that sense, the AKP political elite constructed the Sunni Syrians as extensions of the Turkish self. The politicians called the borders between Turkey and Syria artificial, emphasising the cultural, historical, and religious values common to the Turks and Sunni Arabs (Saracoglu and Demirkol, 2015, p. 305). The Turkish government condemned the EU nations for seeing Turkey as a buffer zone between Europe and the Middle East. Once Russia became a more proactive force in Syria and its overt support to the Syrian regime triggered violence towards civilians in Syria (Ripley 2018, p. 62; Armstrong 2015), Turkey heightened its criticisms of the EU while describing the EU's financial contribution to the cost of Turkey's hosting of Syrian refugees as weak and inadequate. Erdoğan (2016) also warned EU leaders that Turkey was losing patience with the EU's "indifference" on the Syrian refugee issue: "We took people [Syrians] off the buses in Edirne and turned them back. But that would be only a few. After that [...] we will open the doors and say, 'have a good trip'". Still, the AKP political elite also adopted nationalist narratives to present themselves as the defenders of Turkish economic interests. They depicted Turkey as an equal partner of the EU, appealing to the ontological insecurities of the Turkish public. Davutoğlu (2016) argued that his administration did well to defend the economic interests of Turkey even on the issue of Syrian refugee crisis. He depicted his bargaining on the "EU-Turkey refugee deal" as an "economic success" for the Turkish nation even as Turkey called on the EU to contribute more. Erdoğan (2019) was thus pressuring the EU political elite to send further finances to Turkey to meet its commitment of €3 billion in humanitarian aid.

The Erdoğan government also criticised the EU for not supporting Turkey's plans to build "safe zones" in northern Syria. The AKP has depicted Turkey as a liberator for the Syrian refugees and expected financial and political support from the EU nations to build safe zones to resettle the Syrian refugees (Beaumont & Smith 2019; Baynes 2019; Weise 2019). However, Guarascio (2019) stated that most of the EU nations opposed the AKP's plan to forge these safe zones as it would be a cover to displace the YPG Kurds from Northern Syria. Erdoğan (2019) was forthcoming with its criticisms and threats as he called on the EU: "You, European Union come to your senses. If you choose to describe our operation as an occupation movement, our job is easy. We [could] open the doors, we send 3.6 million refugees to you".

In summary, then, the refugee crisis turned into an occasion for the AKP political elite to present themselves as morally superior to EU nations. This was particularly successful insofar as it played upon the ontological insecurities of the Turkish public. The AKP political elite claimed that the European Union, while purportedly intent on promoting human rights and universal values, was giving inadequate support to Syrian refugees. The Erdoğan administration thus used Turkey's protection of Syrian refugees as a narrative tool to reflect a humanitarian face for Turkey that pointedly contrasted with that of the EU nations. To date, this has continued with Erdoğan's (2020) recent criticism of the EU for its "ineffective migration policy": "When the EU countries which have strong economies implied quota for the migrants, we embraced all migrants without looking at their race, religion, language and ethnicity".

4.3 The Hungarian "Humanitarianism" and Securitisation of Migration

The legacy of the Ottoman occupation of Hungary between the 16th and 17th centuries left a perception of Muslims as the "other". Among the list of all "others" in Hungarian political history – such as the Jews, the Habsburgs, the Roma, the Soviets – the Muslim as the other came to play a prominent role in the Fidesz government's approach to the migration crisis. The Hungarian Prime Minister Viktor Orbán thus found it easy to exploit the long-lasting ontological insecurity of nationalist and conservative Hungarian citizens against the presumed Muslim migration. Comparing themselves to the fortress commanders and soldiers fighting against the numerically superior Ottoman forces between the 15th and 17th centuries (Pap & Glied, 2017, p. 124), the Fidesz government imagined their role as heroic soldiers fighting in the bastion of European Christendom against the "illegal entrance" of Muslim refugees into Europe (Gyollai & Korkut, 2019).

Equally, Hungary's political leadership used humanitarian discourse to address the ontological insecurity of Hungarians against the West. The conservative and nationalist Hungarian public audience consider the EU as the extension of Western liberal ideals, which destroyed the cultural homogeneity of a Hungarian society entrenched in Christianity and traditional gender and family relations. Increasingly, the Hungarian right-wing embraced an authoritarian religious nationalism as an alternative to the liberal and democratic values of the European Union. Akçalı and Korkut (2012, p. 611) suggested that Hungary's insecurities with respect to the West date back to the Treaty of Trianon (1920), which saw Hungary endure territorial losses after the First World War. In that respect, Akçalı and Korkut (2012, pp. 610–611) highlighted how Hungarian nationalists considered the East as the benign other, as opposed to the "powerful but corrupt" Western political elites. In time, as Korkut (2014, p. 627) underlined, the culture-nation conceptions of Hungarianness have claimed a cultural supremacy pitched against a threatening "diversity" that they saw originating from Europe. In this manner, it was not only the ethnic and religious diversity that migrants would introduce to Hungary, but also the liberal notion of equality and diversity represented by cosmopolitan Europe that emerged as threats to the ontological security that a homogenous Hungarianness would otherwise express. Below, we explore how the Fidesz government presented its security-focused migration politics as humanitarian while catering to the ontological insecurity that both the Muslim migrant and the cosmopolitan Western liberal other would pose to their imagined, "diversity-averse" Hungarian.

It is puzzling that, despite its highly security-oriented migration policies, the Fidesz political elite still sought to appear both moral and realistic amidst the Syrian refugee crisis and to endeavour to adopt a humanitarian image. While Orbán continuously usurped Christianity to construct the Middle Eastern refugees as "Muslim others", he still proposed that the migration journey risked the lives of Syrian and other refugees and that it was more humanitarian to prevent them from starting their journeys to Europe. Right after Europe's summer of migration in 2015, Orbán (2016a) put this very clearly, as follows: "it is more humanitarian not to accept those [that do not have refugee status into the EU] than having them resided on European territory for a few years and remove them from the European Union territory". According to Orbán (2016a), the Europeans were deceiving the migrants with false promises of integration; keeping them in Hotspots outside the EU territory was a more humanitarian response. In order to keep migrants in their home countries and prevent them from making journeys, Hungary was "giving help where there was a need" through its overseas development assistance (Orbán 2016b). That was why, as Orbán (2018b) argued, a sustainable migration system needed migration management through externalisation.

As the EU's criticism of Hungary's failure to protect asylum applicants increased after 2015 – culminating in 2018 with a proposal calling on the European Council to determine the existence of a serious breach, on Hungary's part, of the values on which the Union is founded (Sargentini Report, 2018) – Hungarian humanitarianism adopted a protective stance towards the safety and security of the Europeans against the migrants. According to Orbán (2018a), "[the EU] had to extend security to its citizens" and "Hungary was required to protect [European] borders" (2018b). The threat of terrorism has concerned Europe and cast its everyday security in doubt (Orbán 2016b). This consequent insecurity was also a result of the failure of those that aspired to European cosmopolitanism, who lured the migrants "into making such dangerous journeys with the promise of welfare"; however, according to Orbán "terrorists hid among them" (Orbán, 2016a). Orbán (2016a) also saw migrant communities as being full of internal conflicts and warned those in Europe that hoped for cosmopolitan integration that "if people with conflicting aims arrive at a community system, country, that will not become integration but chaos" (Orbán 2017a). At a news conference with the then European Council President Donald Tusk in 2015, Orbán emphasised that migrants should stay in Turkey, saying "Turkey is a safe country. Stay there. It's risky to come. It's better for the family, for the kids, for yourself to stay" (Orbán 2017a).

Orbán's "fight for Europe" discourse, presenting integration-focused liberal cosmopolitanism as a true danger for the humanitarian needs of Europeans, resonated further within Hungarian newspapers across a wide ideological spectrum. In 2018 *Magyar Hírlap*, a conservative daily, wrote that "the fight for the European identity and traditions has nothing to do with inhumanity, it is about the love of our own people. Precisely those who support migration are responsible for the death of migrants drowning in water and of the victims of terror attacks in Europe" (Õry, 2018). A "left-wing" opposition daily, *Népszava*, in 2018 also expressed the opinion that migration was something to be defended from in those countries traditionally targeted, while trying to argue why Hungary can be more humanitarian, as follows:

> The Muslim immigration (and any immigration) is disproportionate [for] the target countries Germany, France, Holland, England and the Scandinavian countries, especially in big cities. These countries might have to consider the consequences of ethnic redistribution. This is not the case here, we are not a target country. Thus, it would be sensible, if these target countries tried to defend themselves against migratory flows, even with harsh measures, but we can afford to behave in a more human way. (Gal 2018)

Overall, the Hungarian media scene saw a myriad of references to what went wrong with integration in western Europe and why migration was a danger for European societies (Korkut, 2020). Therefore, The Hungarian government and media constructed refugees as a threat for European societies in an attempt to appeal to the Hungarian public. It was not only that Hungary hosted or was to host so many migrants – it was that those European nations that hosted migrants in their cosmopolitan societies would always have troubles. In this way, Orbán adopted a Christian nationalist view, rejecting what he perceived as liberal, internationalist values of Europe. He also boosted nationalist sentiments by claiming that only the Hungarians have the courage to protect the EU's ethnic and cultural composition (Fekete, 2016, pp. 42–43) in his speech for the Hungarian security services in 2017:

> You are now defending the borders of Europe as it happened for the past 500 years. Protecting ourselves and Europe also. This became the national fate of the Hungarian nation over centuries [...] The era of naivety, illusions and laxity have closed in Europe [...] There are those who think that all

people that come to Europe intend to live here according to our customs and laws. The facts are showing the opposite. Terror attacks, riots, violence, crime, ethnic and cultural clashes raise our attention that those who come here do not want to live our lives, but continue with their own lives, but at the level of European people's quality of life or within those countries that the Brussels bureaucrats intend to distribute them. (Fekete, 2016)

Orbán likewise depicted Hungary as a protector of European identity, and the Fidesz party as the true representor of the European public, unlike the liberal EU establishment. He stated that "Hungary is [EU's] future" (Orbán 2018) and Europe would have done better had it not rejected Hungarian solutions, which, he claimed, had proved themselves to be operational and useful (Orbán 2017b).

The Fidesz government increasingly pursued a Christian identity to claim moral superiority over the EU:

Our success has shown that the period of liberal democracy has come to an end. It has become useless to protect human dignity, to extend freedom, and to guarantee physical security. It already cannot maintain the Christian culture. There are those in Europe who still tinker with it thinking that they can reform it. But they do not understand that it is not that the structure fell apart, but the world has changed. Our answer, the Hungarian answer to the world that has changed, is instead of the liberal democracy that ran into darkness we are to establish 21st Century Christian democracy that guarantee human dignity. (Orbán, 2018)

However, in attacking the forces of cosmopolitanism, Orbán became particularly fixated on George Soros, who had a Hungarian and Jewish background, for his "assumed" role in Europe's refugee crisis. "The Soros Foundation" became one Orbán's favoured tropes: its activities were seen as the source of liberal non-Christian ideals as well as justifications for the "illegal" arrival of Syrian refugees into Europe:

[Europe] first rejected its roots and instead of a Europe that acts with its Christian roots, it turned to building the Europe of Open Society [in reference to Soros Foundation]. In Christian Europe, work had value, humans had dignity, man and woman were equal, the family was the foundation of the nation, nation was the foundation of Europe, and states in their turn guaranteed security. In today's Europe of Open Society, there are no borders. European people are exchanged with migrants, family has become co-habitation that can vary as desired, nation, national self-awareness and national feeling have negative connotations and it is considered to be excessive. In liberal Europe, to be European does not mean anything.

This anti-cosmopolitan cultural politics became a justification for rejecting Europe-wide solutions to the migration crisis. Yet even this rejection was framed as humanitarian, both towards European nations and towards migrants, who risked "perilous journeys" having been lured by Europe's perceived liberal migration agenda. As we mentioned above, an important element of Hungarian humanitarianism was also the protection of Middle Eastern Christians. The Fidesz administration sought to present Hungary as the protector of Middle Eastern Christians – a state that cared about the persecuted Middle Eastern Christians whom Europe had failed. Even if Hungary received widespread international criticism for its failure in refugee protection, the Fidesz government introduced the "Hungary helps!" programme, a humanitarian aid project to provide development aid to Middle Eastern Christian societies. Péter Szijjártó (2019), the Minister of Foreign Affairs and Trade, criticised the process of the Arab Spring for encouraging the Islamist groups that persecuted the Christian minorities. Szijjartó (2019), stated that the persecution of Christians was the last acceptable form of discrimination and that there was a consensus around this in international political discourse. Hence, this double critique of Europe catered to both the ontological security and insecurity of Hungarians simultaneously. That was how Orbán puzzlingly presented Hungary as a true humanitarian nation, for migrants as much as for Europeans, while pursuing highly security-oriented migration politics and authoritarian, illiberal political change at home.

4.4 Conclusion

Our chapter has foregrounded the complexities around terms such as *cosmopolitanism* and *humanitarianism* and showed that they do not have to be reconcilable – rather than being humanitarian, what matters is acting humanitarian. The puzzle here is that Turkish and Hungarian politicians branded themselves as superior humanitarians, despite their politicisation of refugee reception and protection policies and self-serving migration politics. In this chapter we have argued that, rather than what they did for refugees, it was how they opposed what the European Union did that makes the two countries' humanitarian self-branding comparable. We have argued that the way such branding functioned appealed to both the ontological security and insecurity that the Hungarian and Turkish populations felt vis-à-vis Europe. Their respective assessments of what Europe represented prompted Hungarian and Turkish national elites to seek to associate a humanitarian brand with their own states and present Europe as the actual non-humanitarian actor, despite its claims of democracy and respect for human rights.

Therefore, we argue that humanitarian rhetoric served domestic purposes either alongside or beyond how they responded to the needs of refugees. While the Turkish political elite took pride in Turkey's generosity towards the Syrian refugees, they also insisted that this was thanks to Turkey's centuries-long humanitarian tradition (Korkut, 2018). While Turkey was hosting Syrians, they claimed, the EU was building walls, remaining unresponsive, and ultimately failing to meet its humanitarian obligations. The Hungarian narrative was more complex than the Turkish one. Remarkably, the Hungarian government managed to devise its humanitarian brand while failing in its obligations towards migrants. It presented its humanitarianism as a defensive instrument for Europeans as well as an offer for those in need, as long as they did not come to Europe. Its instrumentalisation of humanitarian rhetoric for defensive purposes implied that Hungary was standing to protect Europeans against the Islamism brought by the Middle Eastern refugees. This, they claimed, made Hungary the true humanitarian. Yet, their humanitarianism took on broader connotations, extending to Christians in the Middle East as well as others who were inspired to make perilous journeys to reach Europe. Furthermore, the Hungarian political elite depicted the liberal European notion of integration as delusional, alleging that, in failing both migrants and Europeans, their humanitarianism was founded on false premises.

Our chapter has examined two states on the periphery of Europe or the European Union to argue that it is not necessarily the core European states but also peripheral ones that can shape the parameters of Europeanisation. Overall, humanitarianism has proved to be a subject of extensive politicisation and it appears that states' and political leaders' mobilisation around it does not necessarily serve those in need, but at times might cater to the ontological insecurity that their co-nationals feel due to historical legacies and identity-related factors. We have used two apparently divergent countries to argue that, in exploiting humanitarianism for self-branding against the perceived EU critiques, Hungary and Turkey have converged.

References

Abramowitz, M. I., & Edelman, E. S. (2013). US-Turkish Cooperation toward a Post-Assad Syria: A Paper of BPC's Turkey Task Force. *Bipartisan Policy Center, 9*, 2–36.

Akçalı, E., & Korkut, U. (2012). Geographical Metanarratives in East-Central Europe: Neo-Turanism in Hungary. *Eurasian Geography and Economics, 53*(5), 596–614.

Armstrong, P. (2015). Hundreds of Civilians Killed in Russian Airstrikes in Syria: Amnesty. *CNN*, 23 December. Available at: https://edition.cnn.com/2015/12/23/middleeast/russia-airstrikes-syria-amnesty-report/index.html (accessed 20 October 2020).

Baynes, C. (2019). Turkey's Erdogan Threatens to Send Millions of Refugees to Europe Unless It Backs Syria "Safe Zone". *Independent*, 26 October. Available at: https://www.independent.co.uk/news/world/europe/erdogan-syria-turkey-refugees-safe-zone-kurds-trump-europe-borders-a9172311.html (accessed 25 September 2020).

BBC. (2016). Erdoğan'dan AB'ye mülteci krizi tepkisi: Alnımızda enayi yazmıyor. *BBC News*, 11 February. Available at: https://www.bbc.com/turkce/haber-ler/2016/02/160211_erdogan_omer_celik_multeciler_aciklama (accessed 20 October 2020).

Beaumont, P., & Smith, H. (2019). Erdoğan: I'll Let Syrian Refugees Leave Turkey for West Unless Safe Zone Set Up. *The Guardian*, 5 September. Available at: https://www.theguardian.com/world/2019/sep/05/erdogan-ill-let-syrian-refugees-leave-turkey-for-west-unless-safe-zone-set-up (accessed 22 September 2020).

Beki, A. (2016). Davutoğlu: AB ile Kayserili pazarlığı yaptık. *Hurriyet*, 8 March. Available at: https://www.hurriyet.com.tr/dunya/davutoglu-ab-ile-kayserili-pazarligi-yaptik-40065646 (accessed 22 September 2020).

Bowen, J. (2012). Turkey: Risk Worth Taking for Syria Safe Zones. *BBC News*, 28 September. Available at: https://www.bbc.co.uk/news/world-middle-east-19753795 (accessed 30 September 2020).

Browning, C. S. (2018). "Je suis en terrase": Political Violence, Civilizational Politics and the Everyday Courage to Be. *Political Psychology, 39*(2), 243–261.

Buzan, B., & Diez, T. (1999). The European Union. *Survival, 41*(1), 41–57.

Can, Ş. (2017). The Syrian Civil War, Sectarianism and Political Change at the Turkish–Syrian Border. *Social Anthropology, 25*(2), 174–189.

Çapan, Z. G., & Zarakol, A. (2019). Turkey's Ambivalent Self: Ontological Insecurity in "Kemalism" versus "Erdoğanism". *Cambridge Review of International Affairs, 32*(3), 263–282.

Cop, B., & Zihnioğlu, Ö. (2017). Turkish Foreign Policy under AKP Rule: Making Sense of the Turbulence. *Political Studies Review, 15*(1), 28–38.

Daily News Hungary. (2019). Conference of Middle Eastern Christian Church Leaders Starts in Budapest. *Daily News Hungary*, 29 October. Available at: https://dailynewshungary.com/conference-of-middle-eastern-christian-church-leaders-starts-in-budapest/ (accessed 28 September 2020).

Europarl.europa.eu. (2018). Sargentini Report 7 April. Available at: https://www.europarl.europa.eu/doceo/document/A-8-2018-0250_EN.html (accessed 10 January 2021).

Fekete, L. (2016). Hungary: Power, Punishment and the 'Christian-National Idea'. *Institute of Race Relations*, 57(4), 39–53.

Ferris, E., & Kirisci, K. (2016). *The Consequences of Chaos: Syria's Humanitarian Crisis and the Failure to Protect*. Washington, DC: Brookings Institution Press.

Gal, M. (2018). Not In My Name! *Nepszava*, 10 November Available at: https://nepszava.hu/3011560_not-in-my-name (accessed 15 January 2021).

Gazateduvar. (2019). Erdoğan'dan AB'ye mülteci resti: Güvenli bölge olmazsa kapıları açarız. 5 September. Available at: https://www.gazeteduvar.com.tr/politika/2019/09/05/erdogan-guvenli-bolge-olmazsa-kapilari-acariz (accessed 12 September 2020).

Gazeteduvar. (2019). Erdoğan: Suriye'deki petrolü birlikte çıkaralım. 17 December. Available at: https://www.gazeteduvar.com.tr/politika/2019/12/17/erdogan-suriyedeki-petrolu-birlikte-cikaralim (accessed 13 September 2020).

Guarascio, F. (2019). EU Lawmakers Reject Turkey's 'Safe Zone' in Syria, Eye Sanctions Steps. *Reuters*, 23 October. Available at: https://www.reuters.com/article/us-syria-security-eu-idUSKBN1X21JE (accessed 13 September 2020).

Guida, M. (2008). The Sèvres Syndrome and "Komplo" Theories in the Islamist and Secular Press. *Turkish Studies*, 9(1), 37–52.

Gyollai, D., & Korkut, U. (2019). Border Management and Migration Controls – Hungary Report, Global Migration: Consequences and Response. Available at: https://www.diva-portal.org/smash/get/diva2:1334555/FULLTEXT01.pdf (accessed 25 November 2020).

Haberler. (2019). Cumhurbaşkanı Erdoğan: "Ey Avrupa Birliği kendinize gelin". 10 October. Available at: https://www.haberler.com/cumhurbaskani-erdogan-ey-avrupa-birligi-kendinize-12514211-haberi/ (accessed 12 September 2020).

Hale, W. (2007). *Turkey, the US and Iraq*. London: SAQI.

Howell, K. (2002). *Developing Conceptualizations of Europeanization and European Integration: Mixing Methodologies*, Sheffield, pp. 1–27.

Hungary Today. (2019). Foreign Minister: Hungary Assumes Responsibility for All Christian Communities. 29 October. Available at: https://hungarytoday.hu/foreign-minister-hungary-assumes-responsibility-for-all-christian-communities/ (accessed 25 October 2020).

Izbul, C. (2011). Erdoğan: "Suriye İç Meselemiz, Gereğini Yapmak Durumundayız".
  7 August. Available at: https://www.amerikaninsesi.com/a/erdogan-suriye-ic-
  meselemiz-geregini-yapmak-durumundayiz-127078293/898713.html (accessed
  22 September 2020).

Kinnvall, C. (2004). Globalization and Religious Nationalism: Self, Identity, and the
  Search for Ontological Security. *Political Psychology, 25*(5), 741–767.

Kirisci, K. (2018). *Turkey and the West: Fault Lines in A Troubled Alliance.* Washington,
  DC: The Brookings Institution.

Korkut, U. (2014). The Migration Myth in the Absence of Immigrants: How Does
  the Conservative Right in Hungary and Turkey Grapple with Immigration?
  Comparative European Politics, 12(6), 620–636.

Korkut, U. (2017). Resentment and Reorganization: Anti-Western Discourse and
  the Making of Eurasianism in Hungary. *Acta Slavica Iaponica, 38*, 71–90.

Korkut, U. (2018). The Discursive Governance of Forced-Migration Management:
  The Turkish Shift from Reticence to Activism in Asia. *Journal of Refugee Studies,
  32*(4), 664–682.

Korkut, U. (2020). Conflicting Conceptualisations of Europeanisation – Hungary
  country report, Global Migration: Consequences and Responses – RESPOND
  Working Paper Series; 2020/70. Available at: https://www.diva-portal.org/smash/
  record.jsf?pid=diva2%3A1498927&dswid=937 (accessed 18 January 2021).

Kormany.hu. (2018). Orbán Viktor beszéde a miniszterelnöki eskütételét követően.
  10 May. Available at: https://www.kormany.hu/hu/a-miniszterelnok/beszedek-
  publikaciok-interjuk/orban-viktor-beszede-a-miniszterelnoki-eskutetelet-
  kovetoen (accessed 23 November 2020).

Kormany.hu. (2016a). Orbán Viktor sajtónyilatkozata az Európai Tanács ülését
  követően. 21 October. Available at: https://www.kormany.hu/hu/a-miniszterel-
  nok/beszedek-publikaciok-interjuk/orban-viktor-sajtonyilatkozata-az-europai-
  tanacs-uleset-kovetoen (accessed 4 June 2020).

Kormany.hu. (2017). Orbán Viktor beszéde a XXVIII. Bálványosi Nyári Szabadegyetem és Diáktáborban. 22 July. Available at: https://www.kormany.hu/
  hu/a-miniszterelnok/beszedek-publikaciok-interjuk/orban-viktor-beszede-
  a-xxviii-balvanyosi-nyari-szabadegyetem-es-diaktaborban (accessed
  27 November 2020).

Kormany.hu. (2017a). Orbán Viktor beszéde a XXVIII. Bálványosi Nyári Szabadegyetem és Diáktáborban. 22 July. Available at: https://www.kormany.hu/
  hu/a-miniszterelnok/beszedek-publikaciok-interjuk/orban-viktor-beszede-
  a-xxviii-balvanyosi-nyari-szabadegyetem-es-diaktaborban (accessed
  4 June 2020).

Kormany.hu. (2018a). Orbán Viktor beszéde a miniszterek bemutatásán.
  18 May. Available at: https://www.kormany.hu/hu/a-miniszterelnok/

beszedek-publikaciok-interjuk/orban-viktor-beszede-a-miniszterek-bemu-tatasan20180518 (accessed 25 November 2020).

Kormany.hu. (2018b). Orbán Viktor sajtónyilatkozata a Visegrádi Négyek kormányfőinek és Ausztria kancellárjának csúcstalálkozóján. 21 June. Available at: https://www.kormany.hu/hu/a-miniszterelnok/beszedek-publikaciok-interjuk/orban-viktor-sajtonyilatkozata-a-visegradi-negyek-kormanyfoinek-es-ausztria-kancellarjanak-csucstalalkozojan (accessed 4 June 2020).

Lavenex, S. (2001). The Europeanization of Refugee Policies: Normative Challenges and Institutional Legacies. *Journal of Common Market Studies*, 39(5), 851–874.

Miniszterelnok.hu. (2016b). Magyarország az otthonunk, meg kell védenünk! 29 September. Available at: http://www.miniszterelnok.hu/magyarorszag-az-otthonunk-meg-kell-vedenunk/ (accessed 25 December 2020).

Miniszterelnok.hu. (2017). Orbán Viktor beszéde a határvadászok eskütételén. 12 January. Available at: http://www.miniszterelnok.hu/orban-viktor-beszede-a-hatarvadaszok-eskutetelen/ (accessed 22 November 2020).

Miniszterelnok.hu. (2017b). Orbán Viktor beszéde a határvadászok eskütételén. 12 January. Available at: http://www.miniszterelnok.hu/orban-viktor-beszede-a-hatarvadaszok-eskutetelen/ (accessed 4 June 2020).

Miniszterelnok.hu. (2018). Orbán Viktor beszéde a XXIX. Bálványosi Nyári Szabadegyetem és Diáktáborban. 28 July. Available at: http://www.miniszterelnok.hu/orban-viktor-beszede-a-xxix-balvanyosi-nyari-szabadegyetem-es-diaktaborban/ (accessed 26 November 2020).

Morozov, V., & Rumelili, B. (2012). The External Constitution of European Identity: Russia and Turkey as Europe-Makers. *Cooperation and Conflict*, 47(1), 28–48.

Õry, M. (2018). Végvári Vitézek. 25 July. Available at: https://www.magyarhirlap.hu/velemeny/Vegvari_vitezek-1 (accessed 14 January 2021).

Pap, N. and Glied, V. (2017). The Hungarian Border Barrier and Islam. *Journal of Muslims in Europe*, 6(1), 104–131.

Phillips, C. (2012). *Into the Quagmire: Turkey's Frustrated Syria Policy*. Chatham House London, UK, pp. 2–16.

Reuters. (2015). UPDATE 3: It's Risky to Come to Europe, Hungary's PM Tells Migrants. *Reuters*, 3 September. Available at: https://www.reuters.com/article/europe-migrants-orban-eu-idUSL5N1191FS20150903 (accessed 23 September 2020).

Ripley, T. (2018). *Operation Aleppo: Russia's War in Syria*. Lancaster: Telic-Herrick.

Rumelili, B. (2003). Liminality and Perpetuation of Conflict: Turkish-Greek Relations in the Context of Community-Building by the EU. *European Journal of International Relations*, 9(2), 213–340.

Sabah. (2016). Cumhurbaskani Erdogan'dan AB'ye rest: "BEYEFENDILER RAHATSIZ OLMUS". 12 February. Available at: https://www.sabah.com.tr/galeri/turkiye/gunun-en-cok-okunan-20-haberi-1455295879/14 (accessed 23 September 2020).

Saracoglu, C. & Demirkol, O. (2015). Nationalism and Foreign Policy Discourse in Turkey under the AKP Rule: Geography, History and National Identity. *British Journal of Middle Eastern Studies, 42*(3), 301–319.

Şenbaş, D. (2018). *Post-Cold War Relations between Turkey and Syria*. London: Transnational Press London.

Steele, B. J., & Homolar, A. (2019). Ontological Insecurities and the Politics of Contemporary Populism. *Cambridge Review of International Affairs, 32*(3), 214–221.

Subotic, J., & Zarakol, A. (2013). Cultural Intimacy in International Relations. *European Journal of International Relations, 19*(4), 915–938.

T. C. Cumhurbaskanligi. (2020). Cumhurbaşkanı @RTErdogan, Uluslararası Göç Filmleri Festivali'ne video mesaj gönderdi: "Hüznüyle sevinciyle göç hikâyelerinin etkili bir şekilde anlatılması noktasında sinema çok güçlü bir araçtır". *Twitter*, 21 June. Available at: https://twitter.com/tcbestepe/status/1274752039550099458?ref_src=twsrc%5Etfw%7Ctwcamp%5Etweetembed%7Ctwterm%5E1274752039550099458%7Ctwgr%5Eshare_3&ref_url=https%3A%2F%2Fwww.ntv.com.tr%2Fturkiye%2Fcumhurbaskani-erdogandan-abye-gocmen-elestirisinDh1qc5sWE2Bmh9xHoiVJQ (accessed 25 December 2020).

UNCHR (2021). Operational Portal Refugee Situations. 6 January. Available at: https://data2.unhcr.org/en/situations/syria/location/113 (accessed 20 January 2021).

UNHCR. (2020). The UN Refugee Agency: Global Focus UNHCR Operations Worldwide. Available at: https://reporting.unhcr.org/node/2544?y=2020#year (accessed 8 January 2021).

Weise, Z. (2019). Turkey's Invasion of Syria Explained. *Politico*, 15 October. Available at: https://www.politico.eu/article/8-questions-about-turkeys-incursion-into-syria-answered/ (accessed 23 October 2020).

Wodak, R., & Meyer, M. (2009). *Methods of Critical Discourse Analysis*. London: Sage.

Yenidunyagundemi. (2016). Davutoğlu: Avrupa ülkeleri güvenli bölge ihtiyacını anladı. 24 February. Available at: http://yenidunyagundemi.com/haber/davutoglu-avrupa-ulkeleri-guvenli-bolge-ihtiyacini-anladi--4358.html (accessed 23 September 2020).

About the Authors

Umut Korkut is a professor of International Politics at Glasgow School for Business and Society at Glasgow Caledonian University. He is also a member of the Wise Centre for Economic Justice. Prof Korkut holds expertise in Turkish and Hungarian politics and he has published numerous books and articles on issues covering religion, nationalism, gender, migration, and challenges of liberalisation in European politics. He has previously published two monographs entitled Liberalization Challenges in Hungary: Elitism, Progressivism and Populism (2012) and Politics and Gender Identity in Turkey: Centralised Islam for Socio-economic control (with Hande Eslen-Ziya) (2017). Prof Korkut currently leads the EC Horizon 2020 funded research projects DRad: De-radicalisation in Europe and beyond: Detect, Resolve, Reintegrate project (http://dradproject.com) (2020-2023) and Demos: Democratic Efficacy and Varieties of Populism in Europe (https://demos-h2020.eu/en) (2018-2022).

Email: Umut.Korkut@gcu.ac.uk

Tarik Basbugoglu is a PhD candidate at Glasgow Caledonian University. He researches the impacts of the Syrian Civil War on bilateral relations between Turkey and the US. He focuses on how the AKP (Justice and Development party) political elites use material interests, policy of prestige, and identity-making as discursive tools to appeal the Turkish public and the US political elites during the Syrian Civil War. Tarik Basbugoglu is a member of PSA (Political Studies Association), MESA (Middle East Studies Association), and BISA (British International Studies Association), and presented at the 2020 APSA (American Political Studies Association) annual conference on the topic of the AKP, Twitter, and the Syrian Civil War.

Email: tbasbu200@caledonian.ac.uk

5   Revising Humanitarianism and Solidarity

Migration Management and Peripheral Europeanism in the UK, Poland, and Hungary

James Foley, Daniel Gyollai, and Justyna Szalanska

Abstract

This chapter addresses three cases where governments have adopted explicitly Euro-critical or anti-EU stances linked to migration. The primary aim was to understand how nations that reject the established European narrative of international protection have framed their obligations to alleviate the suffering of war and conflicts. This has been broken into three conceptual areas for comparative purposes: humanitarianism, solidarity, and sovereignty. While observing areas of distinction between these states and the EU, the analysis suggests the difficulties involved in hardened contrasts between a cosmopolitan-humanitarian EU and national-sovereigntist states. Instead, the chapter presents a more nuanced picture of how states have developed distinct accounts of humanitarianism and international order. Moreover, there is considerable evidence that narratives of Europeanness developing on the liminal periphery have been reshaping core notions of "European" identity embodied in the official pronouncements of the Commission.

Keywords: UK, Hungary, Poland, migration

5.1   Introduction

The so-called "refugee crisis" of 2015 served to open European integration to new forms of contestation. While Brexit is the best publicised case, "populist" challenges to a perceived pro-Brussels liberal orthodoxy have

Foley, J. and Korkut, U. (ed.), *Contesting Cosmopolitan Europe. Euroscepticism, Crisis and Borders.*
Amsterdam: Amsterdam University Press 2022
DOI :10.5117/9789463727259_CH05

dominated the last political decade. In the scholarly jargon, an earlier phase of "permissive consensus" gave way to a "constraining dissensus", as leaders were forced to address public grievances towards the EU (Hooghe & Marks, 2009). The UK, Poland and Hungary, the cases considered here, belong to the extreme end of that spectrum: in all three, leaders with anti-establishment mandates have assumed control of government, in part by exploiting discontent at EU migration policy. All rejected the dominant EU narratives of continental "solidarity", "burden sharing", and "humanitarianism" in favour of their own revisionist interpretations. While the UK chose the strategy of "exit", other critical governments pursued the strategy of "voice" (Hirschman, 1970), gaining institutional influence by speaking to a range of grievances – over culture, democracy, and the economic crisis – across the continent with a conservative, civilisational idea of European identity. Equally, as this book has demonstrated, the idea of a European "way of life" in need of "defence" has also entered the ideologies at the heart of the EU's cosmopolitan institutions, including the European Commission. Discourses once associated with avowed Eurosceptics are now central to the imagination of the European project. The periphery of the EU has found mechanisms to exploit the institution's democratic deficit and reshape its legitimising ideas.

This chapter thus compares how governments in the UK, Hungary, and Poland have narrated the challenges of European borders and international obligations of protection. Reflecting the book's overarching project, we sought to break down narrow, stereotypical contrasts between liberal and conservative visions of Europe, and to examine the legitimation process in practice. Our primary aim was to understand how nations that reject the established European narrative of international protection have framed their obligations to alleviate the suffering of war and conflicts. This has been broken into three conceptual areas for comparative purposes: humanitarianism, solidarity, and sovereignty. We explore the extent to which their positions represent a breach with European norms and the uses of these ideological conflicts for various modes or order. A key finding is that, even in more extreme cases like Hungary, there is no direct rejection of humanitarianism as a guiding approach. Instead, the governing parties of Hungary, Poland, and the United Kingdom have taken a revisionist approach to humanitarian questions. Their sense of humanitarian obligations, moreover, has been bound up with national perceptions of the state's alignment in world politics. A further finding is that the apparent breach between European and nation-sovereign approaches risks exaggeration. Indeed, there is considerable evidence that narratives of Europeanness developing on the liminal periphery have been reshaping core notions of "European" identity embodied in the official pronouncements of the Commission.

5.2   Humanitarianism, Solidarity, and Sovereignty

The concepts of humanitarianism, solidarity, and sovereignty developed in our three cases are often defined against a perceived European orthodoxy. However, the boundaries of contestation are often vague because the core concepts have undergone numerous rounds of evolution in response to competing pressures. In general, international humanitarian law (IHL) is a set of rules seeking to limit the effects of armed conflict (Hans, 2019). Asylum policy, in that context, is just one type of humanitarian claim, and while refugee protection is an acknowledged part of the IHL package, most explicit discussions of European humanitarianism centre on conflict reduction, relief work, and the provision of external aid. Given emerging debates, it is crucial to consider that these facets are not mechanically separated. Indeed, the observable trend of European policy, particularly in the cases discussed here, is towards externalising obligations, and towards offshoring refugee management, based on bilateral treaties with third countries (see e.g., Akkerman 2018; Betts & Milner 2007; Mc Namara 2013). These have tended to form part of a pragmatic migration management programme, largely in response to the growing volume of asylum claims. Such efforts have been pursued most vigorously by the most avowedly pro-migration of European leaders, including Angela Merkel (Streeck, 2016). This expanded idea of Europe's humanitarian obligation thus transcends particular "populist" government or challenger states.

This evolution is not altogether new. While all modern humanitarian ideology has foundations in the Geneva Conventions and their additional protocols, they have been continuously reinterpreted to reflect changing historical circumstances. The letter of the Convention inheritance relates to the obligations of sovereign states to individual victims of persecution. Such terms were established with European and particularly Soviet dissidents in mind (see e.g., Whitaker, 1998). Since then, three shifts have transformed humanitarian sentiments towards asylum seekers. Firstly, a shift from persecution, as traditionally defined, to forced migration in the wake of civil wars and other disasters, which has had the consequence of managing larger movements of people as opposed to individual political dissidents. Secondly, relatedly, a geographical shift towards the global south, serving to attach a new stigma to the asylum systems, particularly (though not exclusively) where this has involved migration from Muslim majority nations. Lastly, the development of the European Single Market, with its elimination of internal borders tending to shift the problem of migration management to the transnational level.

Recent contestation reflects the interaction of these three shifts. The EU's objective of open markets, porous internal borders and subsequently a unified "area of freedom, security and justice", in the Lisbon Treaty's terms, came up against the problem of uneven interpretations of humanitarian obligations. This caused friction as states sought to limit certain types of migration, particularly from the global south. There were complaints of "asylum shopping", with claimants supposedly seeking to exploit unevenness of conditions or, having faced rejection, moving to other countries. Conversely, the EU insisted that "asylum must not be a lottery" and that "Member States have a shared responsibility to welcome asylum seekers in a dignified manner, ensuring they are treated fairly and that their case is examined to uniform standards" (European Commission, 2014). These were the rationales behind moves towards a Common European Asylum System (CEAS). However, despite numerous rounds of harmonisation protocols defining obligations with regard to *non-refoulement*, asylum procedures, reception conditions, and qualification standards, asylum remains under the control of Member States, and unevenness embedded in the system. A single area of free movement has not been accompanied by anything approaching a single area of law.

Solidarity has a specific definition in the Charter of Fundamental Rights of the European Union (CFR), where it is listed as a "universal value". However, that definition refers specifically to employment rights. In discussions of asylum, "solidarity" has a separate meaning, referring not to a relationship of right between inhabitants and state power, but rather to a quantitative distribution of international protection obligations between states. A recent press release thus refers to "the concerns of countries at the EU's external borders, which worry that migratory pressures will exceed their capacities and which need solidarity from others" and calls for "fair sharing of responsibility and solidarity [...] for rebuilding trust between Member States and confidence in the capacity of the European Union to manage migration" (European Commission, 2020). As Mitsilegas (2014) observed, this conception of solidarity involves a focus on the impact of migration flows on the state, rather than on the asylum seeker, and that they use the term "burden" to describe increased pressures upon the state – with asylum seekers thus viewed implicitly as a burden to national systems. Solidarity here thus takes the form of what has been deemed and analysed as "burden sharing" – in particular, from a legal perspective, the sharing of the responsibility for increased flows of asylum seekers. As with the logic of abuse underpinning the Dublin system, the logic of burden sharing in effect securitises asylum flows by viewing asylum seekers and asylum seeking in a negative light.

This idea of "solidarity" has obvious overlaps with the broader shift in rethinking humanitarian obligations around asylum. There has been a discernible move from a qualitative relationship between individuals and the state (protection from persecution) towards a quantitative problem of distributing obligations (or "solidarity") (Mitsilegas, 2014). This has been inflamed partly because the European system, particularly the Dublin Regulation, have served to concentrate asylum applications in particular border states. The leaders of the EU's dominant state, Germany, have openly admitted that the system, in Merkel's terms, "doesn't work"; Frank-Walter Steinmeier, then German foreign minister, called for reform of Dublin to ensure "fair distribution" of refugees in Europe (Garcés-Mascareñas, 2015). Conversely, it should be admitted that the countries with the greatest grievances towards migration are not always those facing the greatest "burdens". Indeed, the three states considered in this chapter, which are among the few to elect actively Eurosceptic governments, exemplify that contradiction.

A final common theme is "sovereignty", a concept that plays a central role in the idea of Europe as ontologically liberal. Theoretical debate about the EU order usually rests on this concept. As Bickerton (2012, p. 21) observed, "theorists of integration are divided between those who see sovereignty retained at the national level, only delegated in specific areas to the EU, and those who see in the EU the emergence of a new, pan-European sovereign power" (cf. Bellamy & Castiglione, 1997). The European Union appeals to the principle of "pooled sovereignty", a concept which has defined theoretical debate about the EU's purpose. Equally, critical governments have promised to "restore sovereignty" from the European level, a notion central not just to outright Euro-rejectionists such as the Brexit movement, but also to reformist ideas of a "Europe of nations".

Most ideological claims to sovereignty are not applied with consistency. Thus, all three states considered in this chapter made claims to defend national sovereignty. Equally, all have participated in military interventions (in some cases, on "humanitarian" grounds) that violated the sovereignty of other nations and, indeed, often presented such adventures as alternatives to participating in European humanitarian schemes (Cunliffe, 2020). Indeed, these were precisely the grounds on which former US Defence Secretary donald Rumsfeld defined the contrast between "Old" and "New" Europe

(Anderson 2009; Lansford 2017; Levy et al. 2005). In other words, as discussed elsewhere in this book, they defined their humanitarian obligations specifically towards Christians, and actualise those obligations through sending armed forces to a country that only threatens Hungarian sovereignty in the loosest possible sense of the word. This again highlights the complexity and inconsistency of the interaction between humanitarian obligations and claims to sovereignty.

5.3 The UK

The United Kingdom's exit from the European Union risks overshadowing its longstanding revisionist approach to humanitarianism. However, the tensions that led to "Brexit" have deep historical roots. Britain's shifting approaches to asylum, migration, and Europe reflects its complicated efforts to adjust to its post-colonial role. The narrative of refuge initially served to rationalise liberal-democratic and Cold War opposition to totalitarian regimes, but since the 1990s, in the post-Cold War context, the new asylum seekers from the global south have increasingly been framed as a problem requiring containment (Chimni 1998; Erel et al. 2016). Relationships with the European project have a complex interaction with Britain's image of itself, which cannot always be reduced to introspective nationalism. While British leaders, most notably Thatcher, framed Brussels prerogatives as a threat to British sovereignty, it was often insofar as the UK saw the EU as too narrow, constraining wider global ambitions. Documents seen as key "Brexiteer" manifestos, such as *Britannia Unchained*, are likewise invested in defining a wider world role, rather than retreating into a defensive national unit (Kwarteng et al. 2012; Lakin 2014). Britain's state managers and political managers, in other words, have perceived themselves as belonging to a wider cosmopolitan sphere that transcends Europe, which is further complicated by Commonwealth ties and being part of an American-led military policy. Discourses of humanitarianism are thus shaped by Britain's world role, and the state has repeatedly tried to define its commitments in terms that transcend asylum, to encompass a wider interventionist military and diplomatic policy.

Recent UK approaches to asylum owe much to the long period of centre-left dominance under New Labour (Mulvey, 2011, 2010). This established a compound of liberalism and authoritarianism that has continued to prevail under Conservative governments. On the one hand, New Labour established the Human Rights Act, bringing a range of potential legal protections and recourse to European Court of Justice. This has been a regular point of contention with subsequent Conservative governments, which have often vowed to replace the Act. On the other hand, this emerged alongside an increasingly punitive approach to asylum management, rooted in discourses of the "bogus asylum seeker", which coalesced, crucially, with a relatively permissive approach to European economic migration. The latter type of migration was rationalised on neoliberal grounds as enhancing Britain's economic competitiveness by achieving a competitive labour market and providing firms with access to a pool of highly skilled workers. By contrast, asylum seekers were firmly denied access to the labour market. The mark of differentiation, as researchers have long observed, was the likely racial and cultural background of asylum applicants. The UK here reflected a wider shift in its imagination of asylum seekers, from being heroic victims of political persecution, to a stigmatised mass of migrants from the global south. Equally, New Labour built its legitimation on "War on Terror" security policies that have been linked to the spread of Islamophobic rhetoric (Kundnani 2014; Moosavi 2015). Rhetoric conflicts over asylum also merged into terror-related security discourse.

Subsequently, a succession of Conservative governments has managed the fallout from the Arab Spring and from the Syrian Civil War in particular, which again problematised the UK's relations with Muslim-majority nations. No UK government has presented a theoretical objection to humanitarianism (although "human rights" have been criticised in the particular context of the Human Rights Act), and there has been an emphasis on the asylum system as a distinctive "British tradition": "We are granting asylum to those who need it, consistent with this country's proud tradition of giving help to those who need it most" (May, 2014). After an initially deterrence-focused response, David Cameron's government was forced to issue statements of humanitarian concern: Cameron even argued that "no country has done more than Britain when it comes to help for Syrian refugees" (Prime Minister's Office, 2016). Established efforts were made to frame a balance between humanitarian obligation, on one side, and "burdens" (including security burdens) on the other:

> Britain will always be open to those who are seeking asylum from persecution. That says something very important about the kind of country we are and we should be proud of that too. But excessive immigration brings pressures, real pressures on our communities up and down the country. Pressures on schools, housing and healthcare and social pressures too. (Cameron, 2013)

Nonetheless, the above was founded on a revisionist take on humanitarian purpose. Conservative leaders emphasised that humanitarian aid was best delivered externally, outside of UK borders, often in third countries such as Lebanon. Although the UK was taking a comparatively low amount of asylum seekers, leaders emphasised that the country was providing external humanitarian aid, which was preferable on humanitarian grounds, as it would prevent Syrians fleeing the conflict from undertaking "perilous journeys" to reach European countries. A discourse was thus established in which Britain was combining deterrence against those seeking to journey to Europe, and nonetheless establishing itself as the "most humanitarian" response. In this sense, the aim was to break the link between offering asylum and humanitarianism.

Following internal criticism of the UK response, the government established resettlement schemes targeting the "most vulnerable" refugees – notably the VPRS – as alternatives to the standard asylum system. Resettlement is represented as an approach that is distinctive to the UK, and an alternative to relocation within Europe or to admitting greater numbers of applicants into UK borders: "We will not be taking more refugees – we have our programme of resettling people direct from the refugee camps and that stays the same" (Cameron, 2016). In the UK Government's discourse, their system of resettlement is simultaneously a mechanism of "controlled immigration" and, by their own estimation, a more altruistic approach than comparable European schemes, allowing political leaders to bridge conflicting narratives of humanitarianism and border control. However, a new order of stigma was attached to the spontaneously arriving asylum seekers, as opposed to the legitimate, hand-selected recipients of the resettlement programme. These claims rest on the criterion of "vulnerability", which serves as a critical stance on the established international system for managing refugees. They claim that the existing global asylum "system is geared towards helping those most able to access it, and sometimes manipulate it, for their own ends – those who are young enough, fit enough, and have the resources to get to Britain" and as a result, "support is too often denied to the most vulnerable, and those most in need of our help" (May, 2015). The category of the deserving, hand-selected refugee is, in most cases, built on a contrast with the undeserving, spontaneously arriving asylum seeker.

The aim, as above, was to balance apparent humanitarian commitments with an immigration control agenda. This was sometimes framed in conflict with European institutions, although largely insofar as the latter were attempting to achieve similar ends. On the one hand, the UK must present itself as unusually virtuous, particularly in relation to the EU. On the other hand, controlling migration has been central to the legitimation strategies of both governing parties, and both parties have indulged the idea (not supported by statistics) of a country "over-burdened", having taken on an unfair load relative to others. Equally, the above narratives show that humanitarian moralism and anti-migration deterrence measures can be reframed as compatible objectives.

Thus, the UK had developed a revisionist take on humanitarianism long before Brexit. It officially rejected official EU schemes for "solidarity" based on quotas for Syrian refugees, and instead established an autonomous system, which it rationalised as representing higher humanitarian virtue. The Brexit campaign nonetheless served to heighten themes related to migration management. Themes of sovereignty converged around the slogan of "take back control", and while this had broader meanings, its link to immigration and the asylum system was often explicit. Nigel Farage's unofficial Leave campaign thus released a billboard poster headlined "Breaking Point" picturing a queue of non-white migrants crossing the Croatia–Slovenia border, with a subtitle reading: "We must break free of the EU and take back control". While the official Leave campaign distanced itself from the poster, many critics link Brexit's core themes of sovereignty to growing anti-migrant sentiment.

Brexit has meant the UK's withdrawal from core elements of the European asylum system, such as Eurodac, Dublin, and the various CEAS directives. However, it remains bound by a range of other international agreements, and the UK Government insists that leaving EU systems will not lessen commitments to international protection:

> The UK already has high standards in how we operate our asylum system and we will continue to be a world leader in this area. The UK will of course continue to be subject to the ECHR. (quoted in Gower, 2020)

It is also crucial to remember that the UK debate on migration control was not monopolised by Leave supporters. David Cameron's initial referendum position was built around "reforms" to Europe that partly centred on migration. The ideological leader of the Remain and "People's Vote" movements likewise sought to articulate EU membership with a harder position on external borders, specifically geared to reducing non-white, non-Christian migration. This was Tony Blair's offer to voters discontented with migration and was fully consistent with the New Labour position outlined above. It equally overlaps with the views below: Hungarian and Polish leaders support internal but oppose external EU migration. In terms of actual political forces, the Brexit debate should thus be regarded less as a polarised debate between competing value systems, and more as a point of convergence, based on a clash of competing visions of European border control. While the Brexiteers sought to control external migration unilaterally, through restoring powers to the UK parliament, their opponents sought a multilateral agreement for similar purposes.

5.4   Poland

Poland's relationship to Europe is complicated by its emergence from the communist past, which on the one hand leaves a legacy of national resistance to external domination, and on the other hand has inspired a desire for "catch up" with Western Europe. Since accession to the EU in 2004, parties in opposition and government have become increasingly embroiled in European politics, especially during successive EU crises. Accession coincided with but also helped precipitate transformations in party-political conflict, with the dominant axis shifting from left-versus-right to liberalism-versus-social conservatism. Contestation over "European" identity has been central to the resulting differentiation of political values. Nonetheless, all Polish governments have supported European integration as a matter of national interest. The slogan "a strong Poland in a strong Europe" has been a rallying point for all parties. Conversely, there has cross-party resistance to perceived projects for European federalism and the notion of a "two-speed Europe" (Grosse 2018). During the "refugee crisis", politicians from the largest parties (Law and Justice, Civic Platform, Modern) emphasised protection of the EU's external borders. Equally, there was convergence on the question of "solidarity" as a rule and all parties either distanced themselves from or expressed outright hostility towards refugee relocation mechanisms (Szalanska, 2020).

Crucially, shifts in electoral politics have diverted the Polish state from its earlier quest for modernisation and Europeanisation. Since coming to power in late 2015, the Law and Justice party (Prawo I Sprawiedliwość, PiS) has engaged in high profile conflict with the EU and perceived European ideals. It increasingly frames the EU less as an opportunity for Polish development and more as a threat to Polish sovereignty (Buras, 2017). The ideological roots of this discontent lie in convictions about nation, culture, and Europe shared by party members and a wider social base in a predominantly Catholic nation. Jarosław Kaczyński, the unofficial leader of PiS, articulates a vision of Europe as a confederation of sovereign nation-states, based on a pluralism of value systems (Rzeczpospolita, 2020). The Polish government has turned much of its criticisms on the contrast between the apparent pluralism of liberalism and its actual anti-pluralist consequences. Whenever Poland has been admonished or criticised for its illiberal turn, which has included attacks on minorities and press freedom, Kaczyński appealed to principles of national sovereignty.

The "refugee crisis" of 2015 was a lightning rod for the contestation of Polish and European identities. While the earlier Civic Platform government accepted the proposed quota system for relocating refugees, the Law and Justice party disregarded it when it came to power two months later. It first lowered the admission of refugees to 400, then rescinded plans for Poland to take its first 100 refugees in May 2016 (Łotocki, 2019, pp. 176–177). Based on our analysis of political speeches, PiS's rejection of official EU solidarity was founded on five discursive framings: a rejection of EU decrees; the defence of Polish sovereignty; caring about Polish values; Poland's historical experience of national oppression; and, lastly, disputing the most effective policies for managing the "refugee crisis". The first three framings were direct rejections of the solidarity principle, counterposing it to national needs. The final framing, by contrast, represents a more ambivalent reframing of humanitarianism, with calls to send aid to the asylum seekers' country of origin (Szalanska 2020; Łotocki 2019).

Law and Justice thus explicitly rejected the officially conceived solidarity of the quota system, presenting it as unjust and self-interested. In this narrative, the party drew from wellsprings of Polish identity, especially the earlier legacy of dependence on and resistance to the Soviet Union. Equally, they drew on grievances against another historical oppressor, Germany, with Merkel presented as having made smaller, poorer countries bear responsibility for her own policy errors as Kaczynski (2015, quoted in Szalanska, 2020) stated that "it was a mistake of Merkel, and now she wants to share her mistake with other countries".

Additionally, conflict centred on the cultural and religious background of potential refugees relocated to Poland. Leading PiS politicians Jarosław Kaczyński, Beata Szydło, and Mateusz Morawiecki presented the Muslim origins of asylum seekers as a civilisational threat to the Polish nation, with Kaczyński stating that "a family and the nation [and their safety] should be put first, before others" (Kaczynski 2015 in Szalanska, 2020).

Polish historical experience was also invoked, with Kaczyński arguing that a country that had not participated in colonialism should not bear the same responsibility for civil wars as former colonisers. Kaczynski (2017 in Szalanska 2020) stated that "[Poland] did not exploit the countries from which these refugees come to Europe today, we did not use their labour force, and finally we did not invite them to Europe. We have every moral right to say no. Even more than that, since we are already helping". These rationales were used to counter accusations of having violated the party's Christian morality, with the implied dissonance between charitable obligation and actual parsimoniousness.

Law and Justice likewise promoted overseas humanitarian and development aid as the alternative solution to the crisis with Szydlo (2017, quoted in Szalanska 2020) stating "we are helping and we will be helping – but those, who need help and wait there, in place". This rhetorical framing, eliding humanitarian aid with the value of solidarity was also inscribed in the party program of 2019, which asserted that Poland would be a country promoting freedom, justice, solidarity, and truth in the world. It went on to assert that Poland's solidarity was exemplified by military participation in humanitarian interventions in remote corners of the world. This revision of the solidarity principle went even further when the Prime Minister Morawiecki called for the EU engagement in stabilisation and development of Africa to prevent further migration: "We propose creating a European fund for development of Africa and I declare that Poland wants to participate in such help – in giving a rod instead of a fish – in a greater extent than it stems from our GDP" (Morawiecki 2018, quoted in Szalanska, 2020). In Law and Justice's framing, it was Poland standing for real solidarity; by contrast, the established mode of solidarity, the relocation mechanism between Member States, was presented as a tool of Germany and Brussels.

Polish humanitarian aid was in fact substantially raised from PLN 26 million in 2015 to PLN 173 million in 2017; it subsequently declined to PLN 135 million in 2018 (Supreme Audit Office, 2020). Politicisation of humanitarian aid led to the establishment of a new institution – a Humanitarian Aid Minister[7] – with an appointment for Beata Kempa, a politician openly opposed to admitting asylum seekers. This took questions of distribution out of the hands of the Ministry of Foreign Affairs (MFA). Yet, whereas MFA humanitarian aid was distributed in a measured and well-audited manner, the new Ministry was less bound by guidelines on transparency. According to the Supreme Audit Office, all contracts in the Chancellery were concluded without competitions based on offers placed by NGOs (Supreme Audit Office 2020). An example of its ineffectiveness was a charity action

---

7   The post of Humanitarian Aid Minister existed until December 2019, when Mateusz Morawiecki formed his new government after parliamentary elections.

"Backpacks for Aleppo" launched by the Minister Beata Kempa: the collected backpacks, far from being sent to children in Syria, ended up warehoused in a Polish church.

For the Law and Justice government, these revisionist approaches to humanitarianism and solidarity are part of its "policy of getting up from knees". This nationalism involves having a distinct "Polish voice" in European matters and not surrendering to the will (and ideas) of stronger states like Germany. Their mode of contestation with the EU is explicitly designed to restore collective dignity as the foundation of nationalist revival (Runciman, 2018).

5.5 Hungary

Hungary's recent evolution has been dominated by the figure of Viktor Orbán, Hungary's ultra-conservative prime minister, in post since 2010. In Korkut's interpretation, this decade in power has been based on an alternative narrative of Europeanisation: Orbán believes that liberalism has failed and that future integration should be based on a Hungarian-style civilisational (white, Christian) value system (Korkut, 2020). While Orbán himself remains a contested and marginal figure in mainstream European politics, his rhetorical themes have unarguably exerted influence. Korkut (2020) thus demonstrated overlaps between Orbán's vision and the "European way of life" agenda promoted and endorsed by the Commission's new Pact on Migration and Asylum. However, while Orbán has some marginal ambitions for Europe-wide projects, his rhetoric is fundamentally and solely aimed at domestic audiences.

We have shown elsewhere how the Hungarian government dismantled the entire asylum system and criminalised migration (Gyollai & Amatrudo, 2019; Gyollai, 2019); denied international protection for asylum seekers with respect to the human rights of Hungarians and conditioned humanitarian support for would-be asylum seekers in the country of origin to belonging to Christian communities (Korkut, Terlizzi and Gyollai, 2020); and clashed with the EU on migration related issues that eventually resulted in numerous infringement proceedings (Gyollai and Korkut, 2020). Although indicative of a larger political agenda, none of these issues serve other than domestic electoral purposes. To Orbán, we argue, the ideal of a conflicting or peripheral Europeanism to preserve national sovereignty is merely a cover-up; the Orbanisation of EU policy is a collateral damage of the Hungarian PM's politics. Orbán exploits humanitarianism, migration, and Hungary's responsibilities as an EU Member State to bolster his politics of polarisation. In what follows, we will demonstrate how Orbán's false Christian-nationalism has been used to fuel anti-immigrant, anti-Semitic, and anti-EU sentiments to maintain Fidesz-KDNP dominance in Hungary.

The reconstitution of Hungarian national identity based on in- and outgroup conflicts has always been a core element, if not the organising principle, of Orbán's politics of polarisation. It is confrontational and led by enemy construction (Palonen, 2018; Antal, 2016). Prior to the issue of mass migration, the PM had already successfully instrumentalised the collective memories of the 1848/1956 freedom fights salient to the Hungarian public to gain electoral support. The arrival of the unprecedented number of asylum seekers in summer 2015 served as an opportunity to reinforce the "Us" and "Them" dichotomy by evoking the past memories of the Ottoman conquest (Mendelski 2019; Lamour & Varga, 2017). Fidesz have constructed the image of Hungary as a nation which, although left alone and suffered multitude of traumas, has always been able to fight back and regain its freedom from foreign and/or domestic aggressors. Orbán portrayed himself as a freedom fighter, who single-handedly chased the Soviets out of the country in 1989. Since 2015, he has been simultaneously defending "European Christianity" from the "Muslim invasion", and Hungarian national sovereignty against Europe itself. Most recently, triggered by the EU's new framework to strengthen the rule of law, he has been tirelessly fighting for a "new Brussels Empire" against the "Soros network". Orbán's narrative thus conflates opposition to his politics with opposition to the nation as such.

Orbán's narrative repertoire, "the monopolisation of patriotism", "siege mentality", and "self-isolation" are all instrumental in unifying a community, and simultaneously generating and justifying collective hostility against opponents (Bar-Tal, 2000, Ch. 5-7). Fidesz won a landslide victory at the 2018 general elections with no platform other than the anti-immigrant campaign. Orbán has used this platform to escalate his illiberal policies and introduced a new state of crisis (still in force at the time of writing), that is, the so-called "crisis situation caused by mass migration".

To Orbán, the term "Christian" is a multi-purpose ingroup attribute which, before becoming the synonym for "Islamophobic", has been used as an identifier for voters in opposition to Ferenc Gyurcsány's socialist government. For that matter, Fidesz has never made a secret of its devotion to the cultural legacy of the irredentist and anti-Semitic Horthy era in its (group-) identity politics (Palonen 2018; Kovács 2016). Horthy was the regent of Hungary between 1920 and 1944, who put an end to, and avenged (the

"White Terror") the bloodshed of the 1919 Hungarian Soviet Republic (the "Red Terror"). Fidesz symbolically removed the iconic statue of Imre Nagy from Martyr's Square in Budapest and replaced it with the monument that stood there before the Second World War, erected by Horthy to the memory of the victims of the communist regime. Anti-communist and Christian-nationalist ideologies dating from the interwar period thus form the ideological foundation of the political and policy strategies of Orbán. The new constitution, the "Fundamental Law of Hungary" represents a crystallisation of Orbán's attempt to redefine and re-establish Hungarian national identity in line with the ideological framework of the authoritarian Horthy regime (Kis 2012; Miklóssy and Nyyssönen, 2018).

On the one hand, Fidesz has avoided being overtly anti-Semitic, having rather downplayed Horthy's otherwise well-documented (Bodo 2019; Romsics 2016; Ungváry 2016) role in the persecution of Hungarian Jews, both before and during the Holocaust, and mainstreamed the Christian-nationalist agenda only. This, coupled with Fidesz's kin state activism, is appealing to both conservative and diaspora voters. On the other hand, by denouncing Horthy as a Nazi collaborator, Fidesz would potentially lose its far-right, once-Jobbik voters. Neither the silence of Fidesz when neo-Nazi groups marching in the capital, commemorating the SS breakout attempt during the siege of Budapest in 1945, nor the covert anti-Semitism palpable in narratives scapegoating George Soros for anything of which Orbán disapproves, especially irregular migration, are accidental.

Even by their own standards, Orbán's agendas are built on inconsistencies. Several senior members of Fidesz, including Orbán himself, have been recipients of Soros-funded scholarships. Despite the rhetorical conflicts with the Islamic world, Hungary's residency bond business has had an Abu Dhabi branch; Fidesz sold a residency permit to a key figure of the Bashar al-Assad regime; and Orbán is a returning guest of the Turkic Council, maintaining a good relationship with the President of Turkey. At the opening ceremony of Tomb of Gül Baba, in the presence of President Erdogan, Orbán praised the Ottomans for providing protection to fugitives of the 1848–1849 revolution. The Tomb is an Islamic pilgrimage site in the heart of Budapest, recently restored by funds partly from the Hungarian government.

In his relations with Europe, Orbán's "solidarity" included not just withdrawal from the resettlement quota plan, but also a threat to veto the EU's 2021–2027 budget. This sparring was engineered to establish a narrative for domestic audiences: to discuss his veto in Brussels, Orbán had to venture down into the "Wolf's Lair", but he returned with a "victory over Soros".

5.6   Discussion and Conclusion

There are notable differences between the three cases. Britain's conflicts
with the European Union were a complex compound of two elements: the
state's aspirations to higher global leadership, on the one hand, and the
grievances of voters on the other, the latter including immigration but also
economic and democratic concerns. Both before and after Brexit, political
leaders have presented Britain as a nation of higher humanitarian purposes,
whether achieved through foreign intervention or boutique systems of
refugee relocation. They have sought to transcend divides between anti-
migrant deterrence and humanitarian delivery, in a manner that is not
altogether inconsistent with omewhng EU policy. By contrast, Hungary
and Poland have taken more inflammatory stances on humanitarianism,
drawing on narratives of national oppression under the Soviet Union as
well as an explicitly ethno-religious conception of European identity.
Nonetheless, both states have found, like Britain, that "boutique" humanitarian interventions can be a useful arm of foreign policy. As demonstrated
elsewhere in this book, a central focus of Hungarian policy has been to
reframe humanitarianism as a matter of Christian persecution in Islamic
majority countries. The Polish state has involved itself in a range of military
adventures and has sought to shift the boundaries of humanitarianism
in these terms. All three governments have devised a conception of humanitarianism, which reflects their national histories and their sense of
a wider global mission.

   All three rejected the authority of European institutions over quotas,
and thus officially conceived "solidarity". Britain agreed to take a specified
number, but, crucially, only from camps near the conflict zone. It refused
to engage with redistributing the refugees who had already arrived in
Europe, a mechanism designed to relieve stress on border states. Poland's
conservative government signalled its departure from the established
mode of Europeanisation when they overturned earlier commitments
to relocation. The Hungarian government arguably went furthest, in
actively arranging a plebiscite on the quota system. That referendum
(which ultimately failed to deliver a result due to a limited turnout) was
actively grounded on rejection of the European establishment. As the
BBC reported, Orbán sought to portray himself as the "champion of the
concerns of ordinary Europeans" against the actions of "an unelected,
liberal elite". Observable contrasts exist between these cases, with the
UK appealing (however hypocritically) to a higher humanitarian calling,

while Hungary's plebiscitary approach was built on unabashedly populist contrasts between elites and masses.

Lastly, all appealed to principles of national sovereignty. Yet the seriousness of this aspiration has not been tested. The most trenchant academic critics of the EU's impact on popular sovereignty see the bloc as empowering the domestic state at the expense of domestic citizens. However, Kaczyński and Orbán have themselves centralised authoritarian power, and equally show little desire for exiting European structures. As Bickerton observes, "the 'counter-revolutionaries' have no real desire to leave the EU" (Bickerton, 2020). Instead, their manoeuvres have amounted to scapegoating vulnerable populations for the purposes of domestic posturing and internal EU politicking, while expanding the repressive state over ideologically opponents. Indeed, their narrative of a European federalist elite not only misunderstands the recent evolution of the EU towards inter-governmentalism, it also misconceives how member-statehood amounts to a process of state transformation, and the role this plays in the wider democratic deficit.

If these are the parameters of contestation, we must be cautious about superficial contrasts between an ethical, cosmopolitan European technocracy and its sovereigntist Member States. If we consider the EU largely as a superstate bureaucracy evolving towards its own value system, then the above conflicts assume one type of importance. A dualism is maintained, between the progressive-cosmopolitan level and the regressive-sovereigntist level. Conversely, if the EU is regarded as an inter-governmental bureaucracy, it highlights the interconnected nature of the emerging conservative, civilisational government discourses of Europe and the Commission's "way of life" agenda. This reinforces the conclusion, growing across much of the critical literature, that the EU is primarily a confused reflection of the internal politics of its various Member States. In contrast to national parliamentary bodies, which are designed to manage the inevitability of conflict, EU tends to regard a clash of values as taboo and a problem to be managed out of existence (Anderson 2009; Bickerton 2012; Heisenberg 2005). In this sense, the desire to minimise ruptures like Brexit coalesces with the desire to incorporate dissenters, including populists in the European Parliamentary, but more especially dissenting governments in the more decisive institutions of the European Council. This suggests the peculiarities of EU "cosmopolitanism", which functions less as an outright value system than a mode of containing conflicting value systems, to the point of integrating, clumsily, the illiberal sentiments of challenger governments.

References

Akkerman, M. (2018). Expanding the Fortress: The Policies, the Profiteers and the People Shaped by EU's Border Externalisation Programme. *Transnational Institute* 11.

Anderson, P. (2009). *The New Old World*. London; New York: Verso Books.

Antal, A. (2016). Politikai ellenség és identitás. In Földes, Gy., & Antal A. (eds.) Holtpont (pp. 131-152)

Bar-Tal, D. (2000). *Shared Beliefs in a Society*. London: Sage.

Bellamy, R., Castiglione, D. (1997). Building the Union: The Nature of Sovereignty in the Political Architecture of Europe. *Law and Philosophy*, *16*(4), 421–445.

Betts, A., Milner, J. (2007). The Externalisation of EU Asylum Policy: The Position of African States. Danish Institute for International Studies (DIIS).

Bickerton, C. J. (2020). The Persistence of Europe. *New Left Review*. Available at: https://newleftreview.org/issues/ii122/articles/christopher-bickerton-the-persistence-of-europe (accessed 13 January 2021).

Bickerton, C. J. (2012). *European Integration: From Nation-States to Member States*. Oxford: Oxford University Press.

Bodó, B. (2019). *The White Terror: Antisemitic and Political Violence in Hungary, 1919–1921*. Abingdon: Routledge.

Buras, P. (2017). *Europe and its Discontents: Poland's Collision Course with the European Union*. Available at: https://www.ecfr.eu/publications/summary/europe_and_its_discontents_polands_collision_course_with_the_eu_7220 (accessed 20 September 2020).

Cameron, D. (2013). David Cameron's Immigration Speech. UK Government. Available at: https://www.gov.uk/government/speeches/david-camerons-immigration-speech (accessed 8 January 2019).

Cameron, D. (2016). PM Statement Following European Council Meeting: 18 March 2016. UK Government. Available at: https://www.gov.uk/government/speeches/pm-statement-following-european-council-meeting-18-march-2016 (accessed 23 August 2019).

Chimni, B. S. (1998). The Geopolitics of Refugee Studies: A View from the South. *Journal of Refugee Studies*, *11*, 350–374.

Cunliffe, P. (2020). *Cosmopolitan Dystopia: International Intervention and the Failure of the West*. Manchester: Manchester University Press.

Erel, U., Murji, K., Nahaboo, Z. (2016). Understanding the Contemporary Race–Migration Nexus. *Ethnic and Racial Studies*, *39*, 1339–1360.

European Commission, (2014). A Common European Asylum System. Publications Office, EU.

European Commission. (2020). New Pact on Migration and Asylum. *European Commission.* Available at: https://ec.europa.eu/commission/presscorner/detail/en/ip_20_1706 (accessed 13 January 2021).

Garcés-Mascareñas, B. (2015). Why Dublin "Doesn't Work". *CIDOB.* Available at: http://www.cidob.org/en/publications/publication_series/notes_internacionals/n1_135_por_que_dublin_no_funciona/why_dublin_doesn_t_work (accessed 13 January 2021).

Gower, M. (2020). *Brexit: The End of the Dublin III Regulation in the UK.*

Grosse, T. (2018). Polskie ugrupowania polityczne wobec integracji europejskiej. *The Warsaw Institute Review.* Available at: https://warsawinstitute.org/pl/polskie-ugrupowania-polityczne-wobec-integracji-europejskiej/ (accessed 15 September 2020).

Hans. (2019). International Humanitarian Law. European Civil Protection And Humanitarian Aid Operations. *European Commission.* Available at: https://ec.europa.eu/echo/what/humanitarian-aid/international-humanitarian-law_en (accessed 13 January 2021).

Heisenberg, D. (2005). The Institution of "Consensus" in the European Union: Formal Versus Informal Decision-Making in the Council. *European Journal of Political Research, 44*(1), 65–90.

Hirschman, A. O. (1970). *Exit, Voice, and Loyalty: Responses to Decline in Firms, Organizations, and States.* Cambridge, MA: Harvard University Press.

Hooghe, L., & Marks, G. (2009). A Postfunctionalist Theory of European Integration: From Permissive Consensus to Constraining Dissensus. *British Journal Political Science, 39*(1), 1–23.

Kis, J. (2012). Introduction: From the 1989 Constitution to the 2011 Fundamental Law. In Tóth, G. A. (eds.), *Constitution for a Disunited Nation: On Hungary's 2011 Fundamental Law* (pp. 1–21). Budapest: CEUP.

Korkut, U. (2020). Conflicting Conceptualisations of Europeanisation: Hungary Country Report. RESPOND Working Papers, November 2020.

Kovács, É. (2016). Overcoming History through Trauma: The Hungarian Historikerstreit. *European Review, 24*(4), 523–534.

Kundnani, A. (2014). *The Muslims are Coming!: Islamophobia, Extremism, and the Domestic War on Terror.* London: Verso.

Kwarteng, K., Patel, P., Raab, D., Skidmore, C., & Truss, E. (2012). Britannia Unchained. In *Britannia Unchained* (pp. 100–112). New York: Springer.

Lakin, M. (2014). After Cameron: The New New Right and the Unchaining of Britannia. *Global Discourse, 4*(1), 71–89.

Lamour, C., & Varga, R. (2017). The Border as a Resource in Right-wing Populist Discourse: Viktor Orbán and the Diasporas in a Multi-scalar Europe. *Journal of Borderlands Studies, 35*(3), 335–350.

Lansford, T. (2017). *Old Europe, New Europe and the US: Renegotiating Transatlantic Security in the Post 9/11 Era.* London: Routledge.

Law and Justice (Prawo I Sprawiedliwość) (2019). Program partii Prawo i Spawiedliwość. Polski model państwa dobrobytu. Available at: http://pis.org.pl/dokumenty (accessed 17 December 2020).

Levy, D., Pensky, M., Torpey, J. C., & Torpey, J. (2005). *Old Europe, New Europe, Core Europe: Transatlantic Relations After the Iraq War.* London: Verso.

Łotocki, Ł. (2019). Kryzys imigracyjny w Europie w polskim dyskursie publicznym w latach 2015–2018, Elipsa Dom Wydawniczy, Warszawa.

May, T. (2014). Oral Statement by the Home Secretary on Syrian Refugees. UK Government. Available at: https://www.gov.uk/government/speeches/oral-statement-by-the-home-secretary-on-syrian-refugees (accessed 8 January 2019).

May, T. (2015). Theresa May's Speech to the Conservative Party Conference – In Full. Available at: https://www.independent.co.uk/news/uk/politics/theresa-may-s-speech-to-the-conservative-party-conference-in-full-a6681901.html (accessed 25 July 2019).

Mc Namara, F. (2013). Member State Responsibility for Migration Control Within Third States–Externalisation Revisited. *European Journal of Migration and Law, 15*(3), 319–335.

Mendelski, B. (2019). The Rhetoric of Hungarian Premier Victor Orban: Inside X Outside in the Context of Immigration Crisis. In Ratuva, S. (ed.), *The Palgrave Handbook of Ethnicity.* Singapore: Palgrave.

Miklóssy, K., & Nyyssönen, H. (2018). Defining the New Polity: Constitutional Memory in Hungary and Beyond. *Journal of Contemporary European Studies, 26*(3), 322–333.

Mitsilegas, V. (2014). Solidarity and Trust in the Common European Asylum System. *Comparative Migration Studies, 2,* 181–202.

Moosavi, L. (2015). Orientalism at Home: Islamophobia in the Representations of Islam and Muslims by the New Labour Government. *Ethnicities, 15*(5), 652–674.

Mulvey, G. (2010). When Policy Creates Politics: The Problematizing of Immigration and the Consequences for Refugee Integration in the UK. *Journal of Refugee Studies, 23*(4), 437–462.

Mulvey, G. (2011). Immigration under New Labour: Policy and Effects. *Journal of Ethnic and Migration Studies, 37*(9), 1477–1493.

Palonen, E. (2018). Performing the Nation: The Janus-Faced Populist Foundations of Illiberalism in Hungary. *Journal of Contemporary European Studies, 26*(3), 308–321.

Prime Minister's Office (2016). Unaccompanied Asylum-Seeking Children to Be Resettled from Europe. UK Government. Available at: https://www.gov.uk/

government/news/unaccompanied-asylum-seeking-children-to-be-resettled-from-europe (accessed 25 July 2019).

Romsics, I. (2016). The Antisemitism of István Bethlen and Jewish Policy in the Horthy Era. In Braham, R. L., & Kovács, A. (eds.) *The Holocaust in Hungary: Seventy Years Later* (pp. 27–36). Budapest: CEUP.

Runciman, D. (2018). *How Democracy Ends*. London: Profile Books

Streeck, W. (2016). Scenario for a Wonderful Tomorrow. *London Review of Books*, *38*(7), 7–10.

Supreme Audit Office (Najwyższa Izba Kontroli) (2020). Informacja o wynikach kontroli. Realizacja zadań administracji publicznej w zakresie udzielania pomocy humanitarnej poza granicami Polski. Available at: https://www.nik.gov.pl/plik/id,22718,vp,25417.pdf (accessed 17 December 2020).

Szałańska, J. (2020). Conflicting Conception of Europeanisation. Poland Country Report, Multilevel Governance of Mass Migration in Europe and Beyond Project (#770564, Horizon2020) Report Series. Available at: https://respondmigration.com/wp-blog (accessed 29 January 2021).

Társadalomkritikai tanulmányok Magyarország elmúlt 25 évéről. (pp. 131–152). Budapest: Napvilág.

Ungváry, K. (2016). Master Plan? The Decision-Making Process Behind the Deportations. In Braham, R. L., & Kovács, A. (eds.) *The Holocaust in Hungary: Seventy Years Later* (pp. 105–146). Budapest: CEUP.

Whitaker, R. (1998). Refugees: The Security Dimension. *Citizenship Studies*, *2*(3), 413–434.

About the Authors

James Foley is a lecturer in politics at Glasgow Caledonian University. He received his PhD from the University of Edinburgh, and he is the author of two books on Scottish independence and the British state.
Email address: james.foley@gcu.ac.uk

Daniel Gyollai is a PhD Candidate at Glasgow Caledonian University. His PhD project focuses on the effect of narratives on policing. Daniel is currently a research assistant on the Horizon 2020 project RESPOND: Multilevel Governance of Mass Migration in Europe and Beyond.
Email: daniel.gyollai@gcu.ac.uk

Justyna Szałańska is an Affiliate of the Centre of Migration Research, University of Warsaw, and a Research Assistant at the Collegium of Socio-Economics in SGH Warsaw School of Economics. She is also pursuing her PhD at the Faculty of Political Sciences and International Studies at the University of Warsaw. Her PhD dissertation focuses on a category of national identity and its materialisation in Turkey's foreign policy. In 2009 she received her MA Diploma in International Relations and in 2010 her BA Diploma in Turkish Studies from the University of Warsaw. In 2011 she was a Research Trainee at the BILGESAM, a Turkish think tank. In 2014 she was awarded TUBITAK Scholarship for Foreign Researchers in Turkey, which enabled her to be a Research Fellow at the Center of International and European Research at the Kadir Has University (Turkey) between November 2014 and May 2015. Her research interests focus on European integration, identity issues in Turkey and Europe, citizenship policies, and refugee and asylum seeker protection policies. She has been a key staff member on two Horizon 2020 projects: RESPOND Multilevel Governance of Mass Migration in Europe and Beyond (2017–2020) and Investing in "Welcoming Spaces" in Europe: Revitalising Shrinking Areas by Hosting Non-EU Migrants (2020–2024). She is also a co-author of a short documentary on refugee perception in Poland, "Bez komentarza" ("Without a comment"), produced by the POLIN museum (2016).

6   "Leave a Light on for Scotland"

Examining Cosmopolitan Nationalism in Scotland

Marcus Nicolson

Abstract

This chapter examines the relationship between Scottish nationalism and Europeanness. I investigate pro-European rhetoric as used by the Scottish National Party (SNP) in public discourse and contrast the message of this discourse with survey evidence. Through this Scottish case study, it is revealed that Scottish pro-Europeanness has been contested in public debate over the last decades. Today Scottish nationalism, and support for the European Union, remains more nuanced than many outside observers may conclude. This study reaches three main conclusions. The first point is that a hyperactive politicised Europeanness in macro-level politics has only marginal implications for the wider Scottish public. The second is that Europeanness and nationalist identity are not inconsistent. Lastly, Scotland's mainstream political framing of immigration has been employed to justify Scottish distinctiveness, and garner support for an independent Scotland in Europe.

Keywords: *Discourse, nationalism, Scotland, Brexit, Cosmopolitanism, immigration*

6.1   Introduction and Context

The country case of Scotland provides a unique point of analysis in the context of this edited volume that examines the wider European project crisis and issues of European integration. In a comparative European lens, Scotland is a small nation, with a population of just under 5.5 million people, which has witnessed two lifetime-defining political referenda in the last six years. 2014 saw a national referendum on Scottish independence from

Foley, J. and Korkut, U. (ed.), *Contesting Cosmopolitan Europe. Euroscepticism, Crisis and Borders.* Amsterdam: Amsterdam University Press 2022
DOI :10.5117/9789463727259_CH06

the United Kingdom, which returned a majority "No" vote. Two years later
the Brexit referendum on UK membership of the European Union resulted
in a majority "Leave" vote for the UK. The outcome of the Brexit vote came
as an unexpected result for the wider Scottish electorate, of whom the
majority (62%) had elected to "Remain" in the European Union. There was
a distinct conflict between the result returned from the Scottish public and
those of the wider United Kingdom, who expressed a desire to leave the EU.
Support for Scottish independence, and the governing Scottish National
Party (SNP), has increased in the years since the Brexit vote for a variety of
reasons that I will explain in detail throughout this chapter. In the years
following the vote, macro-level pro-independence political discourse in
Scotland has often been framed around the country's pro-European attitude
and outward-looking international ambitions.

In this chapter I examine the relationship between Scottish nationalism
and Europeanness. In particular, I investigate pro-European rhetoric as used
by the Scottish National Party (SNP) in public discourse. I then contrast
the message of this discourse with survey evidence which shows that the
Scottish public retain attitudes to outsiders that do not differ sharply from
those of other UK nations, including England. Scottish nationalism is often
referred to as a politics that is civic, pro-European, and progressive in nature
(Davidson et al., 2018). However, through this Scottish case study it is revealed
that Scottish pro-Europeanness and other commonly accepted traits of
Scottishness have been contested in public debate over the last decades.
Today Scottish nationalism, and support for the European Union, remains
more nuanced than many outside observers may conclude.

This conclusion is based on three main findings from the case study.
The first point to note is that a hyperactive, politicised Europeanness in
macro-level politics has only marginal everyday resonance for the wider
Scottish public, once we depart from the familiar measure of attitudes to
the EU as being synonymous with openness to outsiders. The second is
that Europeanness and nationalist identity are not inconsistent, and part
of the explanation for Scotland's anti-Brexit stance is that it reflects the
energies of the independence campaign. Lastly, Scotland's mainstream
political framing of immigration has been employed to justify Scottish
distinctiveness, and garner support for an independent Scotland in Europe.
This case study exposes the clear links between Scottish nationalism and
pro-European politics, highlighting that the two are not oppositional forces.
It is important, also, to consider some of the key emerging themes from the
literature in order to delve deeper into the themes of cosmopolitanism and
nationalism, before studying specific examples from the Scottish context in

detail. There is a complex relationship between the two-terms, as outlined in the following section.

6.2 Literature Review

Tom Nairn pioneered the notion of neo-nationalism (1977) in his seminal book *The Break-Up of Britain*, published in the late 1970s. Neo-nationalism, as Nairn defines it, is a politics which is a reaction to increasing transnational trading and a rise in multinational corporations in the globalised world, including the wider European project. Following Nairn's conceptualisation, neo-nationalism is not defined by a retreat from globalisation, as more traditional forms of nationalist politics may be categorised, but is rather a product and catalyst of it. Scottish nationalism, in pursuing its independence in Europe objective, is exemplar of neo-nationalist political thought, with arguments about increased trade and international cooperation forming a critical part of rhetoric in the country. The neo-nationalist perspective has incorporated aspects of a cosmopolitan brand of nationalism which has evolved as states have come to recognise the importance of transnational mechanisms to their chances of economic prosperity.

Calhoun (2003) has stated that "cosmopolitanism" is neither a freedom from culture nor a matter of pure individual choice, but a cultural position constructed on particular social bases and a choice made possible by that culture and those bases. It should be noted that there is an important distinction between the two terms *cosmopolitanism* and *cosmopolitanisation*. Beck and Levy (2013, 6) have specified that "cosmopolitanisation is the mechanism through which nationhood is reimagined". Furthermore, Beck and Levy (2013, 6) suggest that "cosmopolitan nations are reimagined through the anticipation of endangered futures". In the 'risk society' states must adapt to the pressures of contemporary neoliberal competition and develop a cosmopolitan vision of nationhood. In the Scottish example, we will see that pro-European attitudes have been perpetuated in public discourse since the 1980s to further Scottish cosmopolitan nationalism.

Billig (1995) has drawn attention to the everyday, banal features of nationalism whereby nationalist sentiments are demonstrated unconsciously in routine and daily social interactions. Examples can vary widely from national topics of conversation to more self-evident nationalist political behaviour such as flag-waving. In Scotland, comparisons with England form part of the banal nationalist rhetoric. Beck (2002, 28), building on Billig's theory, believes that we have now entered an era of banal cosmopolitanism "in which everyday nationalism is circumvented and undermined and we experience ourselves integrated into global processes and phenomena". What does this all mean for the case of Scottish nationalism? While we see examples of banal cosmopolitan nationalism in the discourse and policies of the Scottish government and other elite political actors in the country, these sentiments must be mobilised among the general population if the country is to succeed in gaining independence. The nationalist movement in Scotland must, therefore, go beyond banal cosmopolitanism to reach its aims.

The purpose of this case study is *not* to investigate the core social movement of Scottish nationalism itself. Instead, I focus on how discourse surrounding Scotland's place in Europe has been used to mobilise, what may be termed as, banal cosmopolitan nationalism in the country, where there has been a gap in the existing resource. Keating (2009, 130) has highlighted that "the SNP's vision of Europe has never been very clear [...] as the European Union develops and deepens, it could gradually replace the United Kingdom as the predominant union and external support system for Scottish self-government". A pro-European stance, however, is not a long-standing preposition in Scottish politics. Rather, political attitudes have evolved considerably since a period of Euroscepticism which surrounded the political debate in the 1970s.

The Scottish National Party (SNP) has been the dominant party in Scottish politics for over a decade. It has been the governing party in the devolved Scottish Parliament in Edinburgh since 2007, supported by the Scottish Greens. In the UK's Westminster Parliament, the party holds 48 out of the 59 Scottish constituency seats. The SNP received the largest percentage of votes with 45% at the 2019 general election (Harvey, 2020). The civic brand of nationalism which the Scottish National Party (SNP) have championed has been described as a nationalism that prioritises place, not race (Moskal, 2015). In other words, Scotland's brand of civic nationalism adopts an ideology that a Scottish national identity is available to anyone moving to the country, regardless of ethnic background. This was encapsulated in the First Minister's comments at a speech in Brussels in 2019:

> We can be Scottish and Polish – or Italian, or Pakistani, and much else besides – and European [...] belief in Scottish independence – [...] [is] about self-government, not ethnicity – goes hand in hand with a belief in internationalism and interdependence. National identity is not, and never should be, an exclusive concept. (First Minister Speech at European Policy Centre, Brussels, 11 June 2019)

Scottish nationalism, particularly as advocated through the policies and discourse of the SNP, has tried to emphasise Scotland's "diverse and progressive" qualities in order to establish itself as an inclusive and civic brand of nationalism (Leith & Soule, 2011). Scotland is personified in this political discourse as a "small, proud, welcoming, open and tolerant country", which has furthered civic nationalist sentiment (Bechhofer & McCrone, 2009). These qualities have been described as making Scotland distinctive from other parts of the UK. However, despite this political rhetoric, non-civic and exclusive criteria, including birthplace and ancestry, continue to determine public perceptions of national belonging and Scottishness (Leith & Soule 2011; McCollum, Nowok, & Tindal 2014). Therefore, macro-level political civic nationalist attitudes to citizenship are not always replicated at a population level and Scottish claims of tolerance are often exaggerated in reporting. A pro-European stance has also been adopted in the rhetoric of the SNP to build support for Scottish independence.

6.3   Pro-European Political Sentiment in Scottish Political and Public Debates

Scotland's desire to remain within the European Union has been used by the SNP as one of the founding arguments to further the case for Scottish independence and foster division with the UK government in recent years. The "independence in Europe" objective has formed a key role in the cosmopolitan nationalism the SNP has advocated since the late 1980s. However, it is important to consider that the SNP was not always a pro-European political party. Until as recently as 1988 the party was highly Eurosceptic (Brown et al. 1998). Dardanelli (2005) has claimed that in 1979 SNP voters were more Eurosceptic than voters of other political parties in Scotland and perceived the European project as a right-wing and capitalist mechanism. Until 1988, the SNP party leadership were against membership in the European Economic Community (EEC) due to the perception that "the EC suffered from 'euro-sclerosis' and inefficiency" (van der Zwet 2015, p. 168). The Scottish electorate believed that the EEC was a neoliberal instrument which would not be of benefit to the wider population. However, when Eurosceptic sentiments began to develop within the Conservative party, the SNP performed a U-turn on its Eurosceptic policy and began to campaign for its new goal of achieving an independent Scotland in Europe (Ichijo, 2004). Scottish First Minister Nicola Sturgeon recently made an appeal to European Union leaders to "Leave a Light on for Scotland" (Sturgeon,

2020) in the hope that an independent Scotland will rejoin the EU as an independent nation in the future.

A pro-European political stance has dominated public debate in Scotland in the years since the Brexit referendum in 2016. In the SNP's Tale of Two Cities campaign (SNP, 2019) promotional video the narrator juxtaposes Edinburgh, home of the Scottish parliament, with London and the Conservative Party-led UK government. Edinburgh is presented as progressive and outward-looking, while London is seen to be stagnating and holding Scotland back from economic opportunity by insisting on a Brexit deal that will negatively impact upon Scotland. Again, the claim is made that "Scotland is being ripped out of Europe against its will" by what is described as an unsympathetic and uncaring "Tory government". By pursuing the UK's departure from the European Union despite the vote returned in Scotland, the narrator claims that "this Tory government has ignored the people of Scotland and ignored the Scottish parliament" (SNP, 2019). Following the message of the video, Scottish voters should therefore vote SNP to ensure a prosperous future and future membership of the European Union. It would appear that such arguments gained traction within Scottish voters, as the 2019 UK general election returned an impressive win for the SNP. Such messages were also repeated in SNP campaign material in advance of the EU parliamentary elections in 2019.

In the lead-up to the European Parliament elections in 2019, Paisley and Renfrewshire South MP Mhairi Black made the claim that Scotland "won't abandon our European neighbours" and urged voters to "vote SNP and keep Scotland at the very heart of Europe" (SNP, 2019). The message of this video is to vote against the pro-Brexit Conservative Party-led UK government and reaffirm Scotland's pro-Europe stance in the political arena. Elsewhere, publicity campaign group Scotland is Now have used Twitter to offer self-proclaimed "love letters to Europe". In a poem recited in one campaign video the narrator states, "as long as Scotland's still here, Europe you are always welcome" (Scotland is Now, 2019). The video blends together poetry with scenes and imagery of Scottish nature, presenting an image of a Scottish cultural identity that is closely linked to a unique sense of geography. The video provides evidence of how pro-European narratives are shared across wider cultural platforms in Scotland, and not limited to what may be thought of as traditional political arenas. The examples are also evidence of the banal cosmopolitan nationalism (Beck, 2002) which can be identified in Scotland.

However, pro-European arguments presented in Scottish public debate are often lacking in definition and substance. Salamone (2020) claims that the media have played a role in limiting debate on the mechanisms and functioning of the EU. For example, there was little discussion in the Scottish media of the €750 billion coronavirus recovery plan, one of the most significant achievements of the EU in recent years. Salamone (2020) thus observes that "while European themes certainly form part of the public discourse [in Scotland], they do not feature to an extent or depth that might be expected, given Scotland's ostensible pro-EU position". Critics have emphasised, therefore, that public discourse around Scotland's place in Europe is often presented in simplified terms, which has at times even overlooked significant achievements of the EU from which Scotland could benefit. This streamlined discourse around Europe has fed into the banal cosmopolitan nationalism that has been promoted by the SNP, and other political actors in Scotland. Easy-to-understand and clear messages form a key part of this, which may partly explain why the SNP chose the slogan "Stop Brexit" in their campaign for the 2019 general election. However, banal cosmopolitan nationalist discourse in Scotland also goes beyond general arguments for EU membership and looks to specific areas, such as immigration, to justify Scotland's differing political attitudes.

6.4   Pro-immigration Discourse and Scottish Civic Nationalism

In the following section I examine Scottish government discourse and policy on migration, where arguments are primarily formed around economic, humanitarian, and cosmopolitan justifications. These justifications are often intertwined in a manner that feed together to further banal cosmopolitan nationalist attitudes in Scotland. Hepburn and Rosie (2017, 242) have highlighted that "elite discourse [...] presents immigrants as key players in an open, inclusive and multicultural Scottish nation". In the wake of the Brexit vote political discourse in Scotland has continued to focus on the economic benefits of EU migrants, and the role they play in maintaining vital public services within what is described as an ageing economy. The following extract provides a clear example of this rhetoric. In January 2020 Scottish First Minister Nicola Sturgeon addressed EU migrants at the launch event for a planned new Scottish visa where she highlighted the important role that EU migrant workers, whom she refers to as "New Scots", play in the Scottish economy:

> the fact that Scotland is now a place people come to, rather than leave, is one of the best things to have happened during my time as an MSP. These

new Scots have made Scotland's population younger – something which
is important to the sustainability of public services. (Plan for Scottish
visa: First Minister's speech 27 January 2020)

In the above example, we can see that pro-immigration discourse in Scotland
is often grounded in terms of the economic contribution that migrants
bring. Sturgeon presents Scotland as a destination country for migrants,
including EU citizens, who have contributed to making the country's population younger. The Scottish Government have repeatedly claimed that the
continued arrival of EU migrants to work in the country are essential if
Scotland is to maintain its public services. More recently, however, the SNP,
as represented by Sturgeon, have included humanitarian arguments for a
pro-immigration stance. These have served to politically position Scotland
in contrast to the firmer migration policy of the UK government in the
Westminster parliament in London. The following example shows how
such economic and humanitarian arguments are intertwined in Scottish
political rhetoric:

In Scotland, we know, we understand that the Westminster approach
to migration – as well as being deeply inhumane – poses an existential
threat to our future prosperity. (Brexit and Scotland's future: First Minister
Nicola Sturgeon's statement, 24 April 2019)

In her statement, Sturgeon suggests that the UK government possess an
inhumane immigration policy which threatens the future of Scotland's
economy. The excerpt illustrates how the UK government are positioned
as a threat to Scotland's economic prosperity in the SNP's discourse.,
albeit largely on economic grounds. The interaction between economic,
humanitarian, and cosmopolitan justifications for migration appears to
compliment the SNP's message that Scotland is a country that welcomes
diversity and is thus more outward-looking than the other Leave-voting
nations in the UK. Similar sentiments are to be found in examples taken
from Scottish public policy.

Pro-immigration policy and discourse has also formed a key part of
the SNP's vision for an independent Scotland. The Scottish Government's
"New Scots 2018-2022" framework has been developed with the objective of
improving integration processes for asylum seeker and refugee arrivals in the
country (Scottish Government, 2018). Further public campaigns, including
Fresh Talent and *One Scotland, Many Cultures*, have sought to promote

Scotland's diversity and share a discourse of tolerance and acceptance towards migrant groups, including EU. These campaigns have also had the objective of highlighting Scotland as a destination country for migrants (Hepburn and Rosie, 2017). However, the SNP government has also been criticised for their consistent reference to the economic contribution of migrants, and overlooking other benefits of immigration, including the cultural and linguistic diversity which newcomer groups bring to the country (Phipps and Fassetta, 2015). Regardless of these criticisms, Scotland has continued to brand itself as a tolerant nation in macro-political discourse, particularly through the SNP.

In contrast to the Scottish Government's pro-immigration political stance, the Scottish public do not appear to share the same welcoming attitudes to migrant groups. A recent YouGov opinion poll found that a large percentage of the Scottish general population believed immigrants, particularly non-Europeans, have a negative impact on the economy (YouGov, 2019). Very similar results were gathered from an English sample group of survey respondents in London. As London is a highly cosmopolitan city with a great number of migrants, it is perhaps less surprising that such levels of anti-migrant feeling were recorded. However, it is particularly alarming that the Scottish sample group reported similar levels of anti-migrant attitudes among both datasets, given the relatively low number of migrants in the country. This again serves to evidence the point that the Scottish and English publics do not have widely differing views on immigration, despite political rhetoric to the contrary.

In a detailed analysis of the Brexit referendum, Sobolewska and Ford (2020, 281) have found that "negative views of migrants and minorities were (and are) roughly as widely held in Scotland as in England and Wales, but they were ignored by the SNP, who directed ethnocentric voters' resentments towards London and the Tories" (2020, p. 281). Moreover, in Glasgow, Clark (2020) has reported that discrimination against Scotland's largest Roma minority migrant groups (of EU membership country origin) in the Govanhill area has increased in recent years. These developments also illustrate that there is a "disjunction between pro-migration rhetoric and anti-immigration sentiments at population level" in Scotland (Sime 2020, 337). These examples highlight that, despite pro-immigration political rhetoric in Scotland, the wider population are not as tolerant and accepting of immigrants as political leaders would have us believe. The Brexit referendum has also been used as a point with which to frame Scottish distinctiveness from other UK nations.

6.5   Reimagining the Scottish Nation-state

In public speeches referring to Scotland's position on Brexit, the First Minister has emphasised that the only hope for a prosperous economic future for Scotland is to rejoin the European Union as an independent nation-state. These arguments have developed considerably since the aforementioned Euroscepticism that characterised the SNP, and Scottish voters, in the 1970s. This position is contrasted with the UK government who are described as pursuing a policy of isolationism. In the following extracts from her speeches, the First Minister outlines her vision for an independent Scotland:

> for the Scottish Government, independence is not about the isolationism that characterises Brexit – instead independence would see us recognizing and embracing our interdependence with other nations. We will always seek to be close allies and partners with our neighbours in Europe. The last two years, to my mind, have underlined the importance of that position. (First Minister's speech at French National Assembly, 19 February 2019)
> The idea of Scottish independence has never been about separatism. It is instead about the right of people to decide the form of government best suited to their needs. That right has never been more important given the threat Brexit poses to the internationalist, welcoming European ethos held by so many people in Scotland. (Nicola Sturgeon, 2 January 2021)

Scotland, in adopting an anti-Brexit political stance, is therefore presented as outward-looking and reliant on the continued support and cooperation of other European nations. The above examples also emphasise how Scottish nationalism is presented as cosmopolitan and pro-European in political rhetoric. As Knight (2017, 240) has stated, "the emergent cosmopolitanism in Scotland appears to be fused with a nationalist agenda". Furthermore, Knight (2017, 240) contends that the First Minister's speeches "carry wide appeal and speak for everyday Scots who oppose the political domination of the Conservative English upper classes". The examples shown demonstrate that the SNP seek to reject this perceived English political domination through a continued support for the European Union which is contrasted with the Eurosceptic views of the Westminster administration. The very construction of Scottish national identity ascriptions also offers an explanation as to why the Scottish public may seek to establish a pro-European political stance.

6.6   Scottish Identity Constructions

One of the most commonly used justifications for claims of being Scottish is a rejection of being English. The vis-à-vis relationship with England becomes has formed an integral part of Scottish national identity ascriptions. McCrone and Becchofer (2015) questioned members of the public on the reasons why they chose to ascribe, or not, to a Scottish identity; identity justifications from the public almost always began with the clause; "I'm Scottish because I'm not English". The link between Scottish national identity constructions and pro-European attitudes can therefore follow a clear trajectory. As Ichijo (2004, 143) neatly summarises, "If being Scottish means not being English, and being English means being Euro-sceptical, being less Euro-sceptical is one way of asserting one's Scottishness".

This is not to suggest that Anglophobia is a prerequisite of support for Scottish nationalism. Rather, an assertion of anti-Westminster politics has been adopted by the SNP to assert Scottish distinctiveness and, what have been termed, egalitarian values (Davidson et al., 2018). Traditional signifiers of Scottishness, including the wearing of tartan clothing and adoption of a distinctive Scottish accent, continue to inform claims to a Scottish national identity. Also, other forms of expression, including a rejection of English political attitudes, can be used to express one's right to a Scottish national identity. Therefore, as Ichijo (2004, 143) has earlier stated, Scottish public opinion on Europe is "conditioned by Scotland's relationship to England and Britain as a whole".

In the year 2020, the SNP have renewed calls for European Union leaders to "leave a light on for Scotland" in the hope that an independent Scotland will rejoin the EU as an independent nation in the future. During the final days of 2020, as the Brexit agreement was slowly finalised, SNP party spokesman Ian Blackford stated:

> Scotland will remain a European nation, we will continue to build strong links, and we will be back to take our place as an independent member of the EU. (Ian Blackford Statement, 31 December 2020)

The debate around European membership is therefore on-going and continues to play a key role in the Scottish governments discourse and policy. Meanwhile, public support for independence in Scotland appears to have grown in the last years in particular. A recent poll conducted by What Scotland Thinks posed the question "How would you vote in a Scottish independence referendum if held now?" to the Scottish public. Of those sampled those supporting a "Yes" vote were recorded at 57%, with "No" recorded at 43% (What Scotland Thinks 2021). While polls can never be a truly accurate illustration of voting intentions, these figures do reflect a significant increase in support for Scottish independence since the 2014 referendum in which "Yes" returned 45% of the vote. It would appear that Nicola Sturgeon is not wrong in her claims that "Brexit has changed the game on Scottish independence" (Sturgeon, 2020).

Recent polling results suggest that support for Scottish independence has further grown in 2020, a year dominated by the Covid-19 health crisis (Curtice, 2020). Public support for independence appears to have been further strengthened by First Minister Nicola Sturgeon's performance during the crisis, as the Scottish public perceive her to have handled the pandemic well (YouGov, 2020). Conversely, public trust in Prime Minister Boris Johnson and the UK government has declined during the same period (YouGov, 2020). Even before the pandemic, polls showed that support for Scottish independence had consecutively continued to grow in the intervening years since the first independence referendum in 2014. It would appear that both Brexit and the Covid-19 crisis have contributed to a rise in nationalist public sentiment in Scotland. It is necessary, however, to revisit one of the main reasons why the independence movement failed the first time round – a perceived social connection to the wider British state among Scottish voters.

Sobolewska and Ford (2020, 251), in their analysis of the two referenda Scotland has witnessed in the past six years, believed that "most Scots also feel a stronger sense of affinity and loyalty to Britain than English feel to the EU". Therefore, in 2014 people in Scotland felt strong connections to their compatriots around the rest of the UK which led to the majority "No" result in the Scottish independence referendum. Conversely, in 2016, voters in England especially did not feel themselves to be connected to Europe and the European Union, which gave rise to the "Leave" result in the Brexit referendum. However, an examination of the aforementioned polls suggests that the divide between Scottish voters and the UK government has continued to grow in the past years, and that the connection between the Scottish public and wider British identities may have shifted somewhat in the years since 2014. The larger question remains over whether a second referendum on Scottish independence will ever be permitted to go ahead and under what terms the UK government would agree to such a request.

6.7   Conclusion

In this chapter I have explored how banal cosmopolitan nationalism (Beck, 2002) in Scotland has been operationalised through public discourse on European Union membership, immigration, and the economy. These examples have illustrated that an anti-Brexit, pro-European, and pro-immigration stance has been adopted by the SNP in Scotland to frame the country as distinctive, outward-looking, and progressive in character. This discourse has helped fuel cosmopolitan nationalist sentiment in the country which has been illustrated to have grown since the first referendum on Scottish independence was held in 2014.

The SNP have been able to forge a niche brand of neo-nationalist politics which has diverted Scottish voters' frustrations away from Eurosceptic sentiment to foster an anti-Westminster and in particular an anti-Conservative political ideology. While the SNP were previously a Eurosceptic party, since 1988 they have sought to establish a cosmopolitan Scottish nationalism with the goal of achieving independence for Scotland while retaining EU membership. Examples provided from SNP discourse and wider public debates have illustrated that Scottish pro-European sentiments are often founded in pro-migration and economic prosperity terms. Such discourse, however, has been limited in terms of developing a broader understanding of the benefits of union membership. Commentators, including Salamone (2020) have stated that "the Scottish public would benefit from a more meaningful European debate, grounded in greater substance and reflection".

In this chapter I have illustrated that the oft-cited political and ideological differences with England, particularly regarding public attitudes to immigration and civic citizenship, are often exaggerated in Scottish political discourse. Evidence has been presented which shows that the Scottish and English public hold broadly similar views on immigration, an issue often cited as an area of contention. Furthermore, the majority of Scots continue to base Scottish citizenship claims on the grounds of ethnocentric criteria, namely birthplace and ancestry. These findings stand in contrast to the so-called progressive and outward-looking Scotland narratives which can be seen in political rhetoric.

At the time of writing, and over four years since the Brexit referendum, the UK has now finalised its departure from the European Union. Scottish Parliamentary Elections were held in May 2021, in which arguments over Scottish membership of the EU played a decisive role in influencing voting behaviour. The SNP has been able to expand on its electoral success of the UK general election in 2019 to form a majority government within the parliament, supported by the Scottish Greens. Europe is a mechanism through which Scotland can brand itself as different from the rest of the UK, as illustrated through the examples provided in this chapter. This Scottish case study has shown that cosmopolitan and neo-nationalist movements are operating alongside the European Union, rather than against it. What might at first appear a contradiction in terms, through the features of globalisation and nationalism, has been shown to be an integral part of the movement for an independence Scotland. The Scottish case will have significant ramifications for other European Member States, dealing with their own instances of minority nationalist movements.

References

Anderson, B. (2006). *Imagined Communities: Reflections on The Origin and Spread of Nationalism*. London: Verso.

Bechhofer, F., & McCrone, D. (2009). National Identity, Nationalism and Constitutional Change. In *National Identity, Nationalism and Constitutional Change* (pp. 1–16). Cham: Springer.

Beck, U. (2002). The Cosmopolitan Society and its Enemies. *Theory, Culture & Society, 19*(1–2), 17–44.

Beck, U., & Levy, D. (2013). Cosmopolitanized Nations: Re-Imagining Collectivity in World Risk Society. *Theory, Culture & Society, 30*(2), 3–31.

Billig, M. (1995). *Banal Nationalism*. London: SAGE.

Brown, A., McCrone, D., Paterson, L., & Surridge, P. (1998). *The Scottish Electorate: The 1997 General Election and Beyond*. London: Palgrave Macmillan.

Calhoun, C. (2003). Belonging in the Cosmopolitan Imaginary. *Ethnicities, 3*(4), 531–553.

Clark, C. (2020). Stay or Go?: Roma, Brexit and European Freedom of Movement. *Scottish Affairs, 29*(3), 403–418.

Curtice, J. (2020). Coronavirus: Views Reflect Underlying Attitudes to Governments. *BBC News*, 26 May 2020. https://www.bbc.co.uk/news/uk-scotland-52801321 (accessed 1 April 2021).

Dardanelli, P. (2005). Democratic Deficit or the Europeanisation of Secession? Explaining the Devolution Referendums in Scotland. *Political Studies, 53*(2), 320–342.

Davidson, N., Liinpää, M., McBride, M., & Virdee, S. (2018). *No Problem Here: Understanding Racism in Scotland*. Edinburgh: Luath Press.

Harvey, M. (2020). A Dominant SNP in a Unionist Scotland? The 2019 UK General Election in Scotland. *The Political Quarterly, 91*(1), 56–60.

Hearn, Jonathan (2007). National Identity: Banal, Personal and Embedded. *Nations and Nationalism, 13*(4), 657–674.

Hepburn, E., & Rosie, M. (2014). "The Essence of the Union...": Unionism, Nationalism and Identity on These Disconnected Islands. *Scottish Affairs*, *24*(2), 141–162.

Ichijo, A. (2004). *Scottish Nationalism and the Idea of Europe: Concepts of Europe and the Nation*. London: Taylor and Francis.

Knight, D. (2017). Anxiety and Cosmopolitan Futures: Brexit and Scotland. *American Ethnologist. 44*(2), 237–242.

Leith, M. S., & Soule, D. P. J. (2011). *Political Discourse and National Identity in Scotland*. Edinburgh: Edinburgh University Press.

McCollum, D., Nowok, B., & Tindal, S. (2014). Public Attitudes Towards Migration in Scotland: Exceptionality and Possible Policy Implications. *Scottish Affairs*, *23*(1), 79–102.

McCrone, D. (2017). *The New Sociology of Scotland* London: Sage.

McCrone, D., & Bechhofer, F. (2015). *Understanding National Identity*. Cambridge: Cambridge University Press.

Moskal, M. (2016). Spaces of Not Belonging: Inclusive Nationalism and Education in Scotland. *Scottish Geographical Journal*, *132*(1), 85–102.

Nairn, T. (1977). *The Break-up of Britain: Crisis and Neo-Nationalism*. London: NLB.

Phipps, A., & Fassetta, G., (2015). A Critical Analysis of Language Policy in Scotland. *European Journal of Language Policy*, *7*(1), 5–29.

Salamone, A. (2020). Scotland's European Debate Will Need Greater Depth in the Years Ahead. (Blog) Available at: https://blogs.lse.ac.uk/europblog/2020/11/30/scotlands-european-debate-will-need-greater-depth-in-the-years-ahead/ (accessed 10 February 2021).

Scotland Is Now (2021). Scotland is Here: Scotland Is Now. *YouTube.* Available at https://www.youtube.com/watch?v=5cMQfoQuAkM (accessed 20 April 2021).

Scottish Government. (2019). Made in Scotland Festival: First Minister's Speech. https://www.gov.scot/publications/made-scotland-brussels-launch/ (accessed 10 February 2021).

Scottish Government. (2019). Brexit and Scotland's Future: First Minister Statement. https://www.gov.scot/publications/first-minister-statement-brexit-scotlands-future/ (accessed 10 February 2021).

Scottish Government. (2019). Brexit and Beyond: Where Next for Scottish-EU Relations: First Minister's Speech. https://www.gov.scot/publications/fm-brexit-beyond-next-scottish-eu-relations/ (accessed 10 February 2021).

Scottish Government. (2019). First Minister's Speech at French National Assembly. https://www.gov.scot/publications/first-ministers-speech-at-french-national-assembly/ (accessed 10 February 2021).

Scottish Government. (2019). First Minister's Letter to EU Citizens in Scotland. https://www.gov.scot/publications/first-ministers-letter-to-eu-citizens-in-scotland/ (accessed 10 February 2021).

Scottish National Party. (2019). Stronger for Scotland: The SNP General Election Manifesto. https://www.snp.org/general-election-2019/ (accessed 10 February 2021).

Scottish National Party. (2019). Tale of Two Cities. Available at https://sw-ke.facebook.com/theSNP/videos/scotlands-for-europe/447877172636899/ (accessed 20 April 2021).

Scottish National Party. (2019). Scotland's Future Lies in Europe. Available at https://www.snp.org/scotlands-future-lies-in-europe/ (accessed 20 April 2021).

Scottish National Party. (2019). Keep Scotland at the Heart of Europe. Available at https://www.facebook.com/watch/?v=347352589317841 (accessed 20 April 2021).

Sime, D. (2020). New Scots? Eastern European Young People's Feelings of Belonging and National Identity in Scotland Post-Brexit. *Scottish Affairs, 29*(3), 336–353.

Sobolewska, M., & Ford, R., (2020). *Brexitland: Identity, Diversity and the Reshaping of British Politics.* Cambridge: Cambridge University Press.

Van der Zwet, A. (2015). Operationalising National Identity: The Cases of the Scottish National Party and Frisian National Party. *Nations and Nationalism, 21*(1), 62–82.

What Scotland Thinks (2021). How Would You Vote in a Scottish Independence Referendum If Held Now? https://whatscotlandthinks.org/questions/how-would-you-vote-in-the-in-a-scottish-independence-referendum-if-held-now-ask/?removed (accessed 10 February 2021).

YouGov. (2018). Where the Public Stands on Immigration. https://yougov.co.uk/topics/politics/articles-reports/2018/04/27/where-public-stands-immigration (accessed 10 February 2021).

YouGov. (2020). Scottish Independence: Yes Leads by 53% to 47%. https://yougov.co.uk/topics/politics/articles-reports/2020/08/12/scottish-independence-yes-leads-53-47. (accessed 10 February 2021).

About the Author

Marcus Nicolson is a current PhD candidate in Social Sciences at GCU. Marcus's study investigates the lived experiences of young adult migrants in Glasgow, UK, using a narrative enquiry research design which incorporates creative research methods. He holds an MA in Intercultural Encounters from the University of Helsinki. Marcus works as the Project Manager for the D.Rad project and has previously managed the AMIF-funded VOLPOWER project, investigating the relationships between volunteering, migration, and social inclusion.

Email: Marcus.Nicolson@gcu.ac.uk

7 Flexible Redefinitions of "Us" and the "Others"

Refugee Politics in the Convergences of Multiple "Crises" in the EU and Greece

Eva (Evangelia) Papatzani and Electra Petracou

Abstract
During the last decade, a wide range of political contradictions concerning Europeanisation has unfolded in Greece, in the convergences of the financial and the so-called refugee "crises". This chapter discusses processes of constructing Europeanisation in interrelation with racism and nationalism, and the ways "new" distinctions and divisions emerge. At the same time that Europeanisation in Greece is in crisis during the period in question, it is strengthened as regards border security policies, the construction of a united "Us" against "the Others" via the "irregular" migration movements, and the questioning of the right on protection, movement, and inhabitance. The chapter analyses specific refugee discourses, politics, practices, by emphasizing on politicians' and media rhetoric, as well as some shortcuts of refugees' daily life in Greece.

Keywords: Europeanisation, Greece, nationalism, refugees

7.1 Introduction

Prior to the Eurozone crisis, most political parties, much of the media and public opinion were broadly united on Greece's participation in the European Union. But that crisis, added to the movement of refugees to Europe via Greek islands in 2015, transformed attitudes to European integration. Greece came under pressure from the so-called "Troika" (the International Monetary Fund, the European Union, and the European Central Bank) to adopt strict

Foley, J. and Korkut, U. (ed.), *Contesting Cosmopolitan Europe. Euroscepticism, Crisis and Borders.* Amsterdam: Amsterdam University Press 2022
DOI :10.5117/9789463727259_CH07

austerity measures, prompting a public backlash that included the election of Syriza on a radical mandate. More recently, grievances against Europe often centre on refugees' and migrants' arrivals, protection, and reception rights. Discourses of "burden", "responsibility-sharing", and "solidarity" became focuses of contestation between domestic and European actors. While there were significant party-political differences, nonetheless all Greek parties challenged European asylum policies. Nonetheless, Greek governments and EU agencies have often coalesced on the security of external borders. Greek discourses on borders thus reflect a combination of nationalism and Europeanisation, with border security portrayed as a crucial "European fundamental value". A succession of crises has thus imposed on Greece a contradictory approach to Europeanisation. While grievances against the EU have intensified, there are equally calls for Europe-wide solutions to Greece's predicaments, and European solidarity in protection against "irregular" migration movements.

In this chapter, we discuss processes of construction of Europeanisation discourses and policies, as they unfold in the context of the multiple "crises" in Greece. We explore how the events of the Eurozone crisis and especially with the arrival of migrants and refugees exposed fractures in the Greek sense of "self" and "other". We highlight discourses, policies, and practices, emphasising the rhetoric of politicians and media, as well as on aspects of asylum seekers' and refugees' daily life in Greece. The chapter is based on research conducted for the needs of the Horizon 2020 Research Programme RESPOND, focusing on the Greek case with a special attention to Lesvos Island, including 34 interviews with refugees and asylum seekers of different nationalities and 14 with stakeholders. It is also based on research conducted on issues of "Europeanisation" based on the analysis of political speeches, newspaper articles, and a survey addressed to the project's stakeholders (Papatzani et al., 2020).

7.2   Refugee Discourses, Politics and Practices in Greece (2010–2020)

Since the establishment of an independent Greek state in 1830, nationalistic discourses have centred on distinctions of "self" and "other". The content of each term has depended on the historical context and consequently those terms have shifting connotations. The Greek "self" may refer to Christians, non-communists, Western Europeans, non-Balkans/Turks, Europeans; while the "other" has variously been Balkan countries, immigrants, economic migrants, and, more recently, asylum seekers. A crucial development in national consciousness was when Greece joined the European Union in 1981, in order to modernise its economy and society; stabilise the democratic regime; and mobilise allies in its conflicts with Turkey. Subsequently, Greek governments tended to support "European integration" and EU enlargement. Until the Eurozone crisis and concomitant Greek financial crisis, most political parties in the Greek parliament – except for the Communist Party (KKE) and the Popular Orthodox Rally (LAOS) – and public opinion were likewise supportive.

During the 1990s, immigration attracted controversy and became a focus of public debate when a considerable number of immigrants, mainly from Central and Eastern European countries, migrated to Greece. Governments responded with draconian measures (Sitaropoulos, 1992), imposing controls on immigrants irrespective of their status (Petracou, 1999), based on policies of exclusion, deportation, institutional racism, and a general public discourse of criminalisation of migration (Ventoura, 2004). As Baldwin-Edwards notes, "the Greek political reaction to irregular border crossings by Albanians en masse in December 1990 was highly negative, and reinforced by near-hysterical reports in the mass media which constructed a stereotype of the 'dangerous Albanian'" (Baldwin-Edwards, 2014, p. 1).

The financial crisis since 2009 had obvious economic repercussions, with sharp falls in employment, income, and living conditions. Its effects reverberated throughout Greek society, adding to already deep inequalities. A series of welfare reforms led to severe restrictions in social protection and affected negatively social rights (Sotiropoulos & Bourikos, 2014), while poverty, social exclusion, and the rate of unemployment increased significantly. According to a Eurostat report, 21.1% of Greeks experience severe material deprivation, the second highest rate among EU Member States (Eurostat, 2018). But the financial crisis also impacted on discourses and politics. As Chryssogelos pointed out "austerity brought about a re-politicisation of a whole range of state-society relations that, under the influence of EU membership, had entailed (or intended) the insulation of Greek political and administrative elites" (2017, p. 9). Political debates on the benefits of bailout and austerity measures resulted in intense conflicts over Europeanisation (Altiparmakis, 2019). Rising social discontent in parallel with the deepening of socioeconomic inequalities shifted the Greek electorate away from the mainstream parties, leading to continuous changes of governments during the early 2010s (Ellinas, 2013).

Thus, in response to the crisis, a large part of Greek society adopted an anti-political stance, rejecting the authority of the establishment. By contrast, mainstream politicians and the media responded by posing a sharp dilemma – anti-Europe versus pro-Europe – positioning themselves in the latter camp and all critics in the former. Opposition to austerity was curtailed by fears of the consequences of "Grexit". Conversely, positive discussions of "Grexit" increased among sections of the Syriza party, and more broadly among the radical left, social movements and groups of intellectuals. Syriza came to power promising to confront the "Troika", to secure an exit from the Greek debt crisis, and to end austerity: but, crucially, without taking the country out of the European Monetary Union (EMU). After five months of negotiations with the EU in early 2015, amid imposed capital controls, Syriza called for a national referendum in which the Greek people had to answer "Yes" or "No" to the deal offered by "Troika". This referendum could have been a point of rupture with the EU, and many media and political actors presented it this way by cultivating fears of disintegration. The result, 62% voting "No" to EU measures, provoked division not only between Greeks and the EU, but also between Greek right and left.

Public grievances were inevitably a breeding ground for cultivating fear of "the Other" as responsible for the crisis. Xenophobia and racism increased substantially (Baldwin-Edwards, 2014). During the early 2010s, "illegals", "undocumented" immigrants from Middle Eastern, Asian, and African countries who had settled in Greece, were often seen as inseparable from the crisis. Specific policies were implemented during the early 2010s in line with the "war against illegal migration" discourse. The most characteristic example was the adoption of the "Integrated Border Management Program for Combating Illegal Immigration" in 2011, whose main objectives were "the protection of both the EU and national borders", and the "reduction of the illegal migration" (Ministry of Citizen Protection, 2011). This programme included – among other projects – the construction of the Evros Fence in the southeast borders of Greece, as well as, from 2012, the launch of the "Xenios Zeus" police "sweep" operations in urban centres. The Evros fence was described as a "technical barrier" that would combat "illegal" migration (Ministry of Citizen Protection, 2011). Despite its cost in a period of economic crisis, "national-level discourse by political actors reveals that the construction of the fence was linked to the wider EU-level migration and border control practices, as well as to the national-level perception of migration as a security issue" (Grigoriadis & Dilek, 2019, p. 171). As far as the Xenios Zeus police operation is concerned, it has been implemented through patrols and raids targeting immigrant populations, with the explicit purpose of combating "illegal migration and criminality" (Xenakis & Cheliotis, 2013). As Kandylis argues, "'sweeping' is used as a symbolic substitute for displacement, denoting some final treatment of a problem of dirtiness and obscuring what comes next" (Kandylis, 2015, p. 830).

Along with the aforementioned policies and discourses, the deepening of the financial and sociopolitical crisis was a catalyst for the re-emergence of extreme right-wing populism, nationalism, and the far-right. This included extreme right-wing populist parties (such as Independent Greeks and Popular Orthodox Rally); the neo-Nazi organisation Golden Dawn (GD); along with the conservative right-wing government of New Democracy (ND). All played a crucial role in the normalisation of racist political and media discourses. There is a significant part of the literature that analyses these political developments, insisting either on the significance of populism or of nationalism and their distinctions in the new political context (Ellinas, 2013; Dinas et al., 2016). In this context, a significant rise in racist violence in urban centres, led mostly by Golden Dawn, was noted. Since 2008, GD chose specific Athenian neighbourhoods as "castles" or "strongholds" where it developed its political agenda and mobilised organisational forces (Dinas et al., 2016). In general, anti-migrant violence has been legitimated through three interlinked strategies: a narrative of "isolated events"; the disavowal of its racialised character; and its rationalisation as a regrettable yet understandable reaction to the threats posed by migration (Karamanidou, 2016). These incidents reduced by half during 2014, after the murder of the Greek antifascist rapper Pavlos Fissas and especially since the start of GD's trial in 2015 (RVRN, 2015)[8]. Yet organised racist attacks and violent incidents, targeting, among others, immigrants, asylum seekers, refugee activists, and NGO workers (Disinfaux Collective, 2020–2021), have not stopped but intensified.

In 2015 a total of 856,723 people arrived by sea from Turkey to the Northeastern Aegean islands, a figure accounting for 80% of total arrivals in Europe (Petracou et al., 2018). By comparison there were just 41,038 sea arrivals in 2014. Since then, refugee arrivals became the focus of migration politics and discourses in Greece. Two subsequent events in early 2016 heightened debates, namely the closure of the so-called Balkan route on 8 March 2016 and the entry into force of the EU-Turkey Common Statement on 20 March 2016. Furthermore, the change of government in 2015 (the Syriza and ANEL coalition government that lasted until 2019) constituted another significant factor for the transformation of the dominant political discourse.

---

8   At 16th of October 2020, the court decided unanimously that Golden Dawn was set up and operated as a criminal organisation.

Since then, discourses of Europeanisation in Greece have been closely linked to the so-called "refugee crisis". In the discourses and the formulation of policies the European values, norms and regulations have been mentioned, directly or indirectly, by different actors either to support their arguments or to highlight national interests. The need for "burden-sharing" and "responsibility-sharing" were themes that cut across all political and media discourses, irrespectively of political positions (Papatzani et al., 2020). The notion of "solidarity" with the countries of first reception was a common issue, both for the Syriza-ANEL coalition and for previous governments (such as the ND government). Criticism of the Dublin Regulation was also a cross-cutting theme, with governments insisting on the need for a new relevant regulation that would be able to redistribute migration burdens more effectively across Europe's Member States. A part of the media, mainly its liberal sections, connected the aforementioned narratives with the importance of the EU "fundamental values" and the principles on which it is built, such as freedom, democracy, and participation. What emerged was an unanimity between different political parties about the need for solidarity, due to the perception that Greece had undertaken the heaviest burden regarding refugee and migrant arrivals. This stance can be seen as a mild tension of Europeanisation, as the calls for solidarity did not reach extreme conflicts but instead found some support from various agents within the EU. This "mild" tension was ultimately based in the interaction of actors who had unequal power within the European Union's decision-making structures.

Migration was also explicitly discussed as a security issue by most political parties (including the Syriza-ANEL coalition government) and by conservative media, with the latter insisting on a discourse that divided Europeans and anti-Europeans. Border security rhetoric and policies focused on two opposite but complementary discussions: narratives on the "Europeanisation" of border security policies; and narratives on the "nationalisation" of border security policies, albeit interconnected with the "European fundamental values". All Greek governments and political actors since 2015 insisted on the need for a European response to Greek border management, in parallel with national initiatives beyond EU decisions, from the part of the conservative governments of early 2010s, such as the construction of the Evros Fence (Papatzani et al., 2020). These seemingly contradicting discourses were noted by Triandafyllidou, who observes "while at the policy level they may be obliged to take a specific course of action, at the discursive level they may embrace or fight Europeanisation depending on what seems the best strategy for winning the voters support" (2014, p. 412).

It should be also noted that after the national elections of 2019, and the conservative turn of the electoral result, a wide range of transformations in policies and discourses were observed. The conservative right government of New Democracy has already made specific reforms in the legal framework on Asylum, Reception and Protection that tighten the protection and reception regime for the applicants of international protection. It has also announced and legislated the establishment of "closed centres" for the reception and accommodation of asylum seekers on both the islands and the mainland, a measure that will lead to the deepening of isolation and confinement of reception regime in Greece, dividing asylum seekers and the rest of population in a stricter way.

7.3   Discourses, Politics and Practices Constructing, Isolating, and Excluding "The Others"

Until 2015, key discourses and politics around migration reflected the context of the economic crisis and the deepening of inequalities. Themes of "illegal migration" (*lathrometanastefsi*) as threats to European democracies also reflected this context. The term "illegals" was the central discourse of right-wing politicians and media actors, and it was a political choice, as the Public Order Minister Nikos Dendias of ND declared in 2013.

> We will not neither hide the terms nor try to make them beautiful. And we also claim the maintenance of the term "illegal" in relation to "irregular" in the European political vocabulary. For us this is absolutely clear. The violation of the Greek and European borders is a criminal offense according to Greek law (Ministry of Public Order and Citizen Protection, 2013).

In this context, a clear distinction was made in dominant political discourses between "legal" immigrants, deserving international protection, and "illegals", towards which "we will not feel sympathetic when we are going to protect our national sovereignty and our borders. It is our right" (Ministry of Public Order and Citizen Protection, 2013). These discourses informed policies and practices of exclusion, deportation, and securitisation, with the ultimate effect of increasing borders control.

After the refugees' arrival in 2015–2016, public discourse and politics shifted from "illegal" migration and "sweeping operations" to the humanitarian aspects of massive refugee movements. During this "turn", the term "illegal migration" was left behind and was replaced by the term

"humanitarian crisis" in the dominant discourse of the Greek government
and of a wide range of other actors (including International Organisations,
the EU, NGOs, and scholars). The shift from "lathrometanastes" to "refugees"
also characterised the public discourses of media and the Syriza-led coalition
government. The Greek "self" was constructed as the local population that
received refugees. Grassroots movements were crucial in bringing about this
change, as a large number of solidarity initiatives as well as spontaneous
solidarity practices expanded and determined the first years of the mass
refugee arrivals. Nevertheless, the closure of the "Western Balkan Corridor"
and the EU-Turkey Statement were crucial for another turn in politics and
discourses that moved from the "humanitarian crisis" to the "problem" of
the "refugee crisis".

Yet while openly racist elements may have receded, a process of division
and categorisation among the refugee population was taking place. The
immigrant "other" was no longer an unspecified mass: they were divided
into those deserving protection, and those not. This was strengthened by the
admissibility procedure on the islands, as part of the EU-Turkey Statement,
in the context of the safe third country concept. The lifting of geographical
restrictions on the islands similarly divided asylum seekers according
to their nationality: again, into categories of deserving and undeserving.
Furthermore, during Syriza's term in office, a "pilot project" known as "Low
profile scheme" was implemented on the islands of Lesvos, Kos, and to a
certain extent on Leros from October 2017 until January 2018, without being
legally defined in legislation. The "Low profile scheme" refers to a highly
systematised and arbitrary practice of detention, as newly arrived persons,
usually single men belonging to particular nationalities, whose country
of origin has low recognition rates EU wide, are placed in administrative
detention upon arrival and remain there for a three-month period. The
project focuses on nationals of Pakistan, Bangladesh, Egypt, Tunisia, Algeria,
and Morocco; the list of countries was expanded to 28 in March 2017, when
the project was rebranded as "Low-Profile Scheme" project (ECRE, 2017).
This project has been characterised as a discriminatory "containment
policy" that functions as a new norm for Greece and a pilot project for the
entire European Union.

Since 2019's change of the government, a new construction of "the
other" began running in parallel. Discourses and politics strengthened
the distinctions between "deserving" and "undeserving", clearly indicating those "deserving" as the real refugees, and those not, as "economic
migrants". Referring to the new law on asylum, the relevant press release
in late 2019 noted that "based on the analysis of statistics on nationalities of

persons arriving in the country, it is our common understanding that this is a migration and not a refugee issue" (General Secretariat of Information and Communication, 2019). As such, the government considers that the "profile of refugee" should be applied only to Syrians and claims that the majority of newcomers are economic migrants. These perceptions are closely related to the increase in push-backs and returns that have been noted since the beginning of ND's term in office, especially on the sea borders, but also at the land borders of Evros.

On 9 September 2020, a huge fire destroyed the Moria Hotspot on the island of Lesvos. Back then, about 13,000 asylum seekers were staying in the Hotspot, in overcrowded, unhealthy, and unsafe conditions. Those living Moria have described it as "the hell of Europe". The night of the fire, people tried to shelter in the fields of the neighbouring area or moved towards the town of Mytilene to protect themselves and their families. The fire continued for the next two days, while asylum seekers sprawled into the surrounding area. For those who tried to reach Mytilene, a barrier was established in the middle of the street, in the area of Kara-Tepe. Police had already closed the road to prevent refugees continue their route towards the city. In the government's press conference that took place during the same day, the Minister Notis Mitarakis insisted on the need for a "sense of safety for both the asylum seekers and the local society" of the island (Ministry of Migration and Asylum, 2020). Furthermore, the government confirmed that it takes all the necessary (police) measures "to prevent the entry of asylum applicants in the town Mytilene for health reasons for the protection of themselves and the inhabitants of the island" (Ministry of Migration and Asylum, 2020). The Covid-19 pandemic was used as a tool for constructing "the other" as dangerous and infected, and the local society of Mytilene as endangered and in need of protection.

Nevertheless, this was not the first time that these kinds of police practices, as institutional and spatial deterrence practices, had been implemented on the part of the police and the government. The perception "the further from local society, the better" has been implemented, though in different ways. Earlier in 2020, during a demonstration of asylum applicants, mainly composed of Afghans living in Moria, police established the same border again. The asylum applicants' main slogan was "Azadi", which means "Freedom", yet they did not manage to reach the town, due to the police presence. Practices of separation, deterrence, and segregation have thus been already established on the islands, since the early 2016, and the establishment of Moria Hotspot. The limited interaction with the Greek population of the island constitutes a planned policy. The spatial isolation of the Hotspot and

the spatial distance between refugees and locals turns into social distance
and boundaries that do not facilitate contacts and relationships with the
local population. In the words of Kingslot, a beneficiary of subsidiary protection that used to live in Moria Hotspot:

> It's difficult, really difficult, I, until now [...] I don't speak Greek. Because
> we are not living with locals. We are not communicating, we are not
> connected with locals. I just speak English. It's how I communicate with
> everyone. It's like, there isn't, I speak only English because we are not
> connected, we are not integrating.

Practices of exclusion and distinction between "self" and "other" are not
merely institutional. In the context of increased racism and xenophobia,
such practices may acquire violent forms, and be implemented by non-
institutional forces. Practices of racist violence are not a new phenomenon
in Greece, yet they were on the rise on the early 2010s, during the electoral
rise of Golden Dawn. Back then, violent attacks were focused on migrants
who had arrived in the country during the mid-2000s, mainly from Middle
Eastern, African, and Asian countries. During recent years, after refugee
arrivals and their temporary – or permanent – settlement in the cities, racist
violence practices redoubled, with new constructions of "otherness" serving
to strengthen racism and xenophobia. Refugees' and asylum applicants'
own experiences invariably involved such practices, in the process of day
to day living in the cities or in their marginal camps.

Ermis is a young applicant for family reunification, staying in urban space
of Athens with his mother, sister, and brother. He lives in an apartment in
central Athens, provided by UNHCR, in the context of the ESTIA program, the
housing program for asylum applicants and applicants for family reunification in Greece. In the block of flats where he stays, both Greeks and previously
settled migrants reside. He narrates that living inside the urban space is
much better than the living conditions in camps in the mainland. One of
the reasons, according to him, is the spatial proximity between refugees and
locals that can enhance positive relationships and solidarity. Nevertheless,
Ermis narrates his story of a racist attack of a group of people against him,
which took place at the outdoor of the building where he used to live:

> In November, I was the victim of a fascist attack. In front of my house,
> about 10 people started hitting me on my head. It was a group of people
> with the same t-shirts and with flags. I already had problems with my
> head, and I was very scared after the attack. I went to the central police

department and I made a complaint. I applied to UNHCR to move me and my family to another house. I avoided walking around home after this incident.

At the same time, refugees encounter racist violence not only when they stay inside urban spaces in the large Greek cities, but also during their everyday movements. Thanasis – Mah, an Afghan beneficiary of international protection that used to work as a cultural mediator, narrates:

> Well, I was coming from the camp, from Elefsina. I was changing shift, I was going back to Elefsina to go to Schisto camp and stay. In the meantime, they stopped me like for motorcycles eight people, they beat me up, some cars that were there left, they called the ambulance, then the police came. [...] I consider them as small children who is just following the orders of the teacher who they work, without thinking why they're doing this, they have no idea. They called themselves Nazis, they had neo-Nazi signs, but they say they were Greek. The same as I said to the local community, if they could think a bit, this refugee population. They don't want to be here so it's not their fault, they forced to be here. What do you expect from them, they can do anything, they have to stay, it's not on their hands. You both have the same goal, so why do you treat them like that? Well, they don't want to be here in this country, that doesn't mean that Greece is bad. Come on, let's live in reality, open your eyes, open your mind, how is the situation. You can see that the refugees are frustrated from the situation and you are more.

7.4   Conclusion

In this chapter, we have discussed refugee discourses, practices, politics, and policies in the context of both the so-called "refugee crisis" and the financial crisis. The role of dominant discourses and politics in Greece during the investigated period was – explicitly or implicitly – to reproduce these different "crises" which seem to emerge as the catalysts for an important shift in discourses, politicising issues of Europeanisation. At the same time, during the period under investigation, massive demonstrations and struggles against austerity measures, as well as counter-discourses and movements of solidarity with refugees, emerged from sizeable social movement mobilisations. Issues of Europe and migration have been politicised, with the referendum of 2015 acting as a watershed event.

Conflicts over Europeanisation are present in discourses, policies and practices surrounding financial and migration issues, yet the contents are often vague, undefined, or contradicting. Thus, in adopting European Union's Directives and Regulations, their implementation largely depends on domestic political and social circumstances or conflicts. In parallel, discourses following the adoption of these policies and their implementation bring issues of Europeanisation to the forefront, yet much depends on the balance of forces between political left and right, especially where refugee issues are concerned. Nonetheless, a homogeneous stance cuts across Greece's political divisions. The need for burden- and responsibility-sharing within the European Union constitutes a characteristic example of such discourses, reflecting Greece's geographical positioning at the boundaries of "Europe".

The chapter has also offered a glimpse of how the contemporary "Other" has been constructed and reproduced, through the emergence of exclusionary dichotomies of those deserving and undeserving of protection; who has the right of movement; and who has the right to inhabitance. Racism against migrants has been a systemic, institutional, and functional tool used by right-wing politicians and conservative media, particularly since the emergence of the financial and migration "crises" in Greece. Racism, which has the "ability" to adapt to new circumstances, has re-emerged, by taking violent forms on the level of everyday life that have an impact on both the migrants and local communities. Divisions of national "self" and "other", while having resilience over time, are taking new forms, depending on the political and social context, by affecting – and being affected by – discourses on Europe and Europeanisation.

References

Altiparmakis, A. (2018). Greece – Punctuated Equilibrium: Restructuring Greek Party Politics. In Hutter, S., & Kriesi, H. (eds.), *Restructuring European Party Politics in Times of Crisis* (pp. 95–117). Cambridge: Cambridge University Press.

Baldwin-Edwards, M. (2014). *Immigrants, Racism and the New Xenophobia of Greece's Immigration Policy.* Mediterranean Migration Observatory, 11, Panteion University, Institute for International Relations, Athens.

Chryssogelos, A. (2017). *Still Europeanised? Greek Foreign Policy During the Eurozone Crisis, Greece.* Hellenic Observatory Papers on Greece and Southeast Europe, 118, Hellenic Observatory, LSE.

Davidson, N., & Saull, R. (2016). Neoliberalism and the Far-Right: A Contradictory Embrace. *Critical Sociology, 43*(4–5), 707–724.

Dinas, E., Georgiadou, V., Konstantinidis, I., & Rori, L. (2016). From Dusk to Dawn: Local Party Organization and Party Success of Right-Wing Extremism. *Party Politics*, 22(1), 80–92.

Disinfaux Collective (2020–2021). Lilliput, Magic Land(?): Sketching the Far Right in Lesvos. Available at: https://bit.ly/38kD8Wt (accessed 15 December 2020).

ECRE (2017). Interview: Asylum Procedure Based on Nationality Rather than on Merit – The Situation of Pakistani Asylum Applicants Under the EU Turkey Deal. Available at: https://bit.ly/3ngLbaR (accessed 15 December 2020).

Ellinas, A., A. (2013). The Rise of Golden Dawn: The New Face of the Far Right in Greece. *South European Society and Politics*, 18(4), 543–565.

Essed, P. (2002). Everyday Racism. In Goldberg, D. T., & Solomos, J. (eds.), *A Companion to Racial and Ethnic Studies*. (pp. 202-216) London: Blackwell.

Eurostat. (2018). Can You Afford to Pay All Your Bills? Available at: https://bit.ly/3003A73 (accessed 16 December 2020).

Fekete, L. (2012). *Pedlars of Hate: The Violent Impact of The European Far Right*. London: Institute of Race Relations.

Fekete, L. (2018). *Europe's Fault Lines: Racism and The Rise of The Right*. London; New York: Verso.

General Secretariat of Information and Communication. (2019). St. Petsas for the Decisions of the Ministry Council, 30 September 2019. Available at: https://bit.ly/2TdNyQl (accessed 15 December 2020) [in Greek].

Goldberg, D. (1993). *Racist Culture: Philosophy and the Politics of Meaning*. Oxford; Cambridge, MA: Blackwell.

Grigoriadis, N. I., & Dilek, E. (2019). Securitizing Migration in the European Union: Greece and the Evros Fence. *Journal of Balkan and Near Eastern Studies*, 21(2), 170–186.

Kandylis, G. (2015). Levels of Segregation, Lines of Closure: The Spatiality of Immigrants' Social Exclusion in Athens. *Local Economy*, 30(7), 818–837.

Karamanidou, L. (2016). Violence against Migrants in Greece: Beyond the Golden Dawn. *Ethnic and Racial Studies*, 39(11), 2002–2021.

Katsambekis, G., & Stavrakakis, Y. (2017). Revisiting the Nationalism/Populism Nexus: Lessons from the Greek Case. *Javnost – The Public*, 24(4), 391–408.

Kaya, A. (2017). Populismo e immigration en la Union Europea. In Arango, J., Mahia, R., Moha D., & Sanchez-Montijano E. (eds.), *La inmigración en el oja del huracán*. (pp. 301-319) Barcelona: CIDOB [in Spanish].

Ministry of Citizen Protection (2011). Presentation at the Ministry Council (6/9) of the Integrated Border Management Program for Combating Illegal Immigration, by Minister Christos Papoutsis. Available at: http://www.hcg.gr/node/1260 (accessed 10 December 2020) [in Greek].

Ministry of Migration and Asylum. (2020). Introductory Statement by the Minister of Migration and Asylum Mr. Notis Mitarakis on the Situation in Moria. Available at: https://bit.ly/3pWS6bc (accessed 12 December 2020) [in Greek].

Ministry of Public Order and Citizen Protection (2013) Press Release. 15 November 2013: Answer of the Minister of Public Order and Citizen Protection Mr. Nikos Dendias to a Topical Question of Ms. Maria Giannakaki MP of DIMAR Regarding Immigration in the Context of the Greek Presidency of the EU. Available at: https://bit.ly/397JxDx (accessed 10 December 2020) [in Greek].

Papageorgiou, I. (2013) The Europeanization of Immigration and Asylum in Greece (1990–2012). *International Journal of Sociology*, *43*(3), 72–90.

Papatzani, E., Leivaditi, N., Ilias, A., & Petracou, E. (2020). Conflicting Conceptualisations of Europeanisation: Greece Country Report. *Zenodo*. DOI: 10.5281/zenodo.4244374.

Papatzani, E. (2021). Encountering Everyday Racist Practices: Sociospatial Negotiations of Immigrant Settlement in Athens, Greece. *International Journal of Urban and Regional Research*, *45*(1), 61–79.

Petracou, E. (1999) *Exploring the Social and Historical Dimensions of Migration in the European Context with Special Reference to the Greek Case*. PhD thesis, Center for Research in Ethnic Relations, University of Warwick, UK.

Petracou, E., Leivaditi, N., Maris, G., Margariti, M., Tsitsaraki, P., & Ilias, A. (2018). Greece – Legal and Policy Framework of Migration Governance. *Zenodo*. DOI: 10.5281/zenodo.1418569.

Rovnyi, I., & Bachmann, V. (2012) Reflexive Geographies of Europeanization. *Geography Compass*, *6*(5), 260–274.

RVRN (Racist Violence Recording Network). (2015). Annual Report 2014. Available at: https://bit.ly/2m7yntI (accessed 25 November 2020).

Sedelmeier, U. (2012). Europeanization. In Jones, E., Menon, A., & Weatherill, S. (eds.), *The Oxford Handbook of the European Union*. (pp. 825-840) Oxford: Oxford University Press.

Sitaropoulos, N. (1992). The New Legal Framework of Alien Immigration in Greece: A Draconian Contribution to Europe's Unification. *Immigration and Nationality Law and Practice*, *6*(3), 89–96.

Sotiropoulos, D., & Bourikos, D. (2014). Economic Crisis, Social Solidarity and the Voluntary Sector in Greece. *Journal of Power, Politics & Governance*, *2*(2), 33–53.

Stavrakakis, Y., Katsambekis, G., Nikisianis, N., Kioupkiolis A., & Siomos, T. (2017). Extreme Right-Wing Populism in Europe: Revisiting a Reified Association. *Critical Discourse Studies*, *14*(4), 420–439.

Triandafyllidou, A. (2014). Greek Migration Policy in the 2010s: Europeanization Tensions at a Time of Crisis. *Journal of European Integration*, *36*(4), 409–425.

Ventoura, L. (2004) Nationalism, Racism and Migration in Contemporary Greece. In
    Pavlou, M., & Christopoulos, D. (eds.), *Greece of Migration: Social Participation,
    Rights and Citizenship*. (pp. 147-170) Athens: Kritiki [in Greek].
Xenakis, S., & Cheliotis, K., L. (2013). Spaces of Contestation: Challenges, Actors and
    Expertise in the Management of Urban Security in Greece. *European Journal
    of Criminology*, 10(3), 297–313.

About the Authors

Eva (Evangelia) Papatzani is a PhD Candidate at the Department of Urban
and Regional Planning, National Technical University of Athens, Greece. She
has participated as a researcher in several European and national research
projects on refugee issues. Her research focuses on the geographies of migrant
settlement, interethnic networks and sociospatial segregation, and urban
transformations.
Email: evaliapap@yahoo.gr

Electra Petracou is Associate Professor in the Department of Geography
of the University of the Aegean. Her teaching experience, research, and
interests focus on movements of populations, asylum, refugee, and migration
issues; global, European, and national policies on borders and migration;
and decision-making on social, political, and international issues. She is
co-director of the Laboratory of Movements on Borders in the Department
of Geography of the University of the Aegean.
Email: ipetr@geo.aegean.gr

8 The Cognitions Underpinning Online Discrimination, Derogatory Sarcasm, and Anti-cosmopolitanism towards Syrians at Europe's Periphery

Bogdan Ianosev and Özge Özdüzen

Abstract

This chapter focuses on the anti-cosmopolitan attitudes surging in Europe and its periphery following the so-called refugee crisis by capturing digital publics as a function of intuitive cognition. It studies the emergence of sarcastic anti-cosmopolitan attitudes on Twitter in this period. The chapter examines #FreeEUForRefugees hashtag – a sarcastic form of online engagement exemplifying a publicly expressed willingness of people in Turkey to "send" Syrian refugees to Europe. The chapter contributes to the literature on contemporary anti-cosmopolitan movements, fed by the global rise of far right and the electoral powers the radical right has gained, whilst presenting evidence to the wider areas of critical social media studies and cognitive psychology behind anti-immigrant attitudes. The chapter analyses how discontent towards and violence against ethnic and racial minorities are legitimised on social media platforms and provides situational conditions for such rhetoric, whilst highlighting the largely automatic cognitive mechanisms likely involved in perpetuating anti-Syrian attitudes.

Keywords: intuitions, essentialising, dehumanisation, discrimination, social media

8.1 Introduction

As discussed throughout this volume, the 2015 humanitarian crisis resulted in the politicisation of "Europe" and its periphery. In this chapter, we assess

Foley, J. and Korkut, U. (ed.), *Contesting Cosmopolitan Europe. Euroscepticism, Crisis and Borders*. Amsterdam: Amsterdam University Press 2022
DOI :10.5117/9789463727259_CH08

online expressions of this politics, with a particular stress on discourses surrounding (Syrian) refugees. In focusing on the anti-cosmopolitan attitudes surging in Europe following the humanitarian crisis, the chapter captures digital publics as a function of intuitive cognition and studies the emergence of sarcastic anti-cosmopolitan attitudes on online platforms in this period. The paper examines #FreeEUForRefugees hashtag – a sarcastic form of online engagement that expresses a Turkish publics' willingness to "expel" or "send" Syrian refugees to EU (European Union) countries. Although Twitter analysis is only one way to study how certain themes are publicly expressed and how users are politicised about specific issues, Twitter itself is widely used as a political space by ordinary users, policymakers, and state actors alike. The chapter contributes to the emerging literature on anti-cosmopolitan movements whilst presenting the likely cognitive pathways leading to such attitudes. It responds to digital publics during a war-like scenario, specifically the Turkish military invasion/occupation of Syria, showing that the occupation amplified the online expression of disgust towards Syrian migrants and bolstered their dehumanisation in the host society. In its analysis of social media data, the chapter uses qualitative content analysis, an important tool in exploring individual-level cognitive processes and effects related to broader message characteristics (Riffe et al., 2019).

The chapter identifies Twitter as a discursive space (Ogola, 2015), which also reflects the discourse produced in dominant/mainstream media (Lindgren and Lundström, 2011), and in other traditional public spheres. The formation, spread and reproduction of digital traces functions to assist the far-right in gaining an audience and to allow stereotypes on ethnic others to gain a wider representation (Crosset et al., 2019), whilst providing them with global linkages (Daniels, 2009). Previous literature on the online political communication practices of racist, far right, and radical right-wing ideas identified them as a "networked phenomenon" and studied how right-wing extremists and those who subscribe to extreme right or racist views exploit online platforms to build a collective identity among the like-minded (see Gaudette et al., 2020; Murthy & Sharma, 2019). Diverging from existing literature, this chapter articulates how right-wing groups/users aim to make a policy change through Twitter communication by sarcastically addressing targeted institutions such as the Turkish government or the EU Commission. Although the posts equally blame the right-wing government AKP's policies, the social media interaction on the subject of refugees promotes and legitimises the widespread appeal of the anti-cosmopolitan and nationalist viewpoints that motivate supporters of the AKP.

The chapter identifies irony and sarcasm as being based on shared cultural codes and knowledge between the imagined and actual audiences and the speaker (Bamman & Smith, 2015), hence relying on implicit presuppositions about shared norms (e.g., jokes about Jews implicitly rely on stereotypes about Jews). Online citizen engagement in policy change is a crucial component of "hashtag activism", especially during global social movements such as the narrative agency in #BlackLivesMatter (Yang, 2016) or the digital "call-out culture" in #MeToo hashtag activism (Mendes et al., 2018). Unlike previous studies on hashtag activism, this chapter investigates rising radical right-wing hashtag activism following the humanitarian crisis and locates this sarcastic online expression as arising from users' "intuitive cognition".

Intuitive cognition broadly refers to the plethora of cognitive processes, which emerged at various points in our evolutionary history, that occur automatically in the form of intuitions, and that have the function of helping humans to successfully navigate their environment in order to survive and reproduce. For instance, within the area of cooperation and collaboration, crucial for human survival, there is the idea that the fruits of a joint venture should be distributed equitably between the parties involved, *as a function of the respective contribution of each member* to that venture. This intuition is largely automatic and effortless, and surfaces as a result of our intuitive "sense of fairness" (Baumard et al. 2013). As a result of this mechanism, any cultural norm reinforcing the intuition of the equitable redistribution of spoils will "ring true", while all blatant violations will elicit a perception of injustice or unfairness. Cognitively, it is difficult to evade the activation of our intuitions since they are, to a large extent, automatic and effortless. They activate once relevant information is perceived, akin to the activation of a fire alarm once smoke is detected (Sperber, 1997, Barrett & Lanman, 2008, Mercier & Sperber, 2017).

Similarly, the cognitive underpinnings implicated in anti-immigrant sentiments and racist online expression, responsible for othering Syrian refugees, arise from the same type of cognitive processing – automatic, implicit, and intuitive. This chapter examines universal intuitive cognitions of coalition building, essentialising, and dehumanisation activated by environmental conditions and cultural representations. We propose that such cognitions drive anti-immigrant attitudes, which feed overt and/or covert racist online expression. Furthermore, by specifying the input conditions that activate our cognitive intuitions and the specific inferences they automatically return (such as the belief that intergroup competition is zero-sum or that outgroups have immutable essences causing their behaviour), we track the emergence of derogatory comments as a function of the intuitive cognitions facilitating said comments. Turkish right-wing populists, along with media outlets, provide ample stimuli which reinforce intuitive views and stereotypes about the new outgroup, Syrians. Additionally, perceptions of outgroup boundaries may vary as a function of the markers by which outgroup members are identified, and these markers often come in the form of stereotypes. Frequently, ethnic populations such Kurds are designated by Turkish right-wing populists as outgroups and, more recently, Syrians have been established as permanent outgroups. We identify the insistence on permanent outgroups as a facet of anti-cosmopolitan attitudes.

Studying cosmopolitanism is significant, partly because the discussions on cosmopolitanism challenge the foundations of traditional nation-state-centred social research (Hannerz, 1990; Roudometof, 2005). The central tenet of cosmopolitanism is the "desiderata" for all human beings to live in one and the same political community (Kleingeld & Brown, 2019). However, natural selection favoured the emergence in humans of automatic cognitions designed to solve recurrent problems of group living and intergroup relations, which inevitably work to partition populations into separate groups. As a result, we are intuitively prone to delineating between ingroups and outgroups, to building coalitions, and to disputing over resources, especially in unfavourable environments (Barkow et al., 1992). These intuitive cognitions connect with other intuitive processes such as the essentialising of outgroups, sometimes resulting in dehumanisation, and work toward hindering the likelihood of any cosmopolitan endeavour. On the other hand, approaching cosmopolitanism requires a higher reliance on less automatic and more effortful and analytic cognitions.

There is a noted opposition between conservative/right-wing beliefs and cosmopolitan/multiculturalist ones. Whereas the former relies on intuitive processing, cosmopolitanism likely requires more abstract considerations and analytic thinking. For instance, an analytic thinking style was linked to liberalism (Saribay and Yilmaz, 2017), while an intuitive cognitive style was linked to conservatism (Eidelman et al., 2012). Moreover, conservatism and intuitive thinking have been associated with anti-cosmopolitan attitudes (Zmigrod, Rentfrown, & Robbins, 2018, Davis & Hollis, 2018). Based on this framework, the first section delineates our methodological perspective, followed by a short section on the refugee settlement in Turkey and its implications for the EU. The rest of the chapter brings empirical evidence for coalitional intuitions and their relationship to online stereotyping, categorisation, and anti-cosmopolitan views.

8.2 Twitter Methodology

Online social interactions may instigate far-right political violence, dehumanisation, and disgust for the outgroup. This chapter analyses how discontent towards and violence against ethnic and racial minorities are legitimised on social media whilst providing situational conditions for such rhetoric (Wahlström et al., 2020). Our data showcases the ways cultural racism unfolds by tracing attitudes expressed towards the humanitarian crisis on online platforms. Empirically, the chapter is based on a case study of the hashtag #FreeEUForRefugees (970 items), retrieved in October 2019 using Python programming language. Our analysis is broadly informed by the data analysed in 2018 and 2019 related to Syrians in Turkey (Ozduzen, Korkut, & Ozduzen, 2020), which consists of an engagement with trending topics on Syrians. Users from Turkey used the #FreeEUForRefugees hashtag as part of the wider #Syrians hashtag, which trended as the number one item in October 2019 on Twitter trends for Turkey (Ozduzen & Korkut, 2020, p. 497), when the Turkish state occupied Rojava cantons in Northern Syria.

A small part of the trending topic of #Syrians included a sarcastic engagement with Syrians in Turkey and the EU: the hashtag #FreeEUForRefugees. This hashtag functions as an emblem of the unfolding of disgust and dehumanisation towards refugees, concealed by sarcastic expression. To study anti-refugee online publics, we undertake a qualitative content analysis of Twitter texts. Anderson and Kanuka (2003) define content analysis as an appropriate method for Internet research such as the analysis of text documents including email or chats. In recent years, both qualitative and quantitative content analyses of Twitter posts are widely used to understand Twitter's location in political expression, such as politicians' use of Twitter for campaigning in political elections (Adams & McCorkindale, 2013). Diverging from previous research, our methodology identifies sarcasm and irony as tenets of humour whilst defining them as linguistic phenomena in dealing with political expression.

8.3 The Historical Background of "Refugee" Settlement in Turkey and Its Relation to the EU

Since the early days of the revolution and the civil war in Syria (2011), the Turkish government AKP (Adalet ve Kalkınma Partisi/Justice and Development Party, 2002–present) has had a so-called open-door policy for the Syrian "guests". Since 2011, approximately 4 million Syrians have reached

Turkey or used Turkey as a gateway to reach Europe. Unlike its nationalist and conservative peers in Europe, the AKP government, a neoliberal and Islamist right-wing party, initially adopted a narrative identifying "Syria as Turkey's internal affair and the Syrians as the Muslim brothers" (Korkut, 2016). The AKP usurped its open-door policy towards Syrians to boost its standing within the "Muslim world" as it projected an image of the "helper" of Muslim communities in dire straits.

The 2016 migration deal between the EU and Turkey, which aimed to manage illicit border crossings, altered Turkey's policy-agenda on and public reactions to refugees. Turkey accepted the return of all newly arriving refugees in exchange for €6 billion. Since then, Turkey has acted as "a protector belt" for the "maintenance" of the EU borders. The AKP has also used its "protection" policy as a trump card against the EU, whilst turning the humanitarian crisis into an opportunity to stay in power (Mccarthy, 2020). Although the EU did not act as a monolithic bloc in handling the crisis (Saatçioğlu, 2020), the EU-Turkey deal is likely to have fed anti-cosmopolitan publics in the EU countries and the EU's periphery. The migration deal between the EU and Turkey inspired a public perspective of Syrians receiving financial help from both the Turkish state and the EU, followed by their stigmatisation as lazy groups that strain the welfare state.

In line with the early official discourse propagated by the AKP, the Turkish public initially treated Syrian refugees as "Muslim brothers" and "guests". However, in the absence of formal refugee protection and integration programmes, this early "humanitarian" response soon evolved into a "securitisation" response (Korkut, 2016). Soon after, Syrians settled down in Turkey. In the meantime, the AKP increasingly securitised the Syrians' presence, which entailed "giving up on its 'humanitarian responsibility'" (Koca, 2016, p. 56). The Syrian refugee settlement in Turkey dates to 2011 but the change of policy and official narrative fed into inter-communal tensions and mob attacks in physical geographies in both rural and urban Turkey and hate speech on online platforms, especially in the last three years (Korkut, 2016; Ozduzen, Korkut, & Ozduzen, 2020). These reactions climaxed when Syrians settled down, opened businesses and/or acquired Turkish citizenship in the absence of protection and integration policies.

On the other hand, Turkey and Russia have been the most active geopolitical actors on the ground in Syria. Basbugoglu, Korkut and Ashraf (2020) point to the processes under which Turkey swiftly and willingly interfered with the domestic affairs of Syria following March 2011 protests and subsequent violent clashes in Syria, where Turkey has political interests and security and economic concerns. For instance, Turkey has conducted three cross-border military operations in Northern Syria with Russian consent since 2016, in which Turkey is primarily driven by the need to counter the perceived threat posed by the YPG (People's Protection Units), the Kurdish forces in Northern Syria (Köstem, 2020, pp. 1–2). One of these military operations against the YPG took place in October 2019, prompting the trending topic of #Syrians on the Turkish Internet-sphere.

8.4 Analysis

8.4.1 Sarcastic Online Anti-cosmopolitanism

The tweets in our sample suggest a free EU for Syrian refugees, the new outgroup in Turkey and Europe. From the outset, this suggestion may appear to be a "gain" for the outgroup (i.e., a new life in the EU countries). However, we propose that the hashtag functions sarcastically as a symptom and symbol of rising anti-cosmopolitan tendencies. #FreeEUForRefugees hashtag also implies a politicisation against the EU. Canefe and Bora (2003, p. 127) show how the radical Turkish nationalism and its parliamentary representative Milliyetçi Hareket Partisi (Nationalist Action Party – MHP) as the prime protagonist of anti-European public discourse, which dispute efforts to fulfil the legal criteria on the full membership in the EU. Today, the AKP's (combined with their pact with MHP) populist and nativist "Muslim nation" project redefines Turkey's national and international identity with an ever-increasing dose of anti-Westernism, denouncing the EU/West for preventing the projected rise of Turkey, and a rejection of the EU Progress Reports (Çınar, 2018, pp. 177–178).

In line with this, tweets denounced and mocked the European refugee resettlement and protection policies, highlighting the spread of Syrians through different European countries to deride the EU's perceived lack of refugee intake. These posts also mocked "civilisation" in Europe whilst designating the EU as an entity that stood against Turkey's ability to thrive The fear of external and internal "enemies" run deep in Turkish nation's psychology, fuelling a language of "external powers" working against Turkey (Polat, 2010, p. 58). These tweets designate Syrians as standing in the way of the changes modern Turkey aims for (Benford & Hunt, 1992). Turkish users ask sarcastic, pejorative, and threatening questions to prospective European publics and nations, such as "are you ready for Syrians?" Turkish users applied this hashtag to spread fake news on EU policies about refugees as the new outgroup, using the hashtag whilst retweeting the most popular tweets with disinformation.

Although most of the #Syrians data harnessed during the occupation of Northern Syria by the Turkish state revolves around bio-racism, the #FreeEUForRefugees sub-dataset includes a divergent sarcastic and ironic tone, which, we argue, reproduces and bolsters "migrant stereotypes" and creates an imagined "Syrian category". Politicised ironic and sarcastic tweets shared among this segment of the Turkish online population, expressing deeply felt opinions on a given topic (Liu et al., 2014), tend to highlight intuitive beliefs and unexamined assumptions. Sarcastic anti-immigrant/refugee posts that also include fake news unfold as a result of cognitive mechanisms such as psychological essentialism and coalitional psychology intuitions.

8.4.2   Coalitional Intuitions, Sarcasm, and Anti-cosmopolitanism

Higher reliance on cognitive intuitions about intergroup relations and categorical ascriptions of outgroup essences can lead to endorsing stereotypes about immigrants and refugees and promote anti-refugee attitudes. Moreover, intuitions of deservingness that originally evolved in our hunter-gatherer ancestors to motivate help-giving in small-scale societies are now informing present-day evaluations of welfare recipients.

Automatic intuitions about coalitions promote zero-sum thinking in context of intergroup relations. They are generated as our brains automatically parse group membership as exclusive, mirroring ancient human evolutionary dynamics. Zero-sum thinking is reflected by the explicit belief that a gain for the outgroup equals a loss for the ingroup (Esses et al., 1998; Boyer and Petersen, 2018). Intergroup competition scenarios, such as those emerging as Syrians were being perceived to contend for Turkish resources, trigger both intuitions of coalitional psychology and intuitions of deservingness that motivate behaviours designed both to protect the resources available to the ingroup against outgroups and to restrict welfare for outgroups (Petersen, 2012).

The tweets in our sample assume that if the outgroup leaves Turkey, the ingroup (Turks) will take back control and have a more prosperous and safe life in Turkey. Rather than a direct speech on "taking back control", the posts indirectly recount the possibility that Turkey would be better off were there no Syrians in Turkey. Likewise, the posts on this hashtag generally depict a fantasy scenario implying that if Syrians had not arrived and settled in Turkey, the ingroups' financial and social conditions would have been much better. The main difference between posts under #FreeEUForRefugees and tweets on the wider dataset (#Syrians) in this period is that the users pretend to be considerate about Syrians in Turkey. The actual gain for the ingroup (e.g., getting rid of Syrians) was masked by an alleged gain for the outgroup (e.g., a better life for Syrians in the EU) through sarcasm and irony. The sarcastic component of the online discourse is informed by the users' intention to "send" Syrians to EU Member States such as France, with an ostensible underlying interest in Syrians' wellbeing. On the surface, these users have a desire to see their "Syrian brother" achieve better social and economic conditions which are, in their view, impossible to be accomplished in the current "temporary" hosting context of Turkey. The users highlight the temporary nature of Syrians' residence in Turkey, although the current conditions for Syrians have not been deemed temporary by the Turkish state or the EU – underlining the background assumption that Syrians constitute a permanent outgroup.

The anti-refugee attitudes in Turkey started not while Syrians were initially being welcomed as "guests", but rather later, when many Syrians made it apparent that they wished to or had to remain. Human coalitional psychology predicts that the presence of a salient outgroup in the proximity of the ingroup triggers the intuition that the outgroup is encroaching on the limited resources available to the ingroup. This was made evident by the decision or obligation (since the migration deal) of many Syrians to remain in Turkey, which resulted with the public perception of Syrians as an adversarial coalition taking away jobs from locals and straining the Turkish welfare state. On the other hand, while still enjoying their temporary "guest" status, Syrian refugees had no citizen rights and would have had a difficult time getting employed or accessing the Turkish welfare state. This "guest" status likely precluded coalitional intuitions from initially activating. However, the later perception of Syrians as an encroaching outgroup – after they decided to stay and open businesses, which suggests them becoming more prosperous and settled – automatically triggered anti-immigrant sentiment. Perceiving Syrians as a contending outgroup likely increased the plausibility of anti-immigrant stereotypes as explicit beliefs.

It was previously found that viewing intergroup competition in zero-sum terms drives anti-immigration attitudes, leading to stereotypes that migrants are either lazy (e.g., they strain the welfare state) or industrious (e.g., they take away jobs), irrespective of the cause for migration (i.e., whether migration was driven by seeking asylum, fleeing war, or by economic reasons) (Esses et al., 2010; Cappelen & Yvette, 2018; Sindic et al., 2018). Syrians are antagonised because by wanting to settle into the local economy, they are perceived as fighting for "Turkish" jobs and resources, even when they create jobs. When a salient outgroup is perceived as prospering, they are perceived as prospering on the back of the ingroup, with locals entertaining the zero-sum intuition that, as the outgroup fares better, the ingroup is losing out. This intuition in turn likely motivates anti-immigrant, anti-refugee attitudes (Esses, 1998; Boyer and Petersen, 2018).

Some of the tweets also recommended Syrians to have fun and open businesses in European capitals so that both Syrians and the EU would prosper. This recommendation was most likely intended as an incentive for the Syrian outgroup to contend for jobs with local populations elsewhere, but not in Turkey. On the surface, the fact that users address the EU to "help" Syrian refugees may look like a cosmopolitan perspective and an openness and solidarity embraced by users from Turkey. However, the tweets that used this hashtag recommended Syrians leave Turkey for the EU countries in order to benefit from and strain their welfare states, and "contaminate" the capital cities of EU countries. Such politicised views expressed online resonate with globally prevalent right-wing and populist attitudes, with an added dimension of sarcasm, as users intentionally turn cosmopolitanism against perceived EU elites.

Additionally, perceptions of an unfavourable environment are triggers for our coalitional intuitions since protecting local resources was key for the survival of ancient human populations. Such perceptions are frequently cued by representations of the economy in dire straits, which commonly function as a proxy for limited resources available to the ingroup. This can be observed in our dataset as well, with some users pointing out that "Turkey is in an economic crisis" and therefore is unable to host Syrian refugees. Alternatively, users perceive the arrival of Syrian refugees in Turkey as the beginning of the economic crisis, which also makes sense in a zero-sum scenario, likely reinforcing the intuitive expectation that the arrival of an outgroup should be associated with a strain on local resources, *if* resources are *perceived* to be scarce.

In their perception of the economic crisis in Turkey, the user expressions in the current dataset provide ample instances where Syrians are referred to as lazy. Similar to the overall dataset that was analysed elsewhere (Ozduzen, Korkut, & Ozduzen, 2020), this sub-dataset associated Syrians with the leisurely practice of smoking waterpipe and eating kebab, which maintains the myth of the lazy oriental subjectIs the imagined modernised Turkish or European, who are depicted as hardworking. Users from Turkey recommended that Syrian men relax and have fun in iconic places in Europe – for example, the Eiffel Tower – by circulating texts and images portraying Syrian men smoking waterpipe and having a leisurely time in European capitals.

Depictions of stereotypical laziness in the context of welfare are intuitively judged by our "deservingness heuristic". This scenario most likely also emerged once Syrian refugees decided to remain in Turkey. When judging the deservingness of welfare recipients, the cognitive mechanism sometimes called the deservingness heuristic automatically computes cues of laziness and effort. Among the cues of activation there is the cue of a perceived need on the behalf of the prospective recipient, which is correlated with an effort to alleviate this need. We are motivated to support welfare for victims of bad luck but to deny welfare to recipients who are perceived as cheating or lazy (Petersen, 2012).

Syrian refugees are described as lazy migrants, which activates the input conditions of the deservingness heuristic, resulting in the intuition that the Turkish host community should deny welfare to Syrian migrants. Interestingly, outgroup stereotypes from our sample were so pervasive that they most likely managed to overwrite the perception of Syrian refugees as victims of unfortunate context – the civil war. This was partly done by emphasising that Syrians were lazy, cheaters, and cowardly. The last of the three attributes, cowardice, was key in informing the perception of Syrians as an undesirable outgroup, inherently lacking in positive attributes. This afforded the typical right-wing habit of blaming the victim for their misfortune. Because Syrian males are supposedly cowards, they are to blame for their refugee status – they did not attempt to alleviate their need – and therefore, despite not being responsible for the civil war, they are not worthy of welfare help.

The ease by which all Syrians are depicted as lazy suggests a certain readiness and effortlessness in viewing Syrian refugees stereotypically. This is usually facilitated by attributing essentialised traits to all Syrian refugees so that every single Syrian mirrors the same traits and behaviours as every other member of the "Syrian category". Stereotyping is intuitive, and right-wing narratives routinely activate our intuitions and heuristics that attribute inherent immutable traits to migrants and ethnic or gender minorities functioning to derogate members of such categories. Stereotyping, intuitive processing, and outgroup derogation come together in the right-wing populist mindset.

Right-wing political attitudes are associated with anti-immigrant sentiment, and right-wing narratives likely reinforce our coalitional intuitions. Because social conservatism is linked to dispositionally perceiving intergroup relations in zero-sum terms (Esses et al., 1998), promoting the exclusion of outgroups, and because at its core, cosmopolitanism involves the inclusion of and tolerance for outgroups, we identify outgroup discrimination and the specific suggestion of "sending" Syrians to Europe, featured in our sample, as an anti-cosmopolitan stance.

Cosmopolitanism is revived today due to the tremendous changes that happened in the 1990s following the fall of communism in the USSR and Central and Eastern Europe. The 1990s were also marked by the arrival of the Internet and the epochal revolution in communication technologies, leading not only to the transformation of everyday life and politics but also capitalism (Delanty, 2012, p. 3). Delanty (2012) describes the new millennium as a period of both cosmopolitan and anti-cosmopolitan movements colliding. Today, many people are reluctant to and resent the disintegration of national identities and try to restore closure and cultural purity, such as the wider anti-immigration and anti-refugee mobilisations across Europe and beyond.

Right-wing populism is incompatible with cosmopolitanism. For instance, in Britain and elsewhere in the West, right-wing populism is linked to an anti-multicultural backlash and promotes conformity to traditional values (Jay et al., 2019). Cosmopolitanism implies the experience of "going beyond the familiar" through the increasing transnational spaces and intermingling with the global context. Although users in Turkey respond to a global humanitarian situation and have, on the surface, offered a transnational solution, the way these users express themselves is anti-cosmopolitan. The collected posts designate the Turks as the deciding agents for the future of the Syrian outgroup in Turkey, Syria, and Europe, thus granting a hierarchical leverage to the ingroup over the outgroup.

8.4.3   Online Stereotypes and Political Conservatism

The affordances of social networking sites – including but not limited to retweets, likes, hashtags, and replies – can reinforce stereotypes based in the essentialisation of outgroups and facilitate a networked form of othering and victimisation of outgroups (see Ladegaard, 2012; Felmlee, 2020). To endorse and share stereotypes on social networking sites is effortless. Wider visibility and reach of online stereotypes reinforce existing societal norms related to outgroups. This is partly facilitated by the fact that traditional norms and socially conservative ideas are largely intuitive and therefore cognitively appealing.

Extensive reliance on cognitive intuitions favours simple narratives that are easier to process, more intuitive, and therefore more easily transmitted (e.g., stereotypes). Participants scoring higher on Social Dominance Orientation (SDO), a measure predicting right-wing conservative attitudes and support for existing norms, are also more likely to see intergroup relations in zero-sum terms (Esses et al., 1998). Political conservatism is promoted by low-effort, automatic processing, and right-wing populist narratives are intuitive as they commonly depict the world in simplistic and easily processable terms (Eidelman et al., 2012; Bergmann, 2018).

Attributing stereotypical traits and behaviours to outgroups is linked to psychological essentialism, a natural and spontaneous cognitive tendency that focuses on within-category similarities and tends to ignore individual differences. Because of this, humans are prone to intuitively believe that category members share an underlying "essence" that is responsible for the central traits and behaviours of each member of that category (Gelman, 2003).

Psychological essentialism is useful for categorising animals and making inferences from minimal encounters with potential predators. Essentialism can at times prove a useful learning heuristic, but can also generate epistemically false beliefs. For instance, essentialism drives children towards reasoning that a baby kangaroo raised by goats will grow up to look and act like a kangaroo, but also that French babies brought up by English-speaking parents will grow up to speak French (Gelman, 2003). To this end, young children also reason as if race is a function of underlying essences, transmitted through biological inheritance, and members of essentialised outgroups often fall victim to stereotyping and prejudice (Hirschfeld, 2001). However, the intuition that we should treat all members of a predator species in the same way is an adaptive precaution. Translated into sociology, this intuition becomes a false belief about the likely behaviours of outgroups.

Intuitions of essentialism routinely inform cultural ideas. Turkish social media users depict the Syrian outgroup, who in their view, look the same, act the same, and eat the same food. These users lump Syrians in a homogeneous category sharing an underlying essence of "Syrianness", even if different ethnic, religious, social, and cultural groups compose this category. Furthermore, our data shows that Turks who employ Syrians in their workplaces or help them out are also lumped together with Syrians and depicted as outgroups. The Turkish users sarcastically recommend the "Syrianised" Samaritan Turks, along with Syrians, should leave Turkey for the EU.

Essentialising Syrian refugees, along with negative stereotypes such as laziness or lack of courage in combat, generates false beliefs such as their alleged incongruity with Turkish culture. In our sample, we found mentions of a supposed cultural mismatch between Turks and Syrians which suggested that Syrians are not well suited to acculturate in Turkey.

Since Syrians are perceived as culturally incongruent, Turkish users are sarcastically hopeful that Syrians can "learn from" European manners and attitudes once the EU opens borders and allows them in. In arguing this, online users from Turkey commonly resorted to stereotypes such as laziness of Syrians, or their alleged lack of "courage" in military warfare. The online publics sarcastically designate Syrians as lumpen proletarians lacking morality (e.g., they could attack "our" women), or lacking civilised manners (e.g., they are loud), whilst marking them as "civilisationally incompetent" people (e.g., they could not build a lasting regime and ran away), who thus should leave Turkey (Buchowski, 2006).

Across our data, Syrians are essentialised as kebab-eating social groups. Although kebab is a fundamental part of all different cuisines in the Middle East, in Turkish users' perception it symbolises the Orient as this food is perceived as having its origins in the more "Eastern" geographical areas and traditions. The same sense of essentialism resonates in the user reactions to Syrian men smoking waterpipe, which for them represents the ultimate marker of civilisational incompetence. By categorising refugees as kebab-eating and waterpipe-smoking groups, the users construct an essentialised identity for refugees that compose of derogatory personal attributes such as backwardness and exaggerated leisure.

8.4.4   Categorisation, Stereotyping, and Dehumanisation

In our data, there is an exclusive sense of "we", referring to Turks. This exclusive "we" addresses the EU countries, leaders, and European publics on collected tweets. A hegemonic and toxic masculine Turkish "teacher"/"role model" figure unfolds underlying the exclusive sense of "we" that primarily says: "if our guests do not know how to go to Europe, we can show them". It is assumed that the outgroup lacks strategies and know-how so the ingroup (Turks) should teach "them" the way. This suggests a level of dehumanisation because denying mental attributes such as "agency" (e.g., forward planning, executive functions) to outgroups is an established facet of dehumanisation (Harris & Fiske, 2011). In addition to dehumanising Syrians, the posts include a level of disgust for other permanent outgroups, especially the Kurds.

Unlike common categorisation and dehumanisation for outgroups as animals, for example in the context of the contemporary anti-refugee media ecology (e.g., the larger #Syrians dataset), our sub-dataset (#FreeEUFor-Refugees) reflects sarcastic dehumanisation of refugees. The users employ irony to covertly dehumanise the figure of the Syrian in Turkey. The online narrative dehumanises the perceived kebab-eating and waterpipe-smoking

Syrian men. One of the most retweeted tweets included an implication of users' willingness to send a mixed kebab of Syrian, Afghan, and Pakistani refugees to France, which functions to dehumanise the outgroups. Users not only lump these different social and racial groups together but also liken them to meat dishes.

This implies that they are perceived as animals, and processed animal meat at that. Given that kebabs are perceived by Turkish users as a marker of "less civilised" oriental outgroups, refugees were referred to as kebabs as a way of summarising essentialised traits projected onto them. Similarly, Syrian men are described as menaces to Turkish society as in this view they reproduce and multiply in numbers. One of the tweets suggested using Syrian men as a birth control tool, which is an illustrative example of dehumanisation: "Let's send handsome Syrian men to Europe and control the world's population". Most evident in the data is a contempt for France as a geographical location and Macron as the "ringleader". Across our data, France appears to be the main location where users from Turkey "wish" to send Syrians to. The dehumanisation towards Syrians is enmeshed with the hostility and contempt for the EU countries and leaders, which are defined as "terrorist-backing" and "impeding Turkey's future" (especially the EU as an imagined entity backing the Kurdish autonomy in Syria).

8.5 Conclusion

This chapter has studied the cognitive underpinnings of the right-wing populist backlash to the "refugee crisis" and highlighted specific intuitive cognitions implicated in anti-immigrant and anti-cosmopolitan online publics. We have identified the ways in which Syrians were categorised and stereotyped using cultural and political indicators. The chapter has argued that a specific type of cognitive processing that is fast, frugal, and intuitive is responsible for othering and derogating Syrian migrants and refugees. We identified universal cognitions of coalition building, essentialising, and dehumanisation, which drive anti-immigrant and racist attitudes and feed online comments and activities among Turkish users. In examining a universal cognition of coalition building, our discussion was based on how the local populist ideology informed the psychology of users from Turkey, such as the fear of the adversarial coalitions external (e.g., France) and internal (e.g., Syrians in Turkey), "enemies" plotting against the interests of the Turkish people. In identifying such discourses, we have located how users in Turkey dehumanised Syrians expressing themselves through tweets that discursively relied on a form of sarcasm embedded in disgust. This, we argue, is representative of the contemporary social media ecology of stereotyping, contempt, and disgust online, specifically towards the global outgroup of refugees in the aftermath of the humanitarian crisis.

The chapter identified the derogatory comments as being a result of the intuitive psychology of online users. Right-wing populists, rising anti-cosmopolitan culture in Europe and Europe's periphery and current media ecology provide ample stimuli fit for the input conditions of the coalitional and the essentialising intuitions of Turkish online users which succeed in reinforcing their stereotypical views about Syrian migrants. Our dataset is significant in that it reflects an added dimension of elaboration of common anti-immigrant stereotypes expressed through ironic and sarcastic commentary. Because irony and sarcasm, as tenets of humour, rely on implicit presuppositions about shared norms, ironic tweets highlight stereotypes and intuitive beliefs that are shared among this segment of online publics in Turkey. Therefore, our chapter presents the novelty of fleshing out the intuitive presuppositions of sarcastic anti-immigrant comments. It thus informs the global mushrooming, legitimisation, and mainstreaming of anti-refugee rhetoric and online activity following the humanitarian crisis, by portraying a snippet of digital stereotypes and categorisation around the now-permanent racial outgroup in Turkey and beyond: Syrian refugees.

References

Adams, A., & McCorkindale, T. (2013). Dialogue and Transparency: A Content Analysis of How the 2012 Presidential Candidates Used Twitter. *Public Relations Review, 39*(4), 357–359.

Anderson, T., & Kanuka, H. (2003). *E-Research: Methods, Strategies, and Issues.* Boston: Pearson Education.

Bamman, D., & Smith, N. A. (2015). Contextualized Sarcasm Detection on Twitter. In *Proceedings of the Ninth International AAAI Conference on Web and Social Media.* Burnaby, CA: PKP Publishing.

Barkow, J., Tooby, J., & Cosmides, L. (1992). *The Adapted Mind: Evolutionary Psychology and the Generation of Culture.* Oxford: Oxford University Press.

Barrett, J. L., & Lanman, J. A. (2008). The Science of Religious Beliefs. *Religion, 38*(2), 109–124.

Basbugoglu T., Korkut, U., & Tasawar, A. (2020). Syria: A New Cold War. *Political Insight, 11*(4), 31–32.

Baumard, N., André, J. B., & Sperber, D. (2013). A Mutualistic Approach to Morality: The Evolution of Fairness by Partner Choice. *Behavioral and Brain Sciences*, *36*(1), 59–78.

Benford, R. D., & Hunt, S. A. (1992). Dramaturgy and Social Movements: The Social Construction and Communication of Power. *Sociological Inquiry*, *62*(1), 36–55.

Bergmann, E. (2018). *Conspiracy and Populism: The Politics of Misinformation.* Cham: Palgrave Macmillan.

Boyer, P., & Petersen, B., M. (2018). Folk-Economic Beliefs: An Evolutionary Cognitive Model. *Behavioral and Brain Sciences*, *41*, 1–51.

Buchowski, M. (2006). Social Thought and Commentary: The Specter of Orientalism in Europe: from Exotic Other to Stigmatized Brother. *Anthropological Quarterly*, *79*(3), 463–482.

Canefe, N., & Bora, T. (2003). The Intellectual Roots of Anti-European Sentiments in Turkish Politics: The Case of Radical Turkish Nationalism. *Turkish Studies*, *4*(1), 127–148.

Cappelen, C., & Peters, Y. (2018) The Impact of Intra-EU Migration on Welfare Chauvinism. *Journal of Public Policy*, *38*(3), 389–417.

Çınar, M. (2018). Turkey's "Western" or "Muslim" Identity and the AKP's Civilizational Discourse. *Turkish Studies*, *19*(2), 176–197.

Crosset, V., Tanner, S., & Campana, A. (2019). Researching Far Right Groups on Twitter: Methodological Challenges 2.0. *New Media & Society*, *21*(4), 939–961.

Daniels, J. (2009). *Cyber Racism: White Supremacy Online and the New Attack on Civil Rights.* Lanham, MD: Rowman & Littlefield.

Davis, J., & Hollis, A. (2018) Theresa May's Brexit Speech Has Shades of Hitler. *The Guardian*, 12 October. Available at https://www.theguardian.com/politics/2018/oct/12/theresa-mays-brexit-speech-had-shades-of-hitler (accessed 17 October 2020).

Delanty, G. (2012). The Idea of Critical Cosmopolitanism. In Delanty, G. (ed.), *The Routledge Handbook of Cosmopolitanism Studies* (pp. 38–46); Oxford; New York: Routledge.

Eidelman, S., Christian, S. C., Goodman, J. A., & Blanchar, J. C. (2012). Low-Effort Thought Promotes Political Conservatism. *Personality and Social Psychology Bulletin*, *38*(6), 808–820.

Esses, V. M., Kay, D., Richard, N. L., & Rupert, B. (2010). Psychological Perspectives on Immigration. *Journal of Social Issues*, *66*(4), 635–647.

Esses, V. M., Jackson, L. M., & Armstrong, T. L., (1998). Intergroup Competition and Attitudes toward Immigrants and Immigration: An Instrumental Model of Group Conflict. *Journal of Social Issues*, *54*(4), 699–724.

Felmlee, D., Rodis, P. I., & Zhang, A. (2020). Sexist Slurs: Reinforcing Feminine Stereotypes Online. *Sex Roles*, *83*(1), 16–28.

Gaudette, T., Scrivens, R., Davies, G., & Frank, R. (2020). Upvoting Extremism: Collective Identity Formation and the Extreme Right on Reddit. *New Media & Society, 23*(12), 3491-3508.

Gelman, A. S. (2003). *The Essential Child: Origins of Essentialism in Everyday Thought.* New York: Oxford University Press.

Hannerz, U. (1990). Cosmopolitans and Locals in World Culture. In Featherstone, M. (ed.) *Global Culture: Nationalism, Globalization, and Modernity* (pp. 237–252). London: Sage.

Harris, L. T., & Fiske, S. T., (2011). Dehumanized Perception: A Psychological Means to Facilitate Atrocities, Torture, and Genocide? *Journal of Psychology, 219*(3), 175–181.

Hirschfeld, L. A., (2001). On a Folk Theory of Society: Children, Evolution, and Mental Representations of Social Groups. *Personality and Social Psychology Review, 5*(2), 107–117.

Jay, S., Batruch, A., Jetten, J., McGarty, C., & Muldoon, O. T. (2019). Economic Inequality and the Rise of Far-Right Populism: A Social Psychological Analysis. *Journal of Community and Applied Social Psychology, 29*(5), 418–428.

Kleingeld, P., & Brown, E. (2019). Cosmopolitanism. In Zalta, E. N. (ed.), *Stanford Encyclopaedia of Philosophy.* Center for the Study of Language and Information. Archived from the original on 14 January 2020; Available at: https://plato. stanford.edu/entries/cosmopolitanism/ Stanford, CA.

Koca, B. T. (2016). Syrian Refugees in Turkey: From "Guests" to "Enemies"? *New Perspectives on Turkey, 54*, 55–75.

Korkut, U. (2016). Pragmatism, Moral Responsibility or Policy Change: The Syrian Refugee Crisis and Selective Humanitarianism in the Turkish Refugee Regime. *Comparative Migration Studies, 4*(1), 1–20.

Köstem, S. (2020). Russian-Turkish Cooperation in Syria: Geopolitical Alignment with Limits. *Cambridge Review of International Affairs, 34*(6), 795-817.

Ladegaard, H. J. (2012). Discourses of Identity: Outgroup Stereotypes and Strategies of Discursive Boundary-Making in Chinese Students' Online Discussions about "the Other". *Journal of Multicultural Discourses, 7*(1), 59–79.

Lindgren, S., & Lundström, R. (2011). Pirate Culture and Hacktivist Mobilization: The Cultural and Social Protocols of# WikiLeaks on Twitter. *New Media & Society, 13*(6), 999–1018.

Liu, P., Chen, W., Ou, G., Wang, T., Yang, D., & Lei, K. (2014). Sarcasm Detection in Social Media Based on Imbalanced Classification. In Li, F., Li, G., Hwang, S., Yao, B., & Zhang, Z. (eds.), *International Conference on Web-Age Information Management* (pp. 459–471). Cham: Springer.

Mccarthy, A. (2020). Turning Crisis into Opportunity? The Syrian Refugee Crisis and Evolution of Welfare Policy for Refugees in Turkey from a Public Choice Theory Perspective. *Critical Social Policy, 41*(1), 111-127.

Mendes, K., Ringrose, J., & Keller, J. (2018). #MeToo and the Promise and Pitfalls of Challenging Rape Culture through Digital Feminist Activism. *European Journal of Women's Studies*, *25*(2), 236–246.

Mercier, H., & Sperber, D. (2017). *The Enigma of Reason*. Cambridge, MA: Harvard University Press.

Murthy, D., & Sharma, S. (2019). Visualizing YouTube's Comment Space: Online Hostility as a Networked Phenomena. *New Media & Society*, *21*(1), 191–213.

Ogola, G. (2015). Social Media as a Heteroglossic Discursive Space and Kenya's Emergent Alternative/Citizen Experiment. *African Journalism Studies*, *36*(4), 66–81.

Ozduzen, O., & Korkut, U. (2020). Enmeshing the Mundane and the Political: Twitter, LGBTI+ Outing and Macro-Political Polarisation in Turkey. *Contemporary Politics*, *26*(5), 493–511.

Ozduzen, O., Korkut, U. and Ozduzen, C. (2020) "Refugees Are Not Welcome": Digital Racism, Online Place-Making and the Evolving Categorization of Syrians in Turkey. *New Media & Society*. *23*(11), 1-21.

Petersen, M. B. (2012). Social Welfare as Small-Scale Help: Evolutionary Psychology and the Deservingness Heuristic. *American Journal of Political Science*, *56*(1), 1–16.

Polat, R. K. (2010). How Far Away from the Politics of Fear? Turkey in the EU Accession Process. In Tunkrova, L., & Šaradín, P. (eds.), *The Politics of EU Accession: Turkish Challenges and Central European Experiences* (pp. 58–72). London; New York: Routledge.

Riffe, D., Lacy, S., Fico, F., & Watson, B. (2019). *Analyzing Media Messages: Using Quantitative Content Analysis in Research*. London; New York: Routledge.

Roudometof, V. (2005). Transnationalism, Cosmopolitanism and Glocalization. *Current Sociology*, *53*(1), 113–135.

Saatçioğlu, B. (2020). The EU's Response to the Syrian Refugee Crisis: A Battleground among Many Europes. *European Politics and Society,* *22*(5), 808-823.

S. A. Saribay & O. Yilmaz (2017). Analytic Cognitive Style and Cognitive Ability Differentially Predict Religiosity and Social Conservatism. *Personality and Individual Differences*, *114*, 24–29.

Sindic, D., Morais, R., Costa-Lopes, R., Kelin, O., & Barreto, M. (2018). Schrodinger's Immigrant: The Political and Strategic Use of (Contradictory) Stereotypical Traits about Immigrants. *Journal of Experimental Social Psychology*, *79*, 227–238.

Sperber, D. (1997). Intuitive and Reflective Beliefs. *Mind & Language*, *12*(1), 67–83.

Wahlström, M., Törnberg, A., & Ekbrand, H. (2020). Dynamics of Violent and Dehumanizing Rhetoric in Far-Right Social Media. *New Media & Society*, *23*(11), 3290-3311.

Yang, G. (2016). Narrative Agency in Hashtag Activism: The Case of# BlackLivesMatter. *Media and Communication*, *4*(4), 13.

Zmigrod, L., Rentfrow, J. P., & Robbins, T. W., (2018) Cognitive Underpinnings of Nationalistic Ideology in the Context of Brexit. *Proceedings of the National Academy of Sciences of the United States of America, 115*(19), E4532–E4540.

About the Authors

Dr **Ozge Ozduzen** is a lecturer in digital media and society in the Department of Sociological Studies at the University of Sheffield. After completing her PhD in media at Edge Hill University (2016), she was a British Academy Newton International Postdoctoral Fellow at Loughborough University London and a lecturer in sociology and communications at Brunel University London. Her research focuses on digital humanities and social sciences, online conspiracy theories, racism, and polarisation, as well as visual politics. E-mail: o.ozduzen@sheffield.ac.uk

Bogdan Ianoşev is a PhD student at the Glasgow School for Business and Society, at Glasgow Caledonian University. He was previously awarded an MA in Philosophy from the University of Bucharest, as well as an MA in Cognitive Anthropology from Queens University, Belfast. He presently works for DEMOS and is researching the cognitive and evolutionary underpinnings of populist discourse surrounding the Brexit referendum for his PhD bogdan.ianosev@gcu.ac.uk

9 Two Sides of the Same Coin

Post-"Refugee Crisis" Debates on Migration and European
Integration in Austrian Party Politics

Ivan Josipovic and Ursula Reeger

Abstract

Over the past decade, immigration and European integration have emerged
as increasingly important policy issues for political parties. In the course
of the so-called refugee crisis of 2015, debates on asylum and border control
coincided with claims over political authority and responsibility in the
European multi-level system of governance. In this chapter, we take up
the case of Austria to study (1) how major political parties positioned
themselves in relation to these issues; (2) which organisational consequences they drew following the crisis; and (3) how they mobilised their
respective electorate for the subsequent national elections of 2017. Based
on a qualitative document analysis, our contribution concludes that,
contrary to arguments put forth by cleavage theory, a traditionally centrist
party benefitted the most from an increased salience of immigration and
EU integration issues. We offer an explanation by linking debates on the
transnational cleavage to literature on populism.

Keywords: cleavage theory, European integration, migration, mobilisation,
populism

9.1 Introduction

Migration and European integration are phenomena that create tensions
between nation-state sovereignty and a transnationally oriented society or a
supranational polity. Scholars have argued that the societal transformations
of the past three decades have created distinct populations of winners and
losers of such an expanding socioeconomic and sociopolitical community

Foley, J. and Korkut, U. (ed.), *Contesting Cosmopolitan Europe. Euroscepticism, Crisis and Borders.*
Amsterdam: Amsterdam University Press 2022
DOI :10.5117/9789463727259_CH09

(Strijbis et al., 2018). Some went as far as proclaiming the arrival of new a political cleavage which supersedes the traditional class-cleavage and economic left–right divisions (Hooghe & Marks, 2018). This cleavage has been referred to as the transnational or globalisation cleavage. In this sense, migration and European integration have been argued to represent new core issues and major drivers of change in political party systems across European member states. While party change is generally assumed to be a slow and incremental process, events like the "refugee crisis" of 2015 can constitute critical junctures that abruptly raise the salience of a particular issue and lead to a lasting reorientation of political parties.

In this chapter, we study how Austria's political party landscape has developed in the aftermath of the 2015 "migration crisis". We seek to understand how four different parties politically responded to the increased level of immigration and how they organisationally adapted and mobilised during the following national elections.

Austria is an interesting case for studying the role of migration and European integration in party mobilisation. It displays a longstanding tradition of grand coalitions between the Social Democrats (SPÖ) and the conservative People's Party (ÖVP), both of which are classical mainstream left and right parties born out of the conflict between labour and capital. However, with the Freedom Party (FPÖ), Austria had also had a far-right party in parliament since 1956, long before immigration and asylum became salient issues in electoral politics. This changed following geopolitical transformations that came about as a result of the Fall of the Iron Curtain in 1989, the Balkan Wars of the 1990s and Austria's imminent accession to the EU in 1995. Among the political parties in parliament, the left-wing Green party was the first to systematically pick up the topic of migration in its political program, even before the FPÖ under Jörg Haider (Gruber, 2012, p. 235). In the early 1990s, the FPÖ began to dispute the SPÖ leadership and its competences in the realm of migration and asylum, initiating a popular referendum against the admission and integration of foreigners (Ausländervolksbegehren) in November 1992. Although the referendum did not succeed, and in fact led to a backlash, with large protests against xenophobia (Lichtermeer, "sea of lights", in early 1993), it marks a point in time when immigration had gradually begun to move from a niche topic to mainstream (Gruber, 2012). Austria's accession to the EU in 1995 introduced the second aspect of an emerging transnational cleavage to domestic party politics. By the time of the eastern EU enlargement in 2004, European integration had become a political subject in its own right but also displayed strong links to what was happening in the context of immigration: increasing intra-EU mobility through Schengen on the one hand and an emerging Common European Asylum System on the other hand.

In the following sections, we will draw on cleavage theory to argue that the "refugee crisis" of 2015 has led to a preliminary peak of saliency of the topics of migration and European integration for domestic party politics. After elaborating on the theoretical framework, we show how those topics were discussed in the Austrian parliament during the peak of the crisis and how the parties under investigation adapted to the new situation in view of the following national elections. Therefore, we draw on secondary literature about the national elections of 2017 and partisan strategies as well as on primary data that was collected and analysed under the Horizon 2020 project RESPOND. The primary data originally consisted of 15 public political speeches in various contexts and by major figures among the SPÖ, ÖVP, FPÖ, and the Greens.[9] This was complemented by parliamentary speeches from the latter half of 2015 indicating the immediate political responses at the peak of the crisis. All these speeches were selected as they contained keywords associated with migration and European integration and were embedded in a larger contextualised speech. We conducted a qualitative analysis (Froschauer & Lueger, 2003), wherein we established argumentative patterns in relation to the division of power in the EU, immigrants as policy targets as well as domestic audiences, and finally policy diagnoses and policy proposals. After providing an encompassing picture of the Austrian case, we use the final section of this chapter to elaborate on their wider theoretical implications related to mobilisation along the transnational cleavage as well as populism.

9.2   Theoretical Framework – Mobilising Along the Transnational Cleavage

Over the past three decades, migration and European integration have both become hotly debated topics in electoral politics of EU Member States. The concurrency of their political career, in public debate and salience as electoral policy issues, is by no means a coincidence. In fact, both topics display some common ground at a deeper level of 21st-century societal transformation. Today, migration and European integration represent the two central issues that constitute what is referred to as the transnational

9   In our project, we did not cover the entire political spectrum in the National Council, excluding the NEOS from the liberal spectrum and Team Stronach from the right-wing spectrum.

or globalisation cleavage (Hooghe & Marks, 2017; Strijbis et al., 2018). The core assumption is that both phenomena shape a newly formed and durable sight of social conflict that essentially revolves around the erosion of nation-state sovereignty. European integration implies a transgression of political authority beyond the nation-state, producing supranational political elites and causing domestic change by creating wider fields of social and economic action but also exposing the population to stronger socioeconomic competition and ethnic diversity. Institutionally, increased migration has been a result of European integration and partly that of international human-rights obligations (Joppke, 1998). It generated greater ethnic diversity and cultural intermixing, further dissolving the myth of a nationally homogenous way of life. Cleavage theory (Lipset & Rokkan, 1967) holds that these social developments disproportionately affect particular societal strata and accordingly translate into changes within political party systems. Populations with a lack of mobile assets and an aversion to cultural pluralism would accordingly display similarly negative attitudes towards European integration and migration, making transnationalism vs. nationalism a key-dimension in their search for representation among political parties (Hooghe & Marks, 2017, p. 110).

While party systems can be assumed as relatively resistant to major changes in both programmatic and organisational terms, episodic shocks lead to far-reaching political transformations (Hooghe & Marks, 2017). Crises, such as that of 2015, are junctures (Lipset & Rokkan, 1967) that create uncertainty, increasing the likelihood of new political challengers establishing themselves and old parties leaving well-trodden paths. A central manifestation of the transnational cleavage has been the rise of the GAL-TAN dimension in party politics (green-alternative-libertarian vs. traditional-authoritarian-national) (Hooghe et al., 2002). This sociocultural dimension has been argued to be an increasingly established second ideological layer of party competition, besides the classical economic left–right division. GAL and TAN parties are usually assumed to be post-class cleavage parties that display a strong coherence within their positions on European integration and migration.

In this vein, cleavage theory leads us to the first hypothesis that guided our research: European integration and immigration should be the primary domain of mobilisation for the far-right FPÖ as well as the Green party in Austria. Exogenous shocks, such as the crisis of 2015, should increase the salience of those topics and play into the hands of these challenger parties. Mainstream parties on the centre-left and centre-right, in the case of Austria two traditional class-parities, Social Democrats and Conservatives, would accordingly rather de-emphasise both issues and programmatically stick to their prior dimensions rather than assert more extreme positions in this new domain (see de Vries & Hobolt, 2012; Green-Pedersen).

The second hypothesis relates to the subsequent question of how political parties mobilise from a programmatic point of view. That is to say: which meaning do they ascribe to the EU and immigration via the asylum system? The GAL and TAN parties were assumed to take more extreme stances. As a classical instance of a populist and radical-right party, the FPÖ could be assumed to object to social change and those who promote it. Radical right parties overemphasise notions of a homogenous national community by furthering discursive divisions between a racialised "us" and "them" (Minkenberg, 2019, p. 465). By contrast, the Green Party could be expected to emphasise collective identity at a transnational level, subscribing to European solidarity and an emancipatory agenda that seeks to further human rights and does not shy away from ethnic diversity (Bergbauer, 2010). The two mainstream parties SPÖ and ÖVP would accordingly take positions that more strongly compromise nation-state sovereignty with European integration and placing conditions on human rights claims while refraining from complete exclusion.

In the next section, we will consider more closely how each of these four parties reacted during the immediate crisis of the 2015, on the one hand by looking at measures taken by the actors in government (SPÖ/ÖVP)[10] and on the other hand by considering parliamentary debates at that time.

9.3   The Summer of Migration as a Critical Juncture and the Electoral Race of 2017

Like many other EU Member States, Austria experienced a sharp increase in asylum applications in 2015, mainly by people from the Middle East and Afghanistan. By early summer, large groups began to reach Austria either on foot or by train and bus via Hungary and Slovenia. This led to a high level of news coverage and debates on the failure of the Dublin Regulation, intra-Schengen border closures, secondary movement of asylum seekers, or the distribution of refugees from the southern hotspots, all of which

---

10   The SPÖ held the chancellor office (Werner Fayman) while the ÖVP staffed both ministries responsible for immigration and immigrant integration and was the party of the Foreign and EU Minister (at that time Sebastian Kurz).

coincided with conflicts over multi-level governance and the future of European integration.

On 5 September 2015, when Hungarian authorities decided to tolerate the onward journey of thousands of refugees, Austria's government adopted a pragmatic approach, allowing or even encouraging people to travel on to Germany. However, the asylum seekers who arrived at Vienna's Westbahnhof (train station towards the west) were among the last to encounter a wave of solidarity and even an Interior Minister (ÖVP) to welcome them. In total, more than 80,000 people applied for asylum in 2015 alone. In the following months, the federal government and particularly the conservative party and its ministers began to turn towards an increasingly harsh rhetoric and restrictive policy measures.

9.3.1   A Struggle for Interpretation – Assuming Position in Parliament

Assessing the parliamentary debates from the second half of 2015, we find, as could be expected, that the Greens and the FPÖ embraced their oppositional role by heavily criticising the federal government's actions from diametrically opposed directions. Both display strong coherence within their respective partisan approach. The FPÖ fostered a discourse that circulated around the concepts of national security and nation-state sovereignty by constructing the admission of refugees as a loss of state control. A reoccurring theme shared among far-right MPs was the government's alleged "open borders" policy, which was argued a threat to citizens as it would enable "bogus refugees" to enter national territory. In fact, as early as September 2015, the FPÖ leader in parliament introduced the terminology of a "state of exception" to the public debate and called for exceptional measures. The very concept of a state of exception relates to the suspension of the normal legal order and the restriction of fundamental rights in the face of a threat to the survival of the state or its citizens (notwithstanding that the German word *Ausnahmezustand* carries a particular undertone related to the German experience of fascism). By contrast, the Greens continued, as in prior years and very consistently, to speak of a humanitarian crisis. For their members of parliament, the event of mass migration raised questions of vulnerability and desperation among a population that had experienced war and poverty and now had to walk all the way through Europe. Besides that, the Greens sought to invoke national traditions of taking up responsibility by pointing towards Austria's role during the time of the Iron Curtain, when thousands of Hungarian, Czech, and Polish people fled to Austria.

Among the two parties in government office, we find that both ÖVP and SPÖ provided less homogenous political stances and arguments compared to the two opposition parties discussed above. Likewise, their policy actions mirrored a mix of adhering to European and international human rights demands while at the same time introducing border controls, establishing border fences, and creating a unilateral admission quota. However, terms of rhetoric, we could observe how both mainstream parties sought to discursively divert responsibility, even though they showed different argumentative patterns.

The SPÖ took a passive role in approving of a humanitarian stance, while pointing out that there was also no technical option not to stand up for human rights. One statement by an SPÖ MP is particularly illustrative of this argument. In response to an FPÖ statement, he argued that he was "glad to belong to a party that has taken a stance for humanitarian aid". However, he did not juxtapose his stance with the philosophy of sovereignty proposed by the FPÖ, but rather with the technical implications of that philosophy: "This means that on the one hand we have the legal good of life. [...] On the other side are the questions: How do you slow down 10,000 people at a border [...] What you are suggesting would only be manageable with the use of gun violence. [...] I consider this condemnable, morally instable and divisive for society".

The ÖVP, on the other hand, sought to deflect responsibility to the EU level. An ÖVP member of parliament for example pointed to the Schengen Borders Code to justify the continuing influx of asylum seekers. He went on: "I hope that today our Chancellor will succeed in getting the European Union one step further. I have already said it before today: we can only solve the problem at European level. In reality, we are also suffering, especially the Minister of the Interior. It is a pity that you confuse the two and denounce the Minister of the Interior".

These arguments, delivered by four parties in the Austrian parliament, are illustrative of the distinct stances that each political actor adopted at the peak of the crisis in relation to immigration (and less explicitly also European integration). During the consecutive months, however, the discourses and practices of the parties in government shifted from humanitarianism towards security and nation-state sovereignty. Particularly the ÖVP exterior minister went on to heavily criticise Germany's policy of "waving through" immigrants, even though the Austrian government itself had initially adopted this pragmatic approach. At several public appearances in front of Austrian and German media, the then Foreign Minister and now Chancellor from the ÖVP sought to juxtapose his own stance with what was constructed as an "open border policy" by Germany. A discourse on national border closure ensued in the context of the erection of a border fence in early 2016, an annual quota for asylum applicants and time limits for the residence status associated with the acquisition of asylum status.

9.3.2   The Electoral Race of 2017

If transnationalism constitutes a new cleavage and if 2015 represents a critical juncture that has the power to reconfigure the political party system along the line of this cleavage, then one would be able to observe changes between parties not only in terms of electoral success and government composition, but also in terms of organisational and programmatic changes within each of these parties.

The most evident transformation can be observed within the ÖVP, where the role of current chancellor Sebastian Kurz and his political vision, setting an emphasis on order and security in relation to immigration, replaced the traditional primacy of economic concerns in the ÖVP. In response to the decline of electoral support for the ÖVP in previous years, its members in provincial organisations and federal associations elected a new head of the party – albeit at the cost of a concentration of authority. As the most popular figure in the party, Sebastian Kurz established conditions for this availability, whereby he would have to retain authority over the political orientation of the party, over the political personnel in the event of at- tainment of governmental power, and over the compilation of electoral lists for the National Council (Puller, 2018). Interestingly, this new internal hierarchy stands in considerable contrast to the rhetorical embrace of social movement terminology. Arguably, the ÖVP's electoral campaign introduced a new visual and rhetorical brand centred around the persona of Kurz, while announcing the "start of a movement" and an "opening of the party" (ÖVP general secretary, 2017). This particularly implied the support of its youth organisation and the introduction of experts and celebrities on their electoral lists. Thematically, the ÖVP narrowed its agenda down to a few topics and primarily sought to mobilise around the project of law-and-order politics in relation to immigration.

As Bodlos and Plescia (2018) showed, during the 2017 electoral campaign the ÖVP mentioned immigration in more press releases than ever before. While the topic's share among other policy issues was at an average of 1.6% between 1999 and 2013, it peaked at 7.6% in 2017 (Bodlos & Plescia, 2018, p. 1357). The party adopted many of the positions of the populist right-wing party FPÖ when it came to immigration and integration (Bodlos & Plescia, 2018, p. 1357). Even though it pursued softer rhetoric, it repeatedly questioned and sought to delegitimise certain groups of asylum seekers as economic migrants, blocking the asylum system for people who would be genuinely in need of help. The example of border controls shows how the ÖVP increasingly positions itself as an EU-sceptical actor in the domain of migration and asylum. According to the party leader, the failure of the EU to protect its external borders called upon national governments to reintroduce intra-Schengen border controls, a measure that in fact aligns with the traditional ÖVP credo of subsidiarity. With this policy approach and a new lead figure, the ÖVP managed to increase its approval rates within a short period of time from an average of 20% to a stable 33%, even after entering the new coalition (Neuwal.com, 2021).

For the social democratic SPÖ the immigration issue proved to be highly divisive. At the 2017 election, the SPÖ remained relatively consistent at an all-time low of 26.9% and immigration issues led to reinforced public debates over an ideological split. On the one hand, political commentators located a party within the right-wing SPÖ emerging around the former defence minister and his regional Burgenland division that governed in a provincial coalition with the FPÖ. On the other hand, a liberal or progressive wing was identified in the circles around former chancellor Christian Kern and his party leader successor Pamela Rendi-Wagner. A new party program developed in 2018 provided a differentiated mix of liberal and restrictive policies (Gruber, 2019). Indeed, the SPÖ found itself caught in the dilemma between liberal elements rooted in a tradition of antifascism on the one hand, and communitarian elements related to the value of solidarity (which is nested in the national welfare state) on the other. In this vein, we found comparably differentiated statements by the former party leader Christian Kern, wherein he acknowledged that many societal concerns relating to immigration are legitimate but added, "it is also clear to us that we cannot answer these questions with populist recipes and slogans". According to him, social democracy would offer "real" policy solutions, part of which includes a reform of the EU.

For the Green party, the 2017 elections fell far short of what could be expected from a rise of the transnational cleavage. They received a mere 3.8% of the votes and dropped out of parliament for the first time since their arrival on the political stage in 1986. Political commentators considered one reason for this failure to be a lack of leadership, given the fact that Eva Glawischnig resigned as head of the party only a few months prior to the elections, due to internal party conflicts. As a consequence, Ingrid Felipe and Ulrike Lunacek were elected as federal Green Party spokeswomen and head candidates for the following elections. During their campaign, the Greens also disproportionately thematised immigration (2017: 9%, mean 1995–2013: 6% of press releases) (Bodlos & Plescia, 2018, p. 1357), primarily taking a liberal stance towards asylum. This is also mirrored in the Greens' prior emphasis on the vulnerability of refugees and their exposure to war and persecution, as well as their inhumane treatment along the EU's external borders. In 2015, for example, Eva Glawischnig referred to the EU's focus on border control "no longer tolerable, for all of us no longer bearable!" Yet this stance, it seems, did not resonate among the electorate. Significant voter flows moved towards the SPÖ, the ÖVP, and the Liste Pilz, not least due to a more restrictive attitude in migration policy. The longstanding member Peter Pilz created the spin-off party "Liste Pilz", which was characterised by a more pragmatic and Islamism-critical stance on immigrant integration and eventually managed to enter parliament.

The populist right wing FPÖ, which in previous decades had a monopoly over the immigration issue, tamed its rhetoric during the 2017 elections and generally benefitted from popular dissatisfaction with the work of the grand coalition (Bodlos & Plescia, 2018, p. 1355). While the topic of immigration had traditionally enjoyed a high saliency in FPÖ campaign communication, it featured in twice as much of the press release material issued in 2017 (13.4%) as it had on average between 1999 and 2013 (6.7%) (Bodlos & Plescia, 2018, p. 1355). Considering political claims made following the crisis of 2015, we find that key politicians from the FPÖ tightly linked asylum to notions of illegality, coining terms like "bogus refugee" or "asylum swindler". Another illustrative rhetoric twist can be found among the speeches of FPÖ member Herbert Kickl, who overturned the classic slogan of solidarity with refugees by "demand[ing] solidarity from those who came to us". In terms of organisational structures, there were no considerable reconfigurations between 2015 and 2017. However, under FPÖ chairman Heinz-Christian Strache, members belonging to duelling fraternities, corps, sororities, or other German national connections acquired the greatest influence in the party over the last decade. Eventually, the FPÖ achieved its second-best election result ever during the 2017 national elections, winning 26% of the vote (Bodlos & Plescia, 2018, p. 1358).

Given the fact that both ÖVP and FPÖ had gained votes and had approached each other ideologically, they unsurprisingly entered coalition negotiations and established a government coalition by December 2017. As a result of a political scandal surrounding potential corruption of FPÖ politicians, this coalition broke apart in May 2019.

9.4 Discussion and Conclusions

Having closely considered the political developments following the Summer of Migration 2015 in Austria, we seek to draw some general conclusions from this specific case. In particular, it appears interesting to inquire into the ideological path and electoral success of the ÖVP, given the fact that cleavage theory suggests mainstream parties would struggle amidst the rise of new issues. In the following, we propose a two-dimensional concept of populist politics, arguing that it adequately captures the empirical evidence at hand and that it might provide explanatory factors for our observations.

Populist politics has been defined by Jan-Werner Müller (2016) as a particular conception of politics, whereby the people (usually defined as fellow nationals) are assumed as a morally sound entity that stands in opposition to corrupted elites or an immoral entity that is considered to be not really part of this people. Poier et al. (2020) further emphasise the dual character of populism as a phenomenon that plays out between the two poles of opportunistic communication strategy (Poier et al., 2020) and ideologically determined topics (Mudde, 2017). Referring to Hartleb's (2014) conception of a horizontal and vertical dimension of populism, they point out how populist politics often intertwine particular substantial elements, such as the antagonism between the people and some governing elites, with formal elements of discursive and organisational kind.

In terms of the former aspect, political actors might emphasise enemy figures within the political system (vertical axis) or within society (horizontal axis). Thus, to a certain extent, they play with the construction of particular identities as means of establishing conceptual relationships between themselves, their electorate, and some type of enemy. Immigrants are a classical example of a horizontal enemy, and asylum seekers who arrive without a priori status are a likely instance for the construction of immoral figures. In Austria, the negative politicisation of immigration (but also the governing elites) has traditionally been the domain of the FPÖ. How could the ÖVP credibly adopt such an approach, given its uninterrupted participation in government, its responsibility for the immigration agenda, and its distinctly pro-European attitude?

Indeed, one of the most striking aspects about the Austrian case is the uneven electoral performance among the SPÖ and the ÖVP, the two parties that had dominated the political landscape for decades. As we could see, during the peak of the crisis, we found passive attempts on both sides to legitimise government actions related to the management of asylum. While the SPÖ illustratively did so by pointing out a lack of alternatives at the level of implementation, the ÖVP argued that EU law left no other options but to adopt those who had lodged an application for asylum. However, as we moved on to the period of the national elections in 2017, we found that, unlike the SPÖ, the conservatives actively sought to mobilise through an active and restrictive stance on immigration and also, less explicitly, the assertion of nation-state sovereignty vis-à-vis the EU.

Considering substantial populist elements, the ÖVP's political approach primarily used immigrants as the main enemy figure. Although softer in its rhetoric, compared to the FPÖ, it frequently sought to delegitimise the arrival of asylum seekers and framed itself as an advocate for the closure of national borders and the so-called Western Balkans Route. Yet this approach conveyed far more than a mere policy preference. As became evident, policy responses related to external immigration to the EU are inevitably tied to particular conceptions of the relationship between Member States, their domestic populations, and the EU as a whole. Favouring intra-Schengen border controls, for example, is likely to be tied to narratives of a failure of the EU to protect its external borders and as in the case of the ÖVP, a related call for the principle of subsidiarity. Austria's Conservatives show how the claim of shutting down borders is not only a policy-oriented measure but may also aim to signal nation-state sovereignty vis-à-vis other state powers. It can be interpreted as a critique of the EU or other regional powers, as in this case Germany, which was frequently framed as a hegemonic power with a liberal approach towards immigration.

Evidently, this is far from saying that the ÖVP had turned into an EU-sceptic party. On the contrary, in 2017 it urged its new far-right coalition partner to quit its open anti-EU attitude. However, our case study shows how political conflicts emerging with the rise of the transnational cleavage play into the hands of conservative to right wing parties, because restrictive stances towards immigration typically go along with an emphasis on nation-state sovereignty, enabling politicians to signal their audience that they alone should be in charge. Unlike the social democratic call for refugee distribution, for example, this approach does not rely on cooperation with other state or supranational entities but enables politicians to claim that once in power, they alone could make a difference. Clearly, this argument also does not explain the ÖVP's success, given its decade long participation in government.

Another aspect of the ÖVP's electoral success amidst the rise of trans-national cleavage pertains to the formal dimension of its populist politics. Poier et al. (2020) name strong and charismatic leaders at the organisational level and the grammar of social movements at the discursive level as central features of populisms. Although the ÖVP was part of the government and carried responsibility for the management of asylum, both at the national and European level, key figures, while vested in the offices of the interior and foreign minister, actively sought to distinguish themselves from both the social democratic coalition partner and the chancellor, as well as the EU arena of asylum policy making. The latter is exemplified by the ÖVP ministers' turn towards multi-lateral cooperation with Western Balkan states in attempt to curb immigration via this transit route. As foreign minister, Sebastian Kurz, who would go on to become chancellor in 2017, had the opportunity to credibly present himself as the future leader of a programmatically renewed party. Thus, we observed how a mainstream party's emphasis on "security and order" fell in line with the election of a new party leader, who had started his career as Secretary for Integration and who had spent prior months criticising EU laws and Member States that had adopted a more liberal stance towards immigrants. It is highly questionable whether the party's thematic shift in focus from economics to immigration alone could have had the same impact during the elections.

Besides its approach of discursively cutting off links to other political elites, the ÖVP sought to foster the image of a party that is strongly linked to the people. Despite being a highly organised party with numerous regional and professional branches, it adopted an issue-oriented mobilisation strategy borrowed from movement politics and placed supporting crowds of "ordinary" people at the centre of public events and campaign visuals. Established party internal elites remained in the background and were partly replaced by experts and celebrities. Thus, it did not come as a surprise that the ÖVPs electoral list was named "List Sebastian Kurz – The New People's Party" (our translation).

Overall, the presence of a charismatic leader, the steeper organisational hierarchy, and the movement character of the electoral campaign add formal elements of populism to its ideological shift (Heinisch & Mazzoleni, 2016). This brings the ÖVP closer to the traditional right-wing populist force in Austria, namely the FPÖ. In this vein, our case study illustrates how mainstream parties are by no means passive spectators to the rise of the transnational cleavage and the challenger parties corresponding to it. Instead, they are able to adopt ideological agendas and strategic approaches typically ascribed to GAL and TAN parties. Thus, our work also feeds into postfunctionalist European integration theory (Hooghe & Marks, 2008), which emphasises nationally mediated politicisation as a counter-dynamic to spill-over effects. This is to say that even the most EU-friendly parties, which rarely challenge supranational integration trajectories, engage in territorial identity politics. They mobilise around EU-relevant policy issues (i.e., asylum seeker admission) and connect their positions to claims over political authority and the question of where this authority should be located. More than any other policy area, migration and asylum appear difficult to detach from implicit politicisation about what the EU is and what it should be.

References

Bodlos, A., & Plescia, C. (2018). The 2017 Austrian Snap Election: A Shift Rightward. *West European Politics, 41*(6), 1354–1363.

DeVries, C., & Hobolt, S. (2012). When Dimensions Collide: Electoral Success of Issue Entrepreneurs. *European Union Politics, 13*(2), 246–268.

Green-Pedersen, C. (2012). A Giant Fast Asleep? Party Incentives and the Politicisation of European Integration. *Political Studies, 60*(1), 115–130.

Gruber, O. (2012). *From Niche to Mainstream: Electoral Politicization of Immigration, Migrant Integration and Ethnic Diversity in Austria.* Dissertation, University of Vienna, Austria.

Gruber, O. (2019). Swimming Upstream? Attitudes towards Immigration in Austria and the Electoral Implications for Progressive Politics. In Funk, M., Giusto, H., Rinke, T., & Bruns, O. (eds.), *European Public Opinion and Migration* (pp. 35-58). Brussels/Budapest/Rome/Paris: FEPS/Friedrich Ebert Stiftung/Fondazione Pietro Nenni/Fondation Jean Jaurès.

Hartleb, F. (2014). *Internationaler Populismus als Konzept. Zwischen Kommunikationsstil und fester Ideologie.* Baden-Baden: International Studies on Populism.

Heinisch, R., & Mazzoleni, O. (2016). *Understanding Populist Party Organisation: The Radical Right in Western Europe.* London: Palgrave.

Hooghe, L., & Marks, G. (2002). Does Left/Right Structure Party Positions on European Integration? *Comparative Political Studies, 35*(8), 965–989.

Hooghe, L., & Marks, G. (2008). A Postfunctionalist Theory of European Integration: From Permissive Consensus to Constraining Dissensus. *British Journal of Political Science, 39*, 1–23.

Hooghe, L., & Marks, G. (2018). Cleavage Theory meets Europe's Crises: Lipset, Rokkan, and the Transnational Cleavage. *Journal of European Public Policy, 25*(1), 109–135.

Lipset, S., & Rokkan, S. (1967). Cleavage Structures, Party Systems, and Voter Alignments: An Introduction. In Lipset, S. & Rokkan, S. (eds.), *Party Systems and Voter Alignments: Cross-National Perspectives* (pp. 1–64). Toronto: The Free Press.

Minkenberg, M. (2019). Between Party and Movement: Conceptual and Empirical Considerations of the Radical Right's Organizational Boundaries and Mobilization Processes. *European Societies, 21*(4), pp. 463–486.

Mudde, C. (2017). Introduction to the Populist Radical Right. In Mudde, C., *The Populist Radical Right. A Reader* (pp. 1-10). New York: Routledge.

Müller, J. (2016). *What Is Populism?* Philadelphia: University of Pennsylvania Press.

Neuwal. (2021). Wahlumfragen. *Neuval.com*. Available at: https://neuwal.com/wahlumfragen/

Poier, K., Saywald-Wedl, & Unger, H. (2020). The Issues of the "Populists". A Media Analysis of Election Campaigns in Austria, Germany, Switzerland, Denmark and Poland. *Zeitschrift für Literaturwissenschaft und Liguistik, 50*, 185–202.

Puller, A. (2018). Die Österreichische Volkspartei unter Sebastian Kurz. *Kurswechsel, 3*, 9–18.

About the Authors

Ivan Josipovic (MA, MSc) is a PhD candidate at the Institute for Political Science of the University of Vienna. He holds degrees in Socioeconomics and Political Science. His fields of interest comprise border and migration regimes, asylum politics, and European integration.
Email: Ivan.josipovic@oeaw.ac.at

Ursula Reeger (Mag. Dr.) is a Senior Researcher at the Institute for Urban and Regional Research of the Austrian Academy of Sciences, Vienna, Austria; her research interests include international migration and its impacts, integration processes (on the labour and the housing market), interethnic relations on the local level, and governance of migration and migrant integration and radicalisation.
Email: Ursula.reeger@oeaw.ac.at

Conclusion

James Foley and Umut Korkut

Populist right rhetoric defines its sovereign people not just against the establishment but against the establishment regarded as servants of foreign intruders: the "hordes" massing around Europe. At worst, as this book has highlighted, this becomes Orbán's Soros conspiracy, where Jewish financiers are plotting to weaken nation-states by flooding them with Islamic immigration. Such narratives increasingly transcend the boundaries of narrow nationalism: as Brubaker suggests, they construe "the opposition between self and other not in narrowly national but in broader civilisational terms" (2017, p. 1191). Naturally they rely on making an implausible equivalence between society's least powerful actors – exiles forced to throw themselves on the mercy of foreign states – and the Davos elite, those supposedly omnipotent "globalisers". As we have shown throughout this volume, these connections have little foundation in fact, and such plausibility as they have issues from the internal hypocrisies of mainstream humanitarian narratives.

Yet, for all their absurdity, these narratives contain a kernel of truth. Philanthropic factions of the jet-setting elite really do imagine an intrinsic solidarity between themselves and the world's oppressed. Academics, statesmen and corporate officials do often position themselves paternalistically towards vulnerable populations – most especially, refugees – and regard themselves as similar insofar as, whether rich or poor, powerful or powerless, influential or voiceless, they all alike transcend borders and boundaries. And this does form a strategy of elite moral differentiation from the "immobile" masses (Birtchnell and Caletrío, 2013). Politically, for those seeking to win mass consent for immigration, the problem here is the obvious deadlock between what Piketty (2018) calls the "Brahmin left" and the (millionaire-funded) populist right; both depend on their apparent opposite for legitimation. Cosmopolitanism, insofar as it presents as an identity without a tribal sense of belonging, thus contains an inherent contradiction; as Žižek observes:

Foley, J. and Korkut, U. (ed.), *Contesting Cosmopolitan Europe. Euroscepticism, Crisis and Borders.* Amsterdam: Amsterdam University Press 2022

DOI :10.5117/9789463727259_CONC

it is easy to note how the "cosmopolitan" intellectual elites, despising local people who cling to their roots, themselves belong to their own quite exclusive circles of rootless elites, and thus how their cosmopolitan rootlessness is the marker of a deep and strong belonging [...] This is why it is an utter obscenity to propose an equivalence between elite "nomads" flying around the world and refugees desperately searching for a safe place where they could belong – the same obscenity as that of putting together a dieting upper-class Western woman and a starving refugee woman (Žižek, 2017).

As Žižek suggests, there are differences in form between the mobility forced on refugees and the openness enjoyed by high-end knowledge producers. Refugees are seeking either a new place to belong, or somewhere to shelter until they can return home; cosmopolitan elites, by contrast, have their sense of belonging precisely in their similarity to peers across the world, and their common differentiation from the domestic working and middle classes. Those differences are far starker than the superficial similarities and emphasising them is crucial to combatting conspiratorial narratives. Centrist politicians who represent the cosmopolitan elite thus have a longstanding habit of treating refugees, at best, instrumentally. In his efforts to save Britain from exiting the EU, Tony Blair proposed negotiations with Brussels aimed at preserving intra-continental freedom of movement by hardening Europe's external borders, specifically against the type of Muslim immigration associated with the asylum system. The problematic refugee becomes the bargaining chip to preserve the economic benefits of open borders. These political complexities are easily lost in impressionistic visions of the nomadic rootlessness of contemporary capitalist subjectivity. For decades, theorists dismissed social class, nationhood, and tradition as "zombie concepts", no longer capable of capturing the liquid nature of social bonds (Atkinson, 2007; Beck, 2007). But this impressionism is ill-suited to capturing the dynamics at play in contemporary Europe, before or after its "populist moment" (Brubaker, 2017). At best, the carceral regulation of refugees represents the dark counterpart to the mobility demanded by elite economic actors.

Refugees sometimes do find themselves living alongside affluent cosmopolitan elites, but never truly "with" them, as highlighted by London's Grenfell Tower fire. *Guardian* reporting noted that the victims "were European migrants, black British, refugees from the developing world – some of them second generation – and asylum seekers, sharing the tower with the poor, white working class of London" (Malik, 2017). In most circumstances, refugees must reckon with others of their kind and the vast social majority in most societies who lives close to the town of their birth: to use a contemporary sociological cliché, the "somewheres" as opposed to the "anywheres" (Goodhart, 2017). *Le Monde* reported a study showing that seven out of ten French people live in the region they were born; and around 60% of British people live within 30 miles of where they lived as teenagers (Scheffer, 2021). To understand the liberal left's failure in building solidarity with refugees, it would thus be more meaningful to start from the connections linking refugees to domestic majorities, rather than building imaginary concepts of cosmopolitan subjectivity. And this highlights the economic and social changes that have transformed European societies.

Globalisation, the foundation of cosmopolitan identity, has always been conjugated as neoliberal globalisation. It is not simply that the two processes coincided historically, but that they were causally connected. Naturally, there is a long-established connection between globalisation and rising inequality (Stiglitz, 2002). But that merely reflects the fact that globalisation was pursued as a deliberate mechanism for prising open closed corporatist national economies, to break trade union and social democratic solidarities. Freedom at a transnational level largely meant freedom of capital and finance, to break with democratic accountability. This is symbolised by the European Union Single Market, a product, it must be remembered, of impeccably Thatcherite origins: Lord Cockfield, Thatcher's appointee to the EC as Internal Market Commissioner, is thus widely considered the "father of the Single Market". Political controversy centres on the quarter of that settlement that allows for freedom of movement to travel and work in other European economies. Yet few consider the remaining three-quarters, which is given over to freedom of markets. The logical connections, however, should be clear. Neoliberal globalisation broke the back of collectivist institutions which, in earlier eras, may have formed the groundwork of a grassroots inter-nationalism. Those links are not merely imaginary political slogans. It should be remembered that Europe's leftist working-class movements have their origins in the sphere of German émigrés, fleeing persecution in their homeland. It is equally no surprise today that the best practical solidarity networks emerge from the remnants of religious organisation in depressed working-class neighbourhoods. And part of the reason that controversy centres on national borders is simply that so many other functions of nation-statehood have been effectively depoliticised: for decades in mainstream politics, only the barest bones of the security state have been objects of ideological contestation. The filtering of debate onto questions of borders is thus symptomatic of what Colin Crouch calls "post-democracy" (Crouch, 2019, 2004).

This book has demonstrated the worrying rise of illiberal leaders ranging from Orbán and Erdoğan to Johnson and Kaczyński. They have been the principal beneficiaries of a decade of interlocking crises. Yet one impression from our research has been the difficulty in mechanically separating "good" cosmopolitans from "bad" populists. A more complex picture emerges from our comparative analysis. Thus, for example, much of the violence in right-wing rhetoric stems from the notion of a "clash of civilisations", with Muslim majority countries sitting on the doorsteps of an expanded Europe. But Islamophobia has lineages precisely in the discourse of open societies: long before 9/11, leading commentators spoke of "Jihad versus McWorld" (Barber, 1992), the contention being that the religion of immigrants, "tribal" in nature, would come into conflict with the cosmopolitan civilisations of the West. Such discourses account for much of the heat attached to contemporary migration debates. And the links becomes more obvious when considering that many are fleeing situations of state breakdown that reflect the earlier phase of Western military interventions, inspired, on their part, by notions of imposing American style consumer freedom and democracy (see e.g., Cunliffe, 2020). The post-Arab Spring phase of embroilment between Euro-America and the Arab world should thus be considered in partial continuity with earlier phases, with ultimate origins in the era of colonial rivalries between European powers. Those projects, far from being narrowly nationalist, were themselves "cosmopolitan" in nature, and their lineage is part of the inherent ambivalence of any European identity.

The crisis of European political identity exposed by post-2015 migration thus deserves to be regarded as a problem that transcends populist right rhetoric. Beneath it lies a crisis of the social state, belying Milward's (2000) earlier suggestion that European integration was strengthening the integration of domestic state and society. Equally, there lies inconsistencies between cosmopolitan aspirations to universalism and the reality of life experienced both by domestic working classes and by migrants to European societies. The evidence thus suggests barriers to European integration that cannot be resolved simply by incorporating the populist right (as with the "way of life" agenda) or by repelling them. For those wishing to build solidarity, it may be worth starting from a perspective of local bonds of solidarity or else inter-nationalism, in the classic meaning of that term, rather than attempting to vault over politics through transnational administration. An open borders agenda ultimately cannot evade an encounter with popular accountability forever. Recent EU history demonstrates that efforts to evade such questions have produced the "way of life" agenda, Frontex and offshoring deals with regimes ranging from Turkey to Mali to Libya.

Debates on borders have assumed a new dimension during the corona-virus pandemic, which now begins to reinforce central questions about Europe's core identity. Within weeks of the pandemic a poll of 12 countries found that all showed majorities in favour of border closures to stem the virus, with the biggest majorities in Asian countries nearby China (India at 79% and Vietnam at 78%), but with majorities in all surveyed European countries (the lowest in the UK, at 51%, the highest in Italy, at 76%) (Ipsos-Mori, 2020a). By November 2020, a survey of 21,000 showed a worldwide majority of 67% favouring closing their country's borders until the spread of Covid-19 was fully contained (Ipsos-Mori, 2020b). In effect, the institutional fabric of globalisation has endured its biggest shock, transcending the earlier Eurozone and 2015 crises.

Whereas the 2015 crisis had seen the politicisation of external borders, the 2020 pandemic problematised internal borders. There were abrupt and internal closures within the Schengen Zone. It was thus observed that "Covid-19 presents the biggest challenge yet to the Schengen system", with its 17 Member States having closed their borders following the initial March outbreak: "the unilateral reintroduction of border checks and border closures has become an accepted part of Member States' toolkits to respond to cross-border emergencies" (Kainz, 2020). While there had been some Schengen closures in 2015, border reversions were almost universal in March 2020. Many EU states were reduced to banning foreign travellers, including those from other member states. Concepts of "solidarity" were thus problematised in new ways. Moreover, whereas the earlier crisis of borders had focused on Europe's "Other", this was defiantly a crisis of the European self.

Our recent research, evolving out of the work of this book, used Twitter datasets to chart how the virus was influencing European attitudes to border openness. In the period when lockdowns struck much of Europe, between mid-March and mid-May 2020, we collected a dataset totalling around 8,000 tweets. We collected tweets with the #Schengen hashtag from France, Italy, Hungary, Germany, and Romania to explore internal border closures and travel controls within the Schengen zone, and to explore emerging post-virus discourses of mobility. We likewise charted data in a variety of languages – Hungarian, French, and Italian as well as English – while exploring articulations of "solidarity" within the #Eurozone hashtag. This analysis took place in the crucial months when lockdowns hit much of Europe, between mid-March and mid-May. Our chief finding was extensive resentment against the removal of border controls for the summer of 2020, particularly in French language tweets. The majority of tweets in French, reaching 90%, considered Schengen mobility a problem and many identified

Schengen as an "infectious zone". Italian tweets narrated Schengen restrictions as a new chapter in a longer story of EU failures, traceable back to the Eurozone crisis. This data backs the survey evidence suggesting growing rejection of "open borders" discourse, which, theoretically, raises new doubts about the liberal ideal of Europeanisation.

Nonetheless, the virus's impact on political consciousness has been far from even. Indeed, somewhat paradoxically, the case for border closures and lockdown measures has been largely led by the technocratic establishment, those who had previously been the most ideologically invested in neoliberal globalisation and "open society" ideologies. The election of Joe Biden as United States president – albeit with a worse than expected majority – may signal a return to a regime of what Žižek characterised as "post-political biopolitics" (Žižek, 2008). Conversely, the pandemic exposed many of the inner ideological tensions in populist right programmes. Their rhetoric had always traded on an inconsistent mixture of appeals to authoritarianism and libertarianism. On migration, for example, they simultaneously led the charge for tougher crackdowns at borders, while also breaking perceived ideological taboos in a spirit of rule-breaking defiance. Many reacted to the virus by gambling on a libertarian approach to the pandemic, dismissing the virus as a "hoax" and lockdown as an establishment assault on personal freedom. Where governments came to power on these terms, they quickly found themselves overwhelmed by events, as with Trump, the UK's Boris Johnson, and Brazil's Bolsonaro.

However, there are risks in over-generalising from these well-publicised cases. Even in Europe's core countries, there are signs of populist right resilience. In February 2021, as this book was being finalised, Marine Le Pen scored her highest ever poll rating, with 48% against 52% for incumbent centrist Emmanuel Macron (Al Jazeera, 2021). Le Pen had avoided the libertarian rhetoric of Anglo-American populists or Italy's Salvini, which had proved an electoral loser. Equally, where the populist right has declined during the pandemic, the relationship is not simply a victory for liberal openness. In some respects, core elements of populist right programme have been achieved precisely in the mainstream response to the coronavirus. After Germany's Alternative for Germany (AfD) fell sharply, an AfD member of the Bundestag complained that the party was suffering because the German establishment had stolen its policies. "The main topics of the AfD – such as a greater stress on German national interests, closed European external borders, support of local small and medium-sized industry – were temporarily realised by the government during the corona pandemic [...] That is why opposition parties always have polling losses in a crisis" (Schutz, 2020).

The AfD, like many populist right-wing parties, responded to this political squeeze with a desperate search for distinctiveness, entertaining conspiracy theories and libertarian anti-mask and anti-vaccination doctrines. But controversy-stoking moves simply served to distance the party from small-*c* conservative supporters.

Having abandoned the European Union, Britain has become a microcosm for tensions about borders, openness, and Europeanism. Yet paradoxes abound. As this book has demonstrated, the principal cosmopolitan narrative in British politics takes the form of the Scottish National Party's minority nationalism, with its nation branding programme stressing an "open and welcoming Scotland". Post-coronavirus, the SNP has thrived through a combination of promoting Europeanness ("openness") and enforcing lockdowns ("closedness"). Their success, as demonstrated here, rests on a peculiar combination of superior administration (over Westminster) and superior cosmopolitan morality (relative to English voters). Yet, as demonstrated in an earlier chapter, the UK state and the English also differentiate themselves against Europe in terms of a higher cosmopolitanism. While Brexit was taken as the quintessential statement of "closed society" attitudes, the UK has remained broadly supportive of immigration. Polls showed huge public support – including majorities from supporters of all parties – for a bill offering automatic British citizenship to passport holders fleeing persecution in Hong Kong (YouGov, 2020). Interestingly, in 30 years, this number has transformed: in 1990, there was vast public opposition across all parties to giving Hongkongers citizenship. British opposition to migration is thus conditional, reflecting both pervasive Islamophobia (a hangover from the earlier War on Terror) and democracy grievances against the European project.

It is thus important not to become overly fixated on the tactical missteps of the populist right. The latter should be regarded as symptomatic of deeper problems of social and system integration: beneath the political crisis of European societies are more fundamental economic failures. In 1975, when the British public voted to retain Common Market membership, Roy Jenkins, then of the Labour Party, was asked to explain the result; he replied that the British people "took the advice of people they were used to following" (Bickerton, 2012, pp. 4–5). This is rather similar to the academic notion of a "permissive consensus". That consensus was never uncontentious: the history of referenda of European integration is a testament to politicisation even during the peak years of globalisation. But insofar as it existed, its foundation, as most theorists of integration observed, was the complacency that comes from rising prosperity. Hence the problems encountered since 2008. The political sacrifices of globalisation can no longer offer consistent payoffs in rising wages and property prices: at least, not for the social majority. After the coronavirus, capitalism without rising incomes could be the reality for some years to come.

The result is that the current ideological crisis of the populist right is inseparable from the European Union's crisis of meaning, on core concepts of freedom and (social) security. Both encounter a bundle of interconnected problems. Core contrasts of open and closed societies that sustained earlier narratives of (anti)-globalisation have lost their everyday relevance. The EU has, with great effort, maintained the mobility of capital and trade within the Schengen Zone, without people mobility. Perhaps more evocatively, the EU's willingness to override sacred open border arrangements was best illustrated by the case of post-Brexit Northern Ireland. During Brexit negotiations, EU officials had centred their moral claims on the Good Friday Agreement and keeping the Irish border open. However, just a month after the post-Brexit regime came into force, the EU was threatening to unilaterally reimpose hard borders on Ireland, based on a trade dispute over vaccinations. Even the most hardened Europhiles were perplexed that the bloc's self-image as the guarantor of open borders was being tarnished over a minor dispute where the UK was, by most accounts, morally in the right. As with the earlier doctrine of "defending the European way of life", the Irish border controversy issued directly from the EU's most cosmopolitan element, the European Commission, under the presidency of Ursula von der Leyen. It was the latest illustration that the crossover between the "populist moment" and the coronavirus era will involve subtlety and complexity.

Despite the pandemic's impact on globalisation, the prospect of the disintegration of Europe looks less likely than five years ago. Challengers of the populist left have been seen off; the populist right challenge has been incorporated and, for now, forced into a damaging retreat. And, paradoxically, the Eurozone may even promote a stronger impulse towards integration despite the evidence of its technical failings. Populists ranging from Syriza to Salvini have foundered when forced to imagine a sovereigntist alternative to the currency union. There may even have been a post-Brexit backlash against Euroscepticism, visible in the last European elections, which reversed trends towards falling turnouts. That said, the "void" separating Member States from domestic populations is only likely to grow during an era of economic breakdown. And solidarity may be better reimagined at the level of "inter-nationalist" exchange, between movements of solidarity with national-popular roots in their respective democratic contexts.

References

Al Jazeera (2021). France's Le Pen, at Record High in a Poll, Proposes Hijab Ban. Available at: https://www.aljazeera.com/news/2021/1/30/frances-le-pen-at-record-high-in-polls-proposes-hijab-ban (accessed 2 August 2021).

Atkinson, W. (2007). Beck, Individualization and the Death of Class: A Critique. *British Journal of Sociology, 58,* 349–366.

Barber, B. (1992). Jihad vs. McWorld. *The Atlantic, 269,* 53–63.

Beck, U. (2007). Beyond Class and Nation: Reframing Social Inequalities in a Globalizing World 1. *British Journal of Sociology, 58,* 679–705.

Bickerton, C. J. (2012). *European Integration: From Nation-States to Member States.* Oxford: Oxford University Press.

Birtchnell, T. Caletrío, J. (2013). *Elite Mobilities.* London: Routledge.

Brubaker, R. (2017). Between Nationalism and Civilizationism: the European Populist Moment in Comparative Perspective. *Ethnic and Racial Studies, 40,* 1191–1226.

Crouch, C. (2019). Post-Democracy and Populism. *Political Quarterly, 90,* 124–137.

Crouch, C. (2004). *Post-Democracy.* Cambridge: Polity.

Cunliffe, P. (2020). *Cosmopolitan Dystopia: International Intervention and the Failure of the West.* Manchester: Manchester University Press.

Goodhart, D. (2017). *The Road to Somewhere: The Populist Revolt and the Future of Politics.* Oxford: Oxford University Press.

Ipsos-Mori (2020a). Majority of People Want Borders Closed as Fear about Covid-19 Escalates. Ipsos. Available at: https://www.ipsos.com/en/majority-people-want-borders-closed-fear-about-covid-19-escalates (accessed 2 September 2021).

Ipsos-Mori (2020b). Majority (67%) of Global Citizens Support the Closing of Their Borders as Few (33%) Believe Covid-19 is Contained. Ipsos. Available at: https://www.ipsos.com/en/majority-67-global-citizens-support-closing-their-borders-few-33-believe-covid-19-contained (accessed 2 September 2021).

Kainz, H. B., and Susan Fratzke, L. (2020). When Emergency Measures Become the Norm: Post-Coronavirus Prospects for the Schengen Zone. Migration Policy Institute. Available at: https://www.migrationpolicy.org/news/post-covid-prospects-border-free-schengen-zone (accessed 2 August 2021).

Malik, N. (2017). Grenfell Shows Just How Britain Fails Migrants. *The Guardian.* Available at: http://www.theguardian.com/commentisfree/2017/jun/16/grenfell-britain-fails-migrants-north-kensington-london-refugee (accessed 2 August 2021).

Milward, A. S. (2000). *The European Rescue of the Nation-State.* London: Routledge.

Piketty, T. (2018). Brahmin Left vs Merchant Right: Rising Inequality and the Changing Structure of Political Conflict. WID World Working Paper 7.

Scheffer, P. (2021). We'd Be Lost without Borders. *UnHerd*. Available at: https://unherd.com/2021/02/wed-be-lost-without-borders/ (accessed 2 August 2021).

Schutz, S., (2020). How the Pandemic Dented the Popularity of Germany's Far-Right AfD Party. *NPR.org*. Available at: https://www.npr.org/2020/12/29/950860206/how-the-pandemic-dented-the-popularity-of-germanys-far-right-afd-party (accessed 2 August 2021).

Stiglitz, J. E. (2002). *Globalization and its Discontents*. New York: Norton.

YouGov (2020). Support for Helping British Passport-Holders in Hong Kong is Rising. *YouGov*. Available at: https://yougov.co.uk/topics/politics/articles-reports/2020/07/01/support-helping-british-passport-holders-hong-kong (accessed 2 August 2021).

Žižek, S. (2017). *The Courage of Hopelessness: Chronicles of a Year of Acting Dangerously*. London: Penguin.

Žižek, S. (2008). *Violence: Six Sideways Reflections*. London: Picador.

Index

Protest and Social Movements

James M. Jasper and Jan Willem Duyvendak (eds): *Players and Arenas. The Interactive Dynamics of Protest.* 2015, ISBN 9789089647085

Isabel David and Kumru F. Toktamış (eds): *'Everywhere Taksim'. Sowing the Seeds for a New Turkey at Gezi.* 2015, ISBN 9789089648075

Johanna Siméant, Marie-Emmanuelle Pommerolle and Isabelle Sommier (eds): *Observing Protest from a Place. The World Social Forum in Dakar (2011).* 2015, ISBN 9789089647801

Robert M. Press: *Ripples of Hope. How Ordinary People Resist Repression without Violence.* 2015, ISBN 9789089647481

Jan Willem Duyvendak and James M. Jasper (eds): *Breaking Down the State. Protestors Engaged.* 2015, ISBN 9789089647597

Christophe Traïni: *The Animal Rights Struggle. An Essay in Historical Sociology.* 2016, ISBN 9789089648495

Mustafa Gurbuz: *Rival Kurdish Movements in Turkey. Transforming Ethnic Conflict.* 2016, ISBN 9789089648785

Marcos Ancelovici, Pascale Dufour and Héloïse Nez (eds): *Street Politics in the Age of Austerity. From the Indignados to Occupy.* 2016, ISBN 9789089647634

Johanna Siméant and Christophe Traini: *Bodies in Protest. Hunger Strikes and Angry Music.* 2016, ISBN 9789089649331

Kerstin Jacobsson and Jonas Lindblom: *Animal Rights Activism. A Moral-Sociological Perspective on Social Movements.* 2016, ISBN 9789089647641

Lorenzo Bosi and Gianluca De Fazio (eds): *The Troubles in Northern Ireland and Theories of Social Movements.* 2017, ISBN 9789089649591

Donatella della Porta (ed.): *Global Diffusion of Protest. Riding the Protest Wave in the Neoliberal Crisis.* 2017, ISBN 9789462981690

Frédéric Volpi and James M. Jasper (eds): *Microfoundations of the Arab Uprisings. Mapping Interactions between Regimes and Protesters.* 2018, ISBN 9789462985131

Konstantinos Eleftheriadis: *Queer Festivals. Challenging Collective Identities in a Transnational Europe.* 2018, ISBN 9789462982741

Julie Pagis: *May '68. Shaping Political Generations.* 2018, ISBN 9789462983755

Matteo Cernison: *Social Media Activism. Water as a Common Good.* 2019, ISBN 9789462980068

Isabelle Sommier, Graeme Hayes and Sylvie Ollitrault: *Breaking Laws. Violence and Civil Disobedience in Protest.* 2019, ISBN 9789089649348

Guillaume Marche: *Sexuality, Subjectivity, and LGBTQ Militancy in the United States.* 2019, ISBN 9789089649607

Aidan McGarry, Itir Erhart, Hande Eslen-Ziya, Olu Jenzen, and Umut Korkut (eds): *The Aesthetics of Global Protest. Visual Culture and Communication.* 2020, ISBN 9789463724913

David Chiavacci, Simona Grano, and Julia Obinger (eds): *Civil Society and the State in Democratic East Asia. Between Entanglement and Contention in Post High Growth.* 2020, ISBN 9789463723930

Haris Malamidis: *Social Movements and Solidarity Structures in Crisis-Ridden Greece.* 2020, ISBN 9789463722438

Elias Steinhilper: *Migrant Protest. Interactive Dynamics in Precarious Mobilizations.* 2021, ISBN 9789463722223

Jannis Julien Grimm: *Contested Legitimacies. Repression and Revolt in Post-Revolutionary Egypt.* 2022, ISBN 9789463722650

Tiago Carvalho: Contesting Austerity. *Social Movements and the Left in Portugal and Spain (2008-2015).* 2022, ISBN 9789463722841